MW01181523

FOR
THE LOVE OF
WILDLIFE

Mufasa van der Merwe
March 1995 – 18 April 1997

FOR
THE LOVE OF
WILDLIFE

by Chris Mercer and Beverley Pervan

To Peter & Johanne

We must learn how to read the love
letters sent to us by the wind & rain,
the snow & moon.

Thank you for your support we "all"
appreciate it.

Chris & Beverley

March 2001

About the production of this book
Photographs: Chris Mercer,
Beverley Pervan and Harnas
Design, typesetting and page layout:
Dee Helling and Sandi Arrenbrecht
Printed and bound by CREDA
Communications (Pty) Ltd Gauteng

The book is typeset in 10 pt Galliard

First published in 2000 by the Kalahari
Raptor Centre in South Africa

ISBN 0-620-26014-9

CONTENTS

ACKNOWLEDGEMENT

We wish to thank Andrew Mercer whose poetry has brought a new dimension to the book.

DEDICATION

We dedicate this book to the waning spirit of wild Africa and especially to its purest essence, the predators, with whom Mankind refuses to live or let live.

NAMIBIA

Kaokoland
Ruacana
Oshakati
Opuwo
Ondangwa
Owamba
Kavango
Rundu
Bagani
Kongola
Katima Mulilo
Caprivi Oos
Etosha Pan
Tsumeb
Sesfontein
Okaukuejo
Tsumeb
Boesmanland
Outjo
Otavi
Grootfontein
Tsumkwe
Damaraland
Grootfontein
Khorixas
Outjo
Hereroland Wes
Kalkfeld
Otjiwarongo
Okarara
Otjiwarongo
Hereroland Oos
Omaruru
Epata
Harnas
Omaruru
Okahandja
Karibib
Karibib
Okahandja
Gobabis
Swakopmund
Windhoek
Gobabis
Walvis Bay
Swakopmund
Rehoboth
Hereroland Oos
Rehoboth
Kalkrand
Aranos
Stampriet
Mariental
Maltahohe
Mariental
Maltahohe
Namaband
Lüderitz
Bethanien
Keetmanshoop
Lüderitz
Seeheim
Aroab
Bethanien
Keetmanshoop
Grunau
Karasburg
Oranjemund
Karasburg
Alexander Bay

SAHARA

Namibia

7

HARNAS

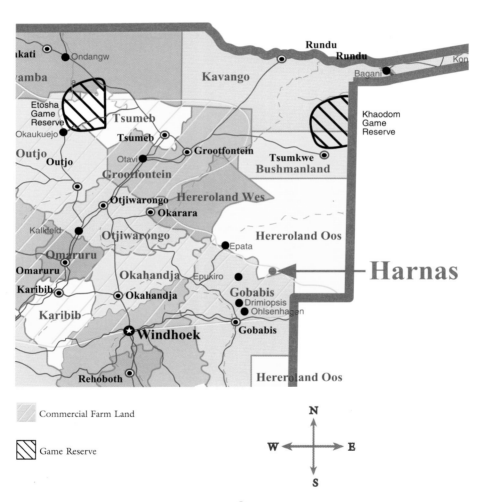

Harnas

Commercial Farm Land

Game Reserve

N
W ← → E
S

8

Part one

THE VANISHING

AND BEAUTY WEARS A COUNTENANCE
WITH THE RADIANCE OF BIRTH.
LIKE A NEW-BORN SCREAMS IN COLOURS
ACROSS THE SPECTRUM OF THE EARTH.

A WORLD WHERE ALL LIFE LISTENS TO
A RHYTHM LIKE A WAVE.
WHICH GATHERS SOUND AND BREAKS UPON
THIS ABUNDANCE THAT GOD GAVE.

EVERY LIFE A CELEBRATION
EVERY VOICE WAS RAISED IN SONG.
EVERY ANGEL HELD THE MELODY
IN HEARTS THAT KNEW NO WRONG.

RESPECT FOR EVERY LIVING THING
AN OATH THE LIVING TOOK.
BUT MAN NOW SWORE WITH OTHERS BLOOD
HIS GUILTY FINGERS SHOOK.

THESE STORMS HAVE RAGED A THOUSAND YEARS
WITH NATURE ON HER KNEES.
HER CHILDREN SCREAM FROM HEADSETS
THROUGH THE SILENCE OF CUT TREES.

NOW BLOOD SEEPS FROM THE HEAVENS
WILL IT DROWN OUR LAST SUNSET?
ABSORBING EVERY COLOUR 'TILL
WE'RE LEFT WITH COLD REGRET.

ON THE BAKING EARTH A MESSAGE
A TIRED MANTRA TO EMBRACE.
WRITTEN IN THE BONES OF THOSE
WHOSE LIVES WE CAN'T REPLACE.

AND FOR THOSE WHO HAVE TO FOLLOW
THROW DUST INTO THE AIR.
FOR EVERY GRAIN THAT WAS A LIFE
BEFORE MAN CEASED TO CARE.

Andrew Mercer

Chapter one

SIMBA

So cry my lonely angel
For what you never had.
For wonders you will never see
For things you'll never have.
You share this sky with emptiness
On broken wings you're falling.
I'm waiting on my knees for you
My lonely angel
Calling.

Andrew Mercer

It was not so many seasons ago that the Great Invasion destroyed Bushmanland. Until that unhappy event, Bushmanland was a wilderness wonderland as ancient and precious as time itself. From Botswana on the eastern side to the Khaodom Game Reserve and Caprivi in the north, an area of five thousand square kilometres was bounded in the West by the white commercial farmlands and the Waterberg Plateau. In the south - Hereroland. Ah, that was where the problem lay, if only they could have known it. Yet how could they have known it, for the untamed inhabitants of Bushmanland lived life and paid their taxes to death from day to day. The apparently limitless expanse of Kalahari sandveld supported a marvellous diversity of flora which we call Acacia Savannah. That in turn supported in a million wondrous, intricate ways a natural celebration of wild people such as only those who have visited the great game reserves of Africa can imagine. Herds of antelope, all uniquely adapted to exploit a particular niche in their environment, grazed and browsed to their hearts' content. Their abundance gave life to the greatest show of predators on earth. The predators provided for the whole range of scavengers who in turn..., well, the whole natural cycle churned along just as Mother Nature intended, with life as a cosmic, omnipresent force which the inhabitants borrowed and gave back to her. A death here sustained a life over there. The life force itself remained strong. It is an atmosphere, this spirit of Africa, that can only survive in wild places where the people live by Nature's rules. It does not exist in places where the human species builds its cities and treats all the other inhabitants of this planet as if they were made of cardboard. Yet they are all people just like you and I, these wild people. They may have different forms from us, but they cry out in pain when they are hurt, and they grieve for lost ones. They shed tears when they are sad or lonely, and show great joy when they are glad.

But some did not see the colour or beauty of Bushmanland. They did not hear the song of the birds or feel the sustaining life force. They regarded the land as "unoccupied" and resolved to occupy it, without realizing - or caring - that unthinking occupation by mankind would destroy it as utterly as would a nuclear bomb. The wild animals, who we prefer to call wild people, had their own history of Bushmanland. For thousands or even millions of years, they had suffered from the poisonous arrows of the small brown people. Then they were hunted by the black people who also killed off the brown people. Then came the murderous white people with the blue eyes and the smoking Mausers in their arms. Finally came the white people with brown eyes who locked up the men with blue eyes in concentration camps and took away their Mausers. The wild people did not care about the colour of the skins or eyes for they knew from tragic experience that the hearts were all the same - as cold and black as onyx.

In this vast paradise which because of its remoteness had not yet been ruined by Man's cruelty and bloodlust, there lived at the time of which we speak, only one pride of resident lions. Of course, in the olden days, dozens of large prides lived in contentment off the millions of antelope who graced the sun-washed plains. By the last decade before the new millennium, the countless herds lived on only in the memory of the elderly and long-lived, and of all the prides of lions which had once filled the life force of the plains with their earth-shattering roars, there was only one left. That was Simba's pride. And the only reason we know about Simba's story today is that hundreds of kilometres away to the south lived an Afrikaans farming family who were different from most other Namibians. The Van der Merwe family loved the wild people and devoted their lives to saving these poor creatures from cruel persecution. They called their farm Harnas Wildlife Sanctuary, and this is their story. But because a love for wild people has interwoven into a rich tapestry the life of the family with those for whom they cared, we must tell the story of the Harnas animals as well. They too have their own point of view.

To see why in 1993 the imprints of Simba's paws came to lie deep in the Omaheke Sandveld near the Harnas Wildlife Sanctuary, we can go back in time to the year 1904. For it was in that year that the German colonial government brought the Herero Insurrection to a decisive end. The Schutztruppe surrounded the Herero forces at the Waterberg Plateau and slaughtered them. During the night a few hundred Hereros managed to break out of the encirclement and they fled east towards British Bechuanaland (now Botswana). With heavy memories of the more than a hundred settlers who were murdered during the uprising, the colonial troops pursued the fleeing Hereros remorse-lessly, hunting them down and killing them. A few scattered groups who survived the retreat contrived after great hardship to reach the protection of British territory, and they settled near the town of Ghanzi which lies to the south of the Okavango Delta. The colonial adventure unfolded, faltered and then unravelled. The government of Namibia came to be decided by popular democratic vote in 1993.

The Herero fugitives of 1904 who had settled around Ghanzi in Botswana still regarded themselves as Namibians. Over the decades they had increased in numbers to tens of thousands and intermarriage with the local Tswana meant that it was difficult to deny a right to vote to anyone who claimed it and who lived in the west of Botswana. SWAPO, the party supported by Russia, China and the United Nations, were strong in the north among the Ovambo but lacked support among the Hereros. To gain their vote SWAPO promised the Botswana Hereros land. But where to resettle them? The obvious place was Hereroland, but the Hereros already there resisted this. Such resistance would have translated into a loss of votes for SWAPO. An alternative had to be found - Bushmanland. Occupied only by a few thousand Bushmen some of whom had anyway worked with the hated colonial government, it was the ideal alternative. It was vast enough to absorb the tens of thousands of voters along with their cattle, goats and donkeys. Behind closed doors in Moscow, Beijing and in the capitals of its regional allies, Angola and Zimbabwe, the political strategy to put SWAPO in power in Namibia was hammered out. How meticulously must the planning have been. How carefully every consideration must have been weighed. All except the interests of the wild people and their habitat needs. The land for votes deal was struck, SWAPO won the election and the authorisation was given. Tens of thousands of Hereros, a good many Tswana and some sharp opportunists who took the chance to be granted some free real estate, streamed into the unspoilt veld, seizing whatever land they desired.

At danger were five thousand virgin square kilometres of Mother Africa; countless exquisite Combretum and Terminalia trees - trees that had adapted over eons to survive in the deep Kalahari sand veld; millions of exquisite animals equally adapted to survive in the summer inferno and billions of tufts of sweet-veld grasses that could endure the light touch of the wild grazers but would be stomped to death under the cloven hooves of the alien cattle, and replaced by the harsh woody thorn bushes. Deprived of their annual harvest of seeds the billions of seedeaters, birds and mammals alike, would quietly perish.

Now clouds of dust rich in iron oxide - the same dust that gives the Kalahari its spectacular red sunsets - rose into the air and hung there in the hot windless atmosphere. Now could be heard the lowing of the cattle herds as they struggled through the yielding soft sand, sinking in up to their fetlocks with each plodding step, the shouts of the drovers and the cracks of the long whips, the roaring of the engines of the lorries and four wheel drive pick-ups, the creaking of the poorly-greased axles of the ubiquitous scotch-carts as they were hauled painfully through the tenacious sand by the straining donkeys, the excited chattering of the piccanins - the children - as they romped and played around the great march, the distant echoes of a rifle shot as meat for the evening meal was procured from Mother Africa's take-away counter. As for the wild people of Bushmanland, they were treated yet again as if they did not exist. For them the noise of the happy intruders was an infernal din from Hell, and the authorisation for the exodus from Botswana, their death warrants.

Into the furthest reaches of Southern Bushmanland marched the invaders. As they went, people peeled off to the left and to the right and spread out in all directions. The new 'pastoralists', as they were now called, settled down to their destructive ways and set about erecting fences to establish their dominion. Lions and stock-farming cannot exist together so at the first sight of lion tracks (spoor) in their vicinity the Hereros would take their rifles, mount their horses and untie the dogs. Then they would simply ride along following the spoor until they found the lions. While the dogs harried and distracted the lions, the horsemen would ride up and shoot them. There was no escape for the lions. In that open savannah there were no mountains or even dense thickets for them to hide in. The soft sand betrayed their every move. Lions are very sensitive to temperature and are quite unable to outrun a horse for long. Indeed in the sort of stunning heat that hammers down on the Kalahari a lion that attempted to do so would very likely have a heart attack before he could be shot. After the kill, the lions would be skinned and the salted skins later processed and either sold for money or kept as a trophy, a symbol of accomplishment.

Although Bushmanland was a non-fenced wilderness and had no formal conservation status, the scientists in the Namibian

15

Department of Nature Conservation had been active in darting and radio collaring the lion population in order to catalogue them and determine the extent of their home ranges. Whilst under sedation the lions were branded for identification purposes. Even today Simba's skin displays an ugly S-shaped scar on his right rear leg. When lions killed livestock belonging to the local Bushmen, the scientist responded by shooting three of the lions themselves. In a paper presented to the South African Veterinary Association in October 1997, one of these scientists, a Dr. Stander, describes the situation in unemotional scientific language.

"Starting in 1993, large-scale settlement of pastoralists (mainly Herero speaking people) occurred in and around TD and on the immediate borders of KGR. The conflict with lions intensified dramatically. So much so that this project was unable to monitor the conflict in any systematic manner. Lions were shot and poisoned secretively and at random, with little information being made available. The rapid encroachment of new people and herds of cattle did not allow for the establishment of personal interaction and collaboration.

The intensity of pastoralism in the vicinity resulted in the almost complete destruction of the Tsumkwe District lion population. Of the 27 lions, nine were killed during 1992. Of these six were killed by pastoralists in Botswana (immediately across the border) and those settling in Tsumkwe District. During 1993 a further ten lions were killed by the same source and by 1995 all the marked and known lions had been destroyed and only two lived in the region. Lions from the KGR did not appear to escape the onslaught of pastoralist settlement in the region. All of the radio-collared lions (N-5) and some of the marked animals (40%) marked in 1992, had been shot just outside the Reserve by the end of 1995. The effect of the pastoralist settlement on the core lion population of the KGR is unknown. Considering some basic ecological characteristics, such as

a) the low lion density;

b) large home range;

c) the relatively small size of the Reserve; and

d) the intensity of pastoralism on the borders, the conflict is expected to have an catastrophic effect on this lion population.

The future of large African carnivores outside conservation areas depends on the views and aspirations of the local people. Only when the local inhabitants live at relatively low intensity and have a particular interest in large carnivores will their future be ensured. In the present study large settlements of pastoralists with large herds of domestic live-stock resulted in a serious conflict of interest, and the subsequent loss of suitable habitat to support a viable lion population."

(TD = Tsumkwe District - southern Bushmanland.

KGR = Khaodom Game Reserve - northern Bushmanland)

For Simba, southern Bushmanland was his home. There he was born and had grown up and there he would have to fight against his own kind to secure for himself a home territory, and with it, his lionesses and their cubs. At the age of three years, Simba was still regarded as a sub-adult male lion, and although he was big - very big - his tawny mane was relatively small. In time, his mane would darken and become bushy. If Fate gave him the time, that is. For humans may expect a comfortable period between birth and death but because of humans, other life forms have no such luxurious expectations. His pride consisted of an adult lion, who may have been his father, and two lionesses. He had two sub-adult brothers and a sister. There were no cubs. This pride formation already showed the effects of excessive hunting. In the few remaining areas of Africa which are free of hunters, the lion prides are much larger and better balanced between adults, sub-adults and cubs. Simba's pride had the characteristic structure of a transient or nomadic population. The pride's home range was southern Bushmanland - five thousand square kilometres. Why was there only one lop-sided pride in such a vast area? Even in the Khaodom Game Reserve to the north, there were five larger prides, and that was only three thousand eight hundred square kilometres. The poisonous hand of the poachers had Bushmanland by the throat.

For Simba, the invaders were now attacking on all fronts. Not only were they decimating his prey animals, leaving him and his family hungry, but when he attempted to live off the only meat now available to him - cattle and goats - he was attacked with dogs, horses and guns and carcasses baited with steel traps. The invaders were too many and they were too strong. His only strategy was to fall back and look for new territory. But where? He could not go north or his small pride would have been savagely treated by the larger prides there. To the south lay the land of the Herero hunter-farmers. It would be certain death for him to try that avenue. The 'pastoralists' were spreading in from the east. There was really no choice. Simba and his small family were forced to move west and in September 1993, they entered the land owned by white commercial cattle ranchers. By this time, the pride had dwindled to just four lions - only his two brothers and a sister had survived.

In Namibia, the arrival of a pride of lions in cattle ranching country - as happens from time to time - is akin to an invasion by armed terrorists. In any society that worships the great god Money the loss, or potential loss, of even one head of cattle is considered to be unacceptable. There was no rest for Simba and his little family. Skilled Bushman trackers were deployed to follow up their spoor. As soon as their general direction had been reported the radios crackled and spoke, and fresh Bushman were dropped off by vehicle several kilometres further on in that direction to pick up fresher spoor and short circuit the process. It was just a matter of time before the lost, wandering family was found. Then the game was on. Once again it took the form of a cavalry charge, only now the pursuing dust cloud contained hideously roaring pick-up trucks instead of baying dogs and thundering hooves. Of course, it made no difference whether the form of conveyance was equine or mechanical. All the riders had the same ruthless cruelty in their breasts, the same inability to adopt a live-and-let-live attitude to others who share our planet. One by one, Simba's remaining family fell to the smoking guns of the ranchers. Harried and hunted, the exhausted lion and his last remaining pride member - his sister - turned south and escaped from the commercial ranching land. The two of them now found themselves in Hereroland, tribal land crowded with little huts, dogs, people and goats. There was no respite for them here. Chased by dogs and men with guns and horses they fled south. His sister was shot near Hochveld and Simba went on alone, the sole survivor of the last pride of lions in all of southern Bushmanland.

An area of land twice the size of Luxembourg had just had its entire lion population exterminated. And nobody had said a word. None of the wealthy and well-connected wildlife organisations had raised a protesting voice. There was no Press Release by the Department of Nature Conservation. Simba's pride and the other wild people of this vast piece of remaining wilderness were allowed to be bludgeoned into oblivion without a single voice being raised in dissent. In October 1993, Simba again entered commercial ranching land, this time in the Omaheke province, very close to Harnas Wildlife Sanctuary and Nature Reserve.

Nic van der Merwe answered the telephone when it rang early one October morning in 1993. It was his neighbour, a Mr. Riedel. He was telephoning to report that one of his cattle had been found that morning. It had been killed and half-eaten by a lion. He wanted to know if Harnas could take care of the situation, or if he should just take his rifle and shoot the lion. Nic begged him not to shoot it. After he had replaced the phone, Nic turned to his wife, Marieta. "It's a lion," he told her. "Someone will shoot it for sure if we do not catch it first." Marieta looked at Nic and pursed her lips thoughtfully. She was the one who had started taking in orphaned and injured animals some twenty-odd years before, and often against Nic's vigorous protests, had built up probably the largest private wildlife care centre in the Southern Hemisphere. She was the rock on which Harnas was founded.

Her three children had all grown up with wildlife as companions and were as comfortable around wild people as a teenage girl with her pony. The two of them sat down in the kitchen and talked. The snag was that although they kept lions in camps, along with all the other big cats of Africa, and had had experience of raising lions from cubs,

19

they had never had to catch a wild lion and therefore lacked both the know-how and the equipment. "We need to do something quick or it will be too late," Nic said at last. "Call the kids." In her usual spontaneous manner, Marieta stood in the kitchen, threw back her head and yelled out at the top of her voice. A Bushman woman answered from the courtyard outside. "Find Nico and Schalk and tell them we need them," she ordered. Nico arrived first. Now in his early twenties, he was a serious young man who would later study Veterinary Science in Pretoria before an assailant's knife would cut short his career in that profession. A big, heavily-built man, he filled the door space as he entered the kitchen. Schalk came sloping in from the back sheds where he had been welding some steel gates for the cages. Not as bulky as his elder brother, he was tall and muscular and would later play international rugby for his country. Marlice, the only daughter, was away at school. "It's a lion," Nic told them. "Riedel's place. He wants to know can we catch it or must he shoot it." Nic never wastes a syllable by way of explanation.

They discussed the difficulties. Even if they succeeded in catching it, they had no suitable cage to contain a wild lion. It would tear apart the electrified wire netting encampments in which their tamer lions were now held. Finding the lion would be hard enough. The tracks themselves would be easy enough to follow but a lion travels prodigious distances at night and the tracks would inevitably cross border fences between farms. "Anyway, Pa," concluded Nico, "we need a high-powered dart gun, and some Zolitol or Rompun." It was perfectly true. Quite apart from the difficulties involved in finding one lion in hundreds of square kilometres of African bush, and bringing such an agile creature to bay, Nico with his interest in veterinary matters was particularly alive to the problems specific to darting wild animals with tranquillizers.

Over the last decade, great strides had been made in South Africa in the medical aspects of tranquillizing such animals; various new drugs had come on to the market, and much bitter experience, at enormous cost to wild lives, had shown what drugs should be used, in what quantities and on which animals.

Too little tranquillizer and it was useless. Too much and the animal died. If it was too hot, or too cold, or the animal had exerted itself too much before being injected, it died. The most popular drug was sold under various brand names but the active component was Ketamine, a powerful dissociative drug which acted upon the peripheral nervous system. Experience had shown that if a strong muscle relaxant such as Xylazine was mixed with the Ketamine in a proportion of three parts ketamine to one part muscle relaxant, there were fewer deaths from capture stress. Muscle relaxant on its own was useless. Or was it?

Darting equipment is very expensive and tricky to use. One system employed air pressure to propel the dart. In theory this sounded good but in practice it meant creeping around the bush with a foot-operated air pump in someone's arms, and pumping away among the thorns while the alarmed quarry made its escape. A more expensive Antipodean device used a .22 calibre blank to create the charge. Halfway down the .22 barrel, there was a join onto a sleeved 10mm barrel in which the dart was inserted. The darts themselves were a cross between an arrow and a syringe. The needle had a rubber or plastic ring over a hole in the side, not the point, of the needle. The front of the barrel of the dart contained the ketamine solution, then there was a rubber piston and at the back of the dart, compressed air which was injected with an ordinary syringe needle. As the dart entered the target animal the rubber sleeve was displaced, thereby opening the hole whereupon the air pressure in the back of the dart forced the solution out of the hole into the animal. Just to prepare the dart for use was a time-consuming exercise that required considerable experience and veterinary knowledge. Harnas at that time had none of these things, but what the Van der Merwe family did have in abundance was the will to save a lion's life and the resourcefulness to overcome any obstacles. The first step was to make sure that the tracks found on Mr. Reidel's farm were indeed those of a lion. The two boys Nico and Schalk drove over to their neighbour's farm that afternoon and verified the spoor. The tracks were at least two days old. It was useless to try to follow them up. The lion could be fifty kilometres away in any direction. They would have to wait for a new sighting.

The following day was a Sunday, and after the home service and Bible readings Nic was surprised to receive a visit from Rudy Britz, his hard-working farm manager. One of the Bushmen had just told him that there were lion tracks on the farm Nicolsrus. The tracks were fresh. This was exciting news, and preparations were made at once for what could be a lengthy follow-up. The vehicles were fuelled and checked, food and water were provided and ropes and canvas sheets were loaded. Two-way radio equipment was installed in all three available bakkies (light pick-up trucks). There were numerous telephone calls to make. The police had to be informed, as were the neighbouring farmers, and permission sought to cross their land if necessary. The Department of Nature Conservation was less than enthusiastic about the capture operation. They had no darting equipment to lend to private individuals and could not understand why the troublesome animal should not simply be shot. The Namibian Broadcasting Corporation was more accommodating and agreed to broadcast regular appeals over the radio to advise people in the Gobabis area of the presence of the lion and to alert them to the follow-up being conducted by Harnas. The Weather Bureau had predicted rain and indeed rain clouds had appeared far away to the North. Nic was well aware of the possibility that rain could spoil the follow-up but took heart from the fact that the snakes, tortoises and monitor-lizards had not yet appeared. These creatures seemed to be better informed than the Weather Bureau about the arrival of the rains. He had no choice, however, but to proceed with preparations even if the whole undertaking was to be at the mercy of the weather.

Dawn broke on the Monday morning a little slower and later than usual, and when Nic went out to see why, sure enough, a bank of blue-grey clouds was rolling in from the north-east, and choking off the rising sun. Squadrons of shapeless grey wisps scudded low across the sky and a stiff breeze was blowing. As soon as Rudy Britz arrived, Nic sent him away with a Bushman to find the direction which the lion had taken - if there was a sustained direction at all. At about 8.00 a.m. Rudy radioed to say that the lion's spoor was heading west - more or less on the line of the district road between Harnas and Gobabis, and a few kilometres to the North of it. It was time to go. Nic climbed into his old Ford Pick-up and started up the powerful five-litre engine. He had welded and bolted some heavy steel bush-bars across the front of the radiator to defend it against outrages by the Omaheke flora of the hard and spiky kind. He took the main road to the south of Rudy's line of travel and cruised slowly along the road, checking for any pug-marks which would show that the lion had turned south. Nico stooped and managed to compress his large frame into the little blue Mazda bakkie and he set off following the sandy track that leads to Epikiro. He would be able to see if the lion had swung to the north. Each of them was accompanied by a Bushman, and had radio contact with the others. Rudy stayed on the prints themselves, bundu-bashing through the scrub, following his tracker who was walking or trotting along the spoor as the terrain allowed. Trailing the lion was easy in the soft sand. A full-grown lion can weigh as much as two hundred kilograms, and his heavy paws press down deep enough to leave an imprint that can be seen by the most myopic of city dwellers.

The trees and shrubs of the Omaheke sandveld formed a formidable obstacle to the follow-up exercise. Although the land appears to be flat, in fact it undulates gently, with shallow red dunes stretching between dry water courses. The vegetation varies with the soil type. The deep Kalahari sand is the home of the yellowwood terminalia, a dense woody forest of small trees which, before the rains force the sap to rise and the brittle, blackened branches to burst out in new shoots, look as if a giant hand has plucked them out of the soft sand and stuffed them back again upside down so that only their roots, bare and withered, are showing. In the richer soil, the bush becomes camelthorn savannah, where these magnificent trees and their great spreading crowns drop nutritious pods and cast deep, cool shade from the relentless sun. Here and there stand groves of smaller camelthorns, while a bewildering variety of sweetveld grasses and the taller bushman grass, grow rank. Everywhere, in varying degrees, the acacia thorn bushes have invaded. The delicate white and yellow lantern-like flowers of the sicklebush hang from the same unyielding branches whose vicious long thorns reach out to rip the flesh of the unwary. The wag-'n-bietjie (Buffalo thorn) and the swarthaak (black hook thorn) carry barbs which can impale an animal in a death grip. How a waterless thirstland as the Omaheke can be endowed with such a stunning variety of grasses, bushes and trees is one of Nature's mysteries.

Thus, across a broad front, the three vehicles made their way westwards, in constant radio contact with each other. For hour after hour, they ground along in the sand and still the spoor led them west. Then late in the afternoon, Nic saw vultures circling some distance ahead and instinct told him that this was the lion's work. Night fell before they could get close enough to look for a carcass and the three vehicles returned to Harnas. Nic telephoned the farmer, a Mr. Hough, who owned the land over which the vultures had been circling, and the two men agreed to meet there first thing the following day, Tuesday. Thinking ahead, Nic also phoned Axel Hartman, the Vet from Otjiwarongo, and went to the considerable expense of hiring him, and his aircraft as well as his darting equipment.

Early on the Tuesday morning, Dr. Hartman's plane arrived, but the weather had closed in, visibility was poor and he decided to leave his plane at Harnas until the clouds lifted. He joined Nic and the others when they drove over to Hough's farm to see what had attracted the vultures. Mr. Hough was a very angry man when he met them and showed them the carcass of one of his cows, killed by the lion. Simba had eaten out the soft intestinal and organ meat, and had also chewed enjoyably on the rump. "I come with you," he told Nic darkly, "and if I see this bloody lion first I shoot him." Fortunately for Simba, his tracks led them eventually out of Hough's farm and into that of the neighbour. At midday, Nico and Dr. Hartman drove back to Harnas to fetch the plane to see if they could spot the lion from the air, but before they could take off, Nic radioed to say that the cloud base had lowered, that it was starting to rain and that the plane could not be used. Axel Hartman flew back to his practice in Otjiwarongo taking his dart gun and tranquillizer darts with him, and he played no further part in the follow-up. Fate however, had arranged a future appointment with him for Simba. Few true wildlife stories ever have a happy ending. Early afternoon found everyone standing under trees seeking shelter from the persistent rain, and Nic called off the search for the day. This time the Weather Bureau had beaten the snakes, tortoises and monitor lizards.

While Nic and the other rescuers were sleeping like the dead after only two days on the lion's spoor, Simba was moving swiftly through the veld, a sinuous tawny form almost invisible against the beige-coloured sand, clumps of whitish, dry grass and tangled thorn bushes. That night he came upon human habitation, a motley collection of shacks and huts, imbued with the smell of wood-smoke, dogs, and most distasteful of all to him, mankind. To avoid this human settlement, he turned south, crossed the wide sandy road and went on doggedly with that urgent stride.

Unlike leopards, lions need each other's company and a lone lion will always seek out his own kind. Poor Simba. Mankind's deadly work meant that there was not another lion left alive any where within hundreds of kilometres of him in any direction.

Halfway between Harnas and Gobabis, which is a distance of about one hundred kilometres, lies a collection of huts around a telephone relay facility called Drimiopsis. A trash-littered rural store, which announced itself engagingly as the 'Katchirua Bread Shopping Centre', had served to attract the attention of sundry itinerant job-seekers, and a number of shanties had grown up around it. A school of sorts had also been established. It was the Principal of this school who received, on the Wednesday morning, a telephone call from a local farmer, one Schoombee, who related to him breathlessly how he had taken two steps out of his home that morning when his eyes had started out of their sockets at the sight of massive paw prints just outside his bedroom window. His wife was so nervous that she had barricaded herself in the house. The Principal

25

was a radio listener and so he was aware of the search and he passed on the information to Marieta at Harnas. She radioed Nic and the team who at that time were patiently tracking the previous night's spoor a good twenty kilometres from Drimiopsis. This message was a lucky break for them because it enabled them to proceed straight to Schoombee's farm thereby saving valuable time. For time was of the essence. The radio broadcasts had also alerted the local hunting fraternity to the presence of the lion and they would also be out looking for him. Nic now decided to employ different tactics. Once one vehicle on the spoor had determined its main direction - and that direction was now to the south, towards Gobabis - the other vehicles went forward several kilometres in that direction and cast about looking to pick up the tracks. Around midday they lost the spoor and spent several fruitless hours walking and driving around before they found it again. When they did, Rudy Britz accompanied by two Bushman trackers took turns to work on it.

In the late afternoon, the prints became so fresh in the rain-dampened soil that the Bushmen refused to work alone and the two of them involved in the tracking started to chatter with unnatural loudness. They had every intention of giving the lion early warning of their approach, so that they would not come upon it suddenly and surprise it. The deliberate noise being made by the two trackers frightened away most of the game animals which would normally have been seen. Even in this commercial farming land, the farmers allowed small herds of kudu or eland to survive so that they could cull them for rations for their labourers, and biltong for themselves, from time to time. There were always, though, the smaller animals, the meerkats and the ground squirrels, to watch them anxiously as they passed by. Now and then, a grey hornbill would fly over with its manta-like wing-beats, emitting its piercing two-tone call. The Bushmen were now plainly terrified and began to 'lose' the spoor with such frequency that Rudy who was a skilled tracker himself, lost his patience with them and sent them back to the vehicle while he continued on his own, picking his way carefully around the formidable clumps of sickle-bush. Presently he came upon yet another fence, and although the prints were now so fresh that he could even see crushed grass stems starting to stand up again in them, he decided that without capture equipment, there was no point in getting any closer. They could begin again early the following day. He turned and started back for his vehicle which was some distance away. Almost immediately he saw something that made his heart skip a beat. There, on top of his own boot prints, were the pugmarks of the lion - following him. The lion had circled back and come up behind him only minutes before.

At this moment, certain thoughts which had been lying undisturbed in the back of Rudy's mind were suddenly projected to the forefront. These included that he was alone and unarmed, that the safety of the bakkie was several hundred metres away and that should he be attacked, he could count upon one certainty - the Bushmen would run away. He stood still, and scanned the surrounding veld with his bush-trained eyes, but could see nothing. No tawny forms or blazing amber eyes. This was no reason to feel secure, for he well knew that a lion can appear - or vanish - like a phantom. With the hair on the back of his neck crawling as negative thoughts crowded in on him, it seemed to take forever to make his way back to the bakkie. "Sunset," he kept thinking, "the worst time for lions." By the time Rudy reached the welcome safety of his bakkie and its two nervously talking occupants, the sun was just an orange watercolour on the distant horizon, and the pointers to the Southern Cross were already twinkling in the darkening sky.

"Nic" he said into his radio, "we are right on top of him now. We catch him tomorrow for sure." From somewhere out in the sombre bush, Nic acknowledged the message with a double click on the handset. The first three days had been painstakingly hardwork with little reward. That was to change on the following day.

Simba was now becoming confused. Although in Bushmanland he had come across human habitation, now whichever way he turned he could not escape it. He had not eaten or drunk water for three days and had travelled over one hundred kilometres during that time. Even his great natural strength and stamina were being taxed. He spent the long night wandering aimlessly first this way then that, searching for prey and water. But there was nothing for him in this prey-desert. The jackals called mockingly. All around him the rufous-cheeked nightjars hiccupped and purred. At least they could still purr. He had long ago forgotten the feeling of deep contentment that allowed him to make that sound. He was still padding along stoically when there was a barely perceptible lightening of the veld. Daylight came creeping back, separating the individual trees and bushes from each other and pouring the colour back in so that the foliage could turn green and become distinct from the grey, fissured branches that supported it. The air was cool and crisp, and at first the sky was still overcast. Then the sun finally broke through the ragged gaps in the mottled patchwork of cloud, sending its cheerful beams slanting across his vision and filling it with vivid colour. The world became alive with birdsong, as if every living bird felt an irrepressible urge to celebrate its survival of the dark dangerous night. Simba found a suitable refuge in some thick grass on the side of a small kopjie (rocky hill) where he could lie down to lick his paws and rest. Even here the poor hunted creature could find no respite, for already the biting flies were landing on him and crawling into his mane. A species of Hippoboscidae that inhabits the Kalahari, these unpleasant insects have evolved a hard carapace which makes them unswattable. Tooth and claw were as helpless against these evolutionary achievements as they were against the technological attainments of the master species. Doomed to endure whatever either chose to inflict upon him, Simba lay down. Soon too his breathing would attract the sand tampans - rapacious little ticks that lurk in the sand - and they would rise in their hordes to the surface of the soil to attack him. When the vestiges of cloud had lost their battle with the sun the last remaining Bushmanland lion lay on the Omaheke sand, the helpless victim of Mankind and the voracious insects that feasted on his blood under the adamantine brilliance of the diamond sky.

At first light on Thursday, Nic and the team started to follow the trail down towards the road between Gobabis and Steinhausen, by the dry riverbed. The Black Nossob river is one of those ribbons of dusty depression that cartographers insist upon tracing in blue on their maps to mislead people into believing that there is actually flowing water in this arid land. The pursuers had been on the spoor for only a couple of hours, when they came across a certain Mr. Kok, who lived near the Steinhausen road. He and his young son had been on their way to town that morning by donkey-cart when they had noticed, to their horror, fresh lion tracks on the sandy road.

Mr. Kok was not a sophisticated man but the sight of the great pugmarks made him realize that there were things that he knew and also things that he remembered. What he knew very well was that lions eat donkeys and, from time to time, their masters too. What he remembered was that it was not as important to go to town that day as he had previously believed. Armed with this fresh realization, he had wrenched his donkeys around and lashed them into a hasty return home. When he saw Nic's pick-up truck approaching, he was very quick to stop it, and tell Nic about the lion tracks. And when Nic asked him if he could be shown the tracks, Mr. Kok forgot about his donkeys and both he and his young son sprang into the back of Nic's bakkie with an alacrity which surprised them all. "Very obliging people" thought Nic, as he drove off for the start of a ride that Mr. Kok and his son would rather, but never would, forget.

Pursuing the indefatigable animal once more, Nic and Rudy noticed that there was now a difference. It was as if the lion had lost his sense of direction. The tracks led this way and that without any clear purpose. The main problem up to now in the follow-up had been the number of fences. Even in Namibia where the average farm is five thousand hectares in extent, the lion had covered such enormous distances that he kept crossing fence lines. Then the team would either have to loosen the tying wires and droppers, lay the fence down, drive over and then repair it, or else one vehicle would have to drive around the camp to try to pick up where Simba had gone out. It was frustrating, tedious work. Hour after hour, on and on went the trail, winding between the stunted sickle bushes and the wag-'n-bietjie thorns, until the tiring pursuers had pawprints branded in their minds. Time dragged on. Morning had been paid for and discarded and it was well into the afternoon when the wandering spoor led into a camp close to the Gobabis road. Nic realised with a start that he had passed the same small kopjie twice, and that the lion was deliberately circling so that he could use the higher ground as a vantage point. Concealed in the rocks and thick grass of the broken hillside he would have a clear, raised view across the open vlei. If he had returned to this spot twice already, Nic had a hunch that he might do so again. Leaving Rudy to continue on the tracks, Nic found some cover and switched off both the engine and his radio. Admonishing to silence the Koks, who were still unsuspecting passengers in the open back of the truck, Nic lay in wait. The minutes ticked past. Time and again he brushed the maddening flies away from his face. From time to time a lower droning tone distinguished a biting fly, such as attacked Simba, from the nuisance and face flies, and Nic had to be alert to trap it with his fingers and then twist off the head. If he ignored it and it bit him, there would be an uncomfortable hard lump there for a day or two.

Just as he was beginning to think that he might have miscalculated, the elder Kok leant over from the back and whispered quietly into his ear, "Look at that horse over there." As Nic's eyes followed the pointing finger, the image of a large lion sitting up in the grass not thirty metres away and looking straight at him flashed full into his gaze. For an instant, they made eye contact. He was big - big enough for Kok to think he was a horse. The watchful, intelligent face was framed by a small mane of golden-brown hair. Then the magnificent big cat turned, and bounded away through the tree-veld. There was no time for Nic to think and even today he cannot explain why he reacted as he did. He started his engine, slammed the pick-up into gear, and stood on the accelerator. The powerful motor spun the wheels, and in no time, Nic was doing eighty kilometres an hour through the bush, smashing down small trees and crushing the bushes under him. His radio microphone had dropped down and draped itself around the steering wheel so that every turn tangled up the lead more and more. And for no explicable reason, he pressed the hooter. The terrified Mr.Kok and his child hung on for dear life to the back of the jolting, bucking truck, as Nic tore through the bundu after the elusive lion. Mr. Kok and his son were at this time in a state of mortal terror. It was not the reckless speed with its attendant risks of hitting concealed rocks or antbear holes that accounted entirely for their unhappy frame of mind. After all, when one came face to face with a lion a certain speed of movement could be expected. Mr. Kok would have approved of the speed, but not the direction. From his point of view they should be crashing away in the opposite direction to that taken by the lion. Any fool knew that. This man was undoubtedly mad. Kok and his son were prisoners in a runaway truck being driven by a lunatic who was trying to catch a man-eating beast.

Nico and Rudy, following up on the lion's spoor, were suddenly confronted with Nic's pick-up, hooter blaring, barrelling past them with the two frightened faces, wide-eyed, in the back. Simba flashed past a mere twenty yards away yet, such is a lion's camouflage, that they never saw him. Surprised at the unforeseen turn of events, and determined not to be left out of Nic's game, they swung around to follow and ran straight into an antbear hole where they stuck fast.

Nic meanwhile carried on racing after the lion, mowing down trees and bushes with the bull-bars. The discordant and continuous chorus of screams from the invitees on the back added an interesting cacophonic dimension to the roar of the engine and the whining of the transmission which was punctuated by the staccato splintering of the Terminalia trees. For nearly a kilometre, Nic kept Simba in sight until the chase neared the road fence, where Nic lost him. He stopped and let the motor idle down, mouth dry and hands wet with the excitement of the chase. Now he had time to disentangle his micro-phone lead, and radio the others, who were busy digging themselves out of the sand. He also had time to say some reassuring words to the Koks who were by now near comatose with sustained fright. The most welcome and reassuring words of all for them was that it was too late in the afternoon to continue the chase, and that it was time for them to be taken home. And it was too late to follow the lion any further that day. Already the sun was merely a molten orb in the west and by the time Nic had found Nico and Rudy, night had fallen and the lights of Gobabis were glittering on the southern horizon.

Nic dropped off the Koks at their home and then he drove the short distance to Gobabis where he had a house. Rudy and Nico also slept that night in town. At last he had caught up with his lion. Now all he had to do was to catch him. That night Nic could dream only of a splendid, awe-inspiring lion with a golden-brown mane. His companions could see nothing but endless paw prints in the sand.

For all that Simba lacked in rest, food and water, he had the indomitable heart of his kind and the untamed spirit of Africa. He was the living epitome of the poet's adage to "go not gently into that good night, but rage, rage against the dying of the light." When the comforting mantle of night had fallen and rendered his pursuers blind whereas he, with his marvellous night vision, was free to go where he chose, he turned east again and padded silently away. He had travelled nearly one hundred and fifty kilometres in just four days. Presently he came to a cattle fence and though he looked over it and could have cleared it with one leap, he chose to dig and tunnel his way under. Pulling the soft sand out with his great forepaws, and scattering it through his legs, he had soon opened a furrow large enough to pull his lithe body through. Then he crossed the road whose pale sand lay khaki in the diffuse light of the half-moon, and dug under the fence on the other side, which gave him access to a wide open piece of low grassland dotted with large trees, almost like a park. The unusual sieve-wire fence under which Simba had just dug gave the clue to where he was. He had entered the game camp of a hunting farm called Ohlsenhagen, a place where wild animals were, in effect, paraded before a paying hunter on land that had been cleared of much of the protective cover, which might have hidden them from the heavy bullets that would smash the life out of them. In his interminable quest for sanctuary Simba could not have chosen a worse place to lie up for the next day.

Friday dawned briskly and urgently, and the capture team was up and about at first light. There was a ribbon of wispy clouds on the eastern horizon, which the morning sun was daubing with molten platinum. The week-long efforts by Harnas to find suitable capture equipment had been partially successful. A farm called 'Welkom', on the road to Buitepos, had a strong steel cage that would hold a lion, and Rudy went off in his diesel bakkie to fetch it as soon as it was light enough for them to see. Also, a local game rancher, a Mr. Coetzee, had some darting equipment and a friend, Sabie van der Spuy, who worked at a local garage, was prepared to perform the darting operation. Unfortunately there was no tranquillizer, nor was any available in Gobabis. All that could be obtained from Windhoek was some muscle relaxant, and there was only enough of that to prepare two darts. Nic could have obtained tranquillizer from Dr. Hartman in Otjiwarongo, but that would have meant postponing the capture attempt for another day. He had seen how far this lion could move in one night. They would just have to make do with what they had. Armed with a borrowed steel cage and two feeble darts containing a muscle relaxant of unknown potency, they set off to catch a wild lion. Nic and Nico made straight for the spot where they had lost the lion on the previous day. Soon after they drove off the tarmac onto the dirt road that leads back to Harnas, Nic spotted fresh earth under the roadside fence, and again instinct made them stop to examine it. Sure enough, they found Simba's diggings and followed his prints across the road and into the Ohlsenhagen game camp. This camp had been partly cleared of bushes and small trees to make hunting easier, but the larger camelthorns and yellowwoods had been left to add character to it. The 'park' was several hundred hectares in area. While Nico started to drive around the perimeter to check if the lion was still in the camp, Nic drove up to the farmstead to speak to the owner. That gentle-man, bemused by the news that there was a wild lion in his hunting camp, weighed up the situation quickly and decided that he had pressing business in Gobabis which would require his attention for most of the day, and he left Nic to it. Nic drove around the eastern and southern border fence line to check for spoor, and was encouraged to see that those fences, though not high, were supported by one strand of electric wire that would shock any animal trying to burrow its way out. He made a mental note of this, knowing that it could prove useful later. After they had searched the perimeter carefully and established that there was no spoor coming out they knew that Simba was still inside. Although the 'park' was wide open with only short grass, they could see nothing even when standing on top of their vehicles to get some elevation. Such is a lion's camouflage that an animal large enough to be mistaken for a horse may disappear in grass only half a metre high.

It was at this crucial time that Nic received some unwelcome visitors and was made to realize again how urgent it was that he capture the lion without delay. Up the entrance road into Ohlsenhagen and in to the very camp where Simba was playing his grim game of hide and seek, rolled a heavy Land Cruiser, painted a dull green. Nic knew very well to whom the vehicle belonged - one of the local hunting brigade - and he sped over to intercept it. Inside were four men, all of them nursing large-calibre hunting rifles. "I heard you was looking for a lion," the driver told Nic. Those radio broadcasts were a double-edged advert, it seemed. Or was it the local grapevine? Whatever, here was a professional hunter, a man who makes his living by killing Nature's children, and he was here on business. "Have you found him?" Nic thought quickly. The man was quite capable of tagging along unwanted until his target was found. "Ja, ja," he answered. "We found his spoor on the other side of the road." He gave careful directions so that the hunter would find the previous day's tracks and watched him drive quickly away, crashing through the gears.

Later that morning Nic was joined by Rudy, Mr. Coetzee, Van der Spuy and a friend. He told them about the hunters and how he had sent them on a

wild goose chase. They started tracking with renewed urgency. How much time would be bought by the false trail which Nic had given the killers was anybody's guess. Simba managed to evade them until mid-afternoon. Nico had followed some fresh tracks into an area so devoid of cover that he felt confident that the lion could not possibly be there. So he brought the vehicle to a halt and opened his door to get out and urinate. The Bushman on the back did the same thing, while Nic's younger son Schalk, who had taken the day off from school to join the search, walked around to the front of the bakkie to have a closer look at the spoor. He had taken only two or three steps forward, when there was an electrifying roar that cut off the urine in mid-flow and loosened the bowels of the Bushman, much to everyone's amusement later. Simba rose from behind the tuft of grass where he had been crouching. His back legs were splayed out and coiled, ready to spring. The front left paw was held up, claws extended, in the position of a boxer about to deliver a left hook. The ears were flattened and the handsome face was creased into a snarl.

The fangs gleamed strong and white from the open jaws of death, but it was the eyes that held Schalk transfixed. The unblinking yellow eyes fairly blazed with intense hatred. For a second or two that seemed like hours to him, the schoolboy stood at the mercy of the harried lion. One spring, one blow or one bite. The warning could not have been more clearly delivered - "leave me alone or else!" Then he was away and the peril was gone. Nico grabbed at the radio with trembling fingers.

For hours they tried to corner him but he managed to elude them every time. The plan was to trap him with the three vehicles against the electric fence long enough to get a dart into him, but he was too agile for them and whenever he sensed that he was trapped, he would double back between the pursuing vehicles, forcing them to turn around and try to round him up again. Later and later into the afternoon went the chase until Nic began to fear that he would be cheated by nightfall yet again. To make matters worse, mechanical problems were starting to occur. The prolific seeds of the Kalahari grasses may be a natural bounty on which most of the ecosystem survives but they have a dismal record for choking up motor car radiators, causing the engines to overheat. Rudy Britz's blue bakkie was worst hit by this problem and often a promising roundup of the lion failed because Rudy had had to switch off his boiling engine.

It should be mentioned that the fence which caused Simba to double back each time was not high and could have been jumped with the greatest of ease. Stories abound of lions surmounting ten-foot high stock fences and springing over them again carrying a heavy ox. These stories may be apocryphal or Simba may have been different from other lions. Certainly, lions are like humans in that their temperament varies one from another. Whatever the reason, Simba steadfastly refused to jump over a fence where he could have done so with ease. But the days and months of being hunted were taking their toll on him and finally the last surviving lion from Bushmanland turned to face his tormentors. He mock-charged Rudy's bakkie - Schalk winding up the window on his side of the vehicle as fast as he could - and then went to ground inside a thicket about ten paces across. There the chase came to an end, with the splendid golden-maned lion at bay, surrounded by three vehicles in a triangle. He had chosen a wag-'n-bietjie (buffalo thorn) tree surrounded by a clump of thick camphor bushes, which the Namibians call Vaalbos. Rudy drove slowly around the bushes, looking for an opening through which the dart could be fired. On the back of his bakkie was the steel cage intended for Simba, but inside the cage was the enterprising Van der Spuy (who worked at the local garage) with his dart gun and the two precious darts. Surely no lion capture has ever been attempted by such unconventional methods. Several times, Simba, mane erect, exploded out at Rudi in a mock-charge, beating the ground with his great forepaws and making a fearsome noise, but Rudy continued to drive around, looking for his chance. At last he found it, a clear view of the crouching back legs. Van der Spuy was no more than five metres away. With shaking hands he prepared his first dart, loaded it, aimed and fired. "What happened, what happened?" called Nic into his radio, dying to know if the dart had gone home. "No good," replied Rudy in a low voice. The dart had struck the lion's back and ricocheted off into the bushes. While everyone held their breath and prayed, Van der Spuy, his teeth chattering in his head, loaded the last dart, and fired. This dart struck Simba high on the back leg - and promptly fell out. Rudy knew from his experience over the years at Harnas that the lion would probably charge in earnest once he felt the sting of the dart. But Simba's response was so quick that it was all over before anyone could really believe what had happened. In one fluid movement, the enraged lion sprang at the bakkie - Van der Spuy cowering in his cage - and crashed into the front left door pillar, which buckled. Then he sank his teeth into the front left fender before springing back to his thorn tree and crouching down again. It was all over in two or three seconds.

"What happened, what happened?" Nic's voice again on the radio. "Ja," replied Rudy, "The dart hit him. But it fell out again. I don't know if the muti went in."

There was nothing to do but wait. Fifteen to twenty minutes, the Vet had advised. Any attempt to manhandle such a fierce and powerful animal would have been suicidal. There were no more darts. So they waited, desperately looking for signs that the drug was taking effect. And while they waited, daylight was ebbing away. No one was quite sure how to tell whether the muscle relaxant was working or how long the effect would last if it was. They discussed what to do over the radios. Rudy's suggestion that Nic should reverse his large pick-up truck into the thicket to see if this would provoke a charge caused yells of disagreement from those on the open back of it. It was decided that Rudy should perform this manoeuvre himself, because van der Spuy had the protection of the steel box-cage. As for Rudy in the flimsy cab of the little bakkie, he could look after himself. Sticking his neck out - in every sense of the expression - of the open window, Rudy reversed his vehicle into the bushes, with Van der Spuy whispering instructions into his hand held radio. "Go back.....keep going.....a little left...no my left.....alright your left....other left .... slowly...stoooop. STOP!" It seemed that their communications were at fault, because Rudy contrived to reverse so close to the recumbent lion that it was able to clamp its teeth onto the cage, which was jutting out of the back of the bakkie. "Too far, too far," was the urgent message from Van der Spuy. Simba's limbs might have been paralysed, but his jaw muscles were working just fine.

At this critical and highly-charged moment, Rudy's diesel bakkie, whose engine had been boiling like a tea kettle for some time, stalled, and refused to start again. "Nya...nya...nya...nya...," went the motor while Rudy grimly tested the integrity of the starter.

"Nya...nya...nya............nya............nya". The starter began to show the strain and to turn the engine slower and slower. So there sat the rescuers with a semi-paralysed lion attached by his teeth to a cage containing the man who worked at the local garage, on a stalled motor vehicle. Then there was a loud backfire that made everyone - nerves already strained - jump, and a cloud of blue-black smoke preceded the blessed sound of the engine running again. "The hell with it," thought Rudy, and drove steadily forward, pulling Simba out of the thicket by the lion's teeth. He pressed the transmit button and called Nic. "It's working. His legs are weak. Bring your truck quick."

Nic reversed his Ford towards Simba, who by now had released his grip on the cage. There was more than a little anxiety and vociferous protest from his exposed passengers as Nic propelled them towards the angry lion. But when the tailgate was positioned over the grumbling, fulminating animal, the thick canvas tarpaulin could be spread out and lowered over him. Someone suggested that four men stand on the corners of the canvas to hold it down, a suggestion that was rejected out of hand. Once his head had been covered with the tarpaulin, Simba became more tractable and Rudy was able to tie his forepaws together with thick rope, and attach his back legs to another. The steel cage was then lifted down and placed behind the thundering mound of canvas that was shoved and dragged backwards into the cage. They had done it, but just in time, for only two minutes after they had heaved the weighty cage and its royal occupant onto Nic's brown pick-up, Simba stood up groggily and threw himself against the bars with such force that the whole vehicle rocked from side to side. "Hell, he could make a noise, that lion," observed Nic later. "I never knew such an angry one. He really hated people."

The triumphant team made their way back to Harnas with their prize. Nic struggled to control the vehicle, for every time they passed anyone on the road the mere sight of a human being would provoke Simba to hurl himself about, and the vehicle would rock precariously and swerve all over the road. It was dark by the time they got back to Harnas. There they had built a solid brick structure with steel bars, a sanctum just right for this occasion. Someone lay on the roof and pulled up the sliding door of the cage after Nic had backed the cage right up to the gate, and seeing a dark refuge available to him, Simba sprang into it. Then they left him alone with water and meat on a floor thickly strewn with hay, so that his stress level could come down. But it never did. The slightest sight of a human being, no matter how far away, would send him into a frenzy of growling and roaring, and attacking the steel bars of his jail. Capture might have robbed Simba of his freedom but it never took from him his indomitable spirit, his hatred for all humanity or his wild untamed character. He remained the noble King of Beasts even under these conditions right up until the day he died.

It was never Harnas' intention to keep Simba in jail. Nic had only wished to save him from the trigger-happy mob and then return him to the wild. But now he discovered that there was no available wilderness. Nic contacted everyone he knew or could think of, looking for a place where Simba could be released. But he found that nobody wanted a wild lion. Nic might have been selling leprosy for all the response he received to his letters and telephone calls. An unnatural 'S' shaped scar could be seen on Simba's right rump and Nic passed this information on to the Department of Nature Conservation while pleading in vain for somewhere to release Simba. "Oh, then he is one of Dr. Flip Stander's lions," an official told him matter-of-factly. "Flip was doing some research on lions in Bushmanland and he darted several lions and branded them. Put radio collars on them to study their movements. That sort of thing. Flip is in London now but he'll be back in two months. Talk to him." So Simba had to remain in prison, with Harnas his reluctant gaoler, until the return of the Nature Conservation official who was 'responsible' for the lion.

While Harnas and Simba together awaited the return of Dr. Stander from England, Nic tried to think of different alternatives. He tried introducing Simba to the pride of lions in his large camp, in the hope that Simba would integrate with them, but they rejected the newcomer fiercely. Lion prides will attack and kill any intruding lion or lioness. Then Nic built a large, open-air enclosure for Simba around a Karee tree to give him more freedom in natural surroundings but when they released him into it he flung himself at the fence so angrily that they had to manoeuvre him back into his jail before he broke through and escaped. Nic shrugged his shoulders. All he could do was to feed Simba and make him as comfortable as possible while they waited. How long this unsatisfactory situation might have lasted is hard to say, but Fate intervened to bring it to an unexpected and violent end.

40

Early one morning just before Christmas 1993 the staff at Harnas were rudely awoken by the clamour of a terrible commotion. Nic and Max, the tour guide, were the first to arrive at Simba's sanctum from where the uproar was emanating. They found that they had come upon a battlefield. Simba, mauled and bleeding copiously from several wounds, was under attack by the resident pride. He had retreated into a corner of his cage, trying to protect his back, and was snapping right and left as the feints and rushes came at him. But for all his courage he was one against five and as fast as he parried one attack, another got through and opened up yet another wound. The pride had dug a tunnel under the wire of their enclosure, somehow avoiding or ignoring the strand of high-voltage electricity that was designed to prevent this. Then they had succeeded in breaking open the steel sliding gate, invaded the cage and set upon Simba.

Max, who was Rudy Britz's nephew, was the first to react. He picked up a plastic hosepipe and belaboured the bars, shouting and swearing until by sheer force of personality, he managed to chase the truculent lions out of Simba's cage. As they scrambled back under the wire into their own camp, Max ran forward to shut the open gate quickly, for Simba, full of fight despite his wounds, was trying to follow their retreat and carry the fight back to them. Max slipped as he slammed the gate shut, and his foot slid under the fence into the hole which the lions had dug and became trapped there. To pull his foot out, he had to take a grip on the steel bars and when he did so the furious Simba attacked his fingers, leaving scars which Max bears today with pride.

Wounds made by a lion or any meat-eating predator for that matter, almost always go septic, and once again Axel Hartman had to fly down to Harnas, this time to operate on Simba. Simba was darted and the Vet cleaned out the wounds and sutured them. The deepest wound was on his back and that was already showing signs of infection. During the operation, the lion vomited and Max became afraid that too much tranquillizer had been used. When it was over, Max folded a towel under the lion's great head, and pulled the tongue out to make sure that he did not swallow it. Then he came back every few minutes to check that Simba was all right. Half an hour later, he noticed a peculiar look on the lion's face and called the Vet. But it was too late. Simba was dead. All the efforts to save him had come to nought. Poor Simba. After all the suffering which he endured looking for his own kind, the Fates ordained that when he finally did meet some, that they would kill him.

Whether he died from an overdose of drugs, or from his wounds or from shock or stress does not matter now. All that really matters now is that a magnificent, untamed person has vanished from this world, and the world is a poorer place for it. It also matters that the people who should have been protecting his habitat failed to do so. And it matters most of all, that in the most land-rich country in the world, less than one and a half million people in 800,000 square kilometres of land, there is nowhere for refugees from persecution, like Simba, to live out a normal life in their natural habitat where they must employ their God-given strength and speed. Nobody wants a wild lion.

The Simba affair taught the people at Harnas some valuable lessons. There was a crying need for them to have adequate darting equipment, and they purchased an expensive state-of-the-art dart gun which they have had to use on numerous occasions since then.

Rudy Britz decided that he would take precautions to prevent his bakkie from overheating at critical moments, so he removed the radiator from its normal place and re-located it in the back, behind the cab, where it is safe from grass seeds but now vulnerable to low lying camelthorn branches.

Simba's body was sent to a taxidermist near Windhoek and he now finds himself placed in the dining room at Harnas, with one paw raised in a threatening gesture and a perpetual snarl on his face. This is appropriate for he now shows to mankind the only face that the master species ever showed him - endless aggression.

Chapter two

THE VAN DER MERWE FAMILY

I feel the hand of God here
In everything I see,
In harmony with nature's law
Yet still an anomaly.
For man must live in two worlds
That shall not ever meet,
And though he tries to balance them
These worlds lie at his feet.
And although he is yet shackled to
The routine of his life,
His heart still soars with birds of prey
And wheels in endless flight.

Andrew Mercer

To the west of the Omaheke province where the friendly Terminalia and Acacia trees shelter the sands with cool shade, lies a barren, forbidding gravel desert which stretches through the Khomas Hochland to the Namib itself - surely the driest place on Earth. All creatures who wish to survive in this treeless anvil on which the sun hammers so viciously must pay the price to Nature. Biologists call that price adaptation. Summer air temperatures soar well above 40 degrees Celsius (104 Fahrenheit) and the temperature of the ground reaches 70 degrees Celsius (160 Fahrenheit). Strange things start to happen. Grasses become poisonous; the few stunted bushes which detect a browsing animal not only infuse their leaves with Tannin - a deadly poison - but also release pheromones into the air to warn others of their kind who will at once toxify their own leaves.

The magnificent desert oryx antelope have evolved a sophisticated air conditioning system for cooling the blood that runs to the brain. Other antelope such as the eland store body heat during the day and release it at night. Birds such as the sandgrouse can fly for sixty kilometres, squat in water to wet their sponge-like abdominal feathers and then fly all the way back to their nest to bring water to the chicks. There are beetles which spray pungent organic acids into the faces of their predators, and Parabutus scorpions equipped with stings more potent than the lethal neurotoxin of the mambas and cobras. Most animals simply become nocturnal. All natural creatures must adapt or die and the same applies to humans. Even the religions that come to us out of the deserts of the old world preach an eye for an eye and a hand for a theft. A man who chooses to live out his life in such a land becomes in time a reflection of his surroundings - hard, unforgiving and steeped in Old Testament faith.

There was such a man who lived with his wife in this brutal land. For fifteen long, hard years he and his wife had worked to build up a ranch on a rugged expanse of sand called Tennessee. And for fifteen long, lonely years they had been trying for a child. Finally this Afrikaans farming couple was blessed by the birth of a daughter, whom they named Marieta. This, their only child, was destined to become the rock upon which Harnas Wildlife Sanctuary was founded and the Mother of all the wild people who found refuge there. Her father was the product of his own upbringing and environment, a patriarch who governed his family, his labourers and his farm with a Bible in one hand and a sjambok (whip) in the other. He was not a cruel man, but rather an iron-hard disciplinarian with no time for affection and no tolerance for weakness. Indeed, he was disappointed that his only child was a girl, for he would have preferred a son who could have become his foreman, and help him to run the farm. Knowing that his daughter would inherit the farm and wanting her to be tough

Marieta van der Merwe, the mother of Harnas

enough to run it on her own when he was gone, he treated her as if she were a boy. From an early age, the little girl was expected to learn how to manage the ranch, and he took her with him wherever he went.

In the mornings, Marieta's father would rise, get dressed in his blue overalls and take up his stick. His daughter would also put on her overalls and take up her own little stick. Then they would drive down together to the sheep kraal, and work on the flock, taking off ticks, dosing them and counting them. Mid-morning would find them home for breakfast, after which it was off to the cattle post to do the same with the cattle, and then whatever field or fencing work needed to be done. After lunch, her father usually retired to his office to do his bookwork and Marieta was free to go and swim in the dam with her dogs, or go to her tree-house, or spend some time with her mother. Whining was not allowed. When she was four or five years old, he over-heard her complaining to her mother that she had nothing to do. He made her take a spade and dig a hole in the ground. It was a boiling hot day, and she was weeping and pleading with him as she toiled away. When he felt that the hole was deep enough for her to have learnt the lesson never to complain, he made her fill it in again.

Marieta loved animals from the very beginning and it is easy to understand why this should be so for an only child living on a remote farm. As a baby, the black dog, Lissie, who had been given to her as a birthday gift, slept in her cot with her. The house was full of dogs and when the family travelled to town, the dogs came too, crammed into the car. When the little girl had time to play, her companions were the dogs. Poor Lissie had to learn to climb up to the tree-house, for Marieta used to bully her and bite her until she did. Her mother came home from church one day to find the dogs all seated on chairs in a circle around her daughter, who was reading to them from the Bible. They had all been dressed up in Marieta's parents' clothes, and she received a hiding for reading to dogs from the Bible, which her mother evidently regarded as a blasphemy. If Marieta went off her food her mother found that if she put it on a tray on the floor and fed the dogs at the same time, her daughter would get down and eat because her companions were also eating. At seven years of age, her father sent her to boarding school at Witvlei, about forty-kilometres away, telling her that she would 'get soft' if she remained with her mother.

What a desolate place is Witvlei. A few neglected government houses scattered around a petrol filling station in a wasteland alongside the main tar road between Windhoek and Gobabis. The school building, there was only one, sat and brooded austerely on a bleak, stony hillside. For some odd reason the toilets had been planted a considerable distance away towards the top of the hill where they were used more as a public convenience by the local troops of baboons than by the school children. Wherever there are baboons, there will always be leopards to prey on them. A visit to the toilet was a terrifying thing for a small girl with any sort of imagination.

This was the start of a very unhappy time in Marieta's life, partly because of the bullying which she received from a bigger, older child, one of the neighbour's daughters, and partly because of the severity of the discipline. Hard as it might be for first-world people to believe, the weapon for enforcing discipline at Witvlei School, which had a total of only twelve pupils in all - was a skeer-strop. This consisted of a piece of wood about half a metre long which was nailed to a strip of leather which the teacher held in her hand. The indiscriminate use of such a sadistic instrument on so little a girl is horrifying enough, but if one adds to this the fact that her father approved of the discipline which she received at Witvlei School, then one begins to understand how Marieta could later laugh off injuries received from wild animals which would have traumatised persons who had not had to survive such a tough upbringing.

When the small child had to endure a beating with the skeer-strop, she would often - not unnaturally - wet her pants. One day after such a painful and unhappy occurrence, she was obliged to ask permission to go to the toilets. As the woebegone little Marieta made her way up the lonely mountain side to the toilet block, she was shivering with fear. Timidly, she pushed open the door, and a large baboon who had been exploring the toilets, and defecating all over them,

47

leapt past her with a loud roar, causing the petrified girl to poop in her dungarees. When she had recovered from her fright, she sat in the toilet, crying, until eventually, her teacher arrived to find out what had happened to her. "What have you done here?" demanded the flinty old woman sternly, looking around at the soiled walls. "Please Miss" wailed Marieta, "There was a big baboon and he frightened me, so I mess my pants. Now I can't go back or the other children will laugh at me."

The old lady dragged the miserable, smelly little girl by her hair to a nearby dam, pushed her into the water and made her clean herself up. Then she used some deodorant from her handbag to disguise the olfactory evidence of the mishap, and took the now heavily perfumed child back to class. "At least she never told the other children why I came back in soaking wet clothes," relates Marieta.

Even with the best of intentions it was hard to avoid the beatings. She was given a cooking pot which contained meat, and told to clean it, but was not told what to do with the meat inside, and was too shy to ask. Marieta tipped out the meat and cleaned the pot as she had been told. Then she proffered the shiny clean pot to the teacher. "But…. The meat. I gave you meat!" exclaimed the old lady. The tone was enough to signal the little girl what was coming to her. Instinctively she turned and made a run for it. "Catch her!" ordered the voice of authority, and the other boys and girls gleefully joined in chasing Marieta across the veld until they had captured her and returned her with malicious expectation to the teacher, who was waiting with the skeer strop. Every third weekend, her father would come and fetch her home, and there would be her Lissie, and the other dogs, to greet her. One weekend she refused to be taken back to school and hid away from her parents. "What is the matter?" her mother asked, but Marieta had been taught too well by her father about fighting her own battles and not complaining, and she refused to talk about the bullying and the beating. Her mother had to prise the story out of the other children before she was able to tackle the problem, and the bullying finally came to an end.

Heaven knows that Marieta's mother tried to bring some tenderness into her daughter's life, and would perform little maternal duties like rubbing cream into the child's hands and chapped lips when she came home from school during the cold winters. But the father's influence dominated and when her mother died from an attack of asthma when Marieta was fourteen years of age, that was the end of any softness or warmth. To cap a wretched year, her companion Lissie and all the other dogs died when they were fed poisoned meat by one of their neighbour's labourers. But a portent of the future came in the form of a Vervet monkey that was given to her by some relatives who lived at Upington in South Africa.

Only a year after the death of her mother, her father remarried a widow with five children. Marieta, after being the only child for fifteen years, was suddenly confronted with five step-brothers and sisters. Her step-mother showed favouritism to her own children; when she baked cookies, it was for her children, not Marieta; when she put coins into the socks at Christmas, it was in their socks, not hers. Marieta could not stand them. As for her father, he resolved the disputes between Marieta and her new siblings in his usual harsh and unsympathetic manner. At the first hint of squabbling, he would move the furniture in the kitchen against the walls to form an arena, and make them fight it out. Any child not fighting hard enough would get a klap (blow) from him. The young girl would have to fight it out with fists against boys older than her, under the critical gaze of her only parent. Marieta did not have an easy childhood. By the time she arrived at Gobabis School in standard four, she was tough and rebellious. There she met Nic van der Merwe through her room-mate, who was his girlfriend.

Nic was also an only child who had grown up on a farm. But his friends were the children of the Bushmen who worked on the farm. His early years were spent in the wild and in the company of Bushmen, while his father built up a ranching empire. The elder Nic van der Merwe was a stereotypical cattle baron who had started out as a truck driver and never looked back. The ranches that he lined up in his sights fell like dominoes to him - Nicolsrus,

Hinda, Swakana, Greatrex, Harnas, forty-six thousand hectares (approximately one hundred thousand acres) in all, making him one of the wealthiest landowners in Namibia.

Nic's father never saw a problem that could not be surmounted. When his son reached the age of eight, and refused to go to school without his Bushmen friends, a problem arose. He could not send blacks to a 'white' school since Namibia was in those days administered by apartheid South Africa. He simply bought a house in Gobabis and moved his wife and son into it so that Nic would not have to board. Every morning after breakfast young Nic would assemble his Bushman friends and the little gang would march off to the school gates. Leaving his friends to play outside, Nic would go in for classes. At lunch time he would go out to play with his friends instead of staying inside the school grounds with the other white children. Sometimes, he bunked classes to go and smoke cigarettes with them under the railway bridge, or go to a local policeman's house where he learned to play guitar.

Later on in his school career, Nic's mother and the little Bushmen went back out to Nicolsrus, and he became a boarder in the hostel. Although the rules only permitted boarders to go home every third weekend, Nic would phone his father every weekend. "Please Pa, won't you fetch me this Sunday?" "Now you know that I am not supposed to. Why should I break the rules for you?"

"If you fetch me, I'll give you the black Dairy cow, the one that belongs to me. Ag please, Pa."

"Alright, but if I fetch you, the cow is mine. O.K?"

Then on the Sunday afternoon, his father would give him back the black cow and the pantomine would be repeated with the ownership of the cow being transferred back and forth every weekend.

Neither Nic nor Marieta was bookish and as soon as they could they left school. Marieta went home to help her father run Tennessee and her life settled into a routine of working the farm all week, and spending weekends with Nic in Gobabis. Nic joined the Police Force. Marriage was the next step. Against the odds he succeeded in obtaining the consent of the old patriarch for the hand pof his daughter. Nic and Marieta were married in Gobabis when they were only twenty years old, and set off together to explore married life. Destiny was waiting patiently to lead them to Harnas but the young couple had first to pay some dues to life and experience. Although their parents both ranched large tracts of land, Nic's salary as a fresh constable was pitiful. He had to supplement his meagre income by playing in a band, while Marieta had to take employment as a civilian at Gobabis Police Station.

They tell jokes about salaries in the South African Police Force. One of them goes like this.

A farmer was being bankrupted by a large troop of baboons who were eating all the mealies that he planted. Nothing he tried could stop them and in desperation he called Van der Merwe (Readers must know that all South African jokes involve Van der Merwe just as all English jokes have an Irishman as their butt, and Scandinavians direct their humour at the Norwegians). Anyway, this Van der Merwe agrees for an extortionate sum of money to get rid of the baboons, and he walks unarmed across the veld into the mealie lands, where the onlookers watch as he assembles the baboons in a semi-circle around him. He says something to the baboons, and they all fall about laughing, holding their stomachs and rolling around on the ground. Then he says something else, and now they start to cry, holding on to each other for support as their eyes stream with tears. Then he starts to address them again and this time, the whole troop turns as one, and gallops away over the hills and over the horizon never to be seen again. Van der Merwe returns to claim his fee, and the onlookers beg him to reveal his secret. "What did you tell the baboons?" they asked again and again until at last he capitulates. "Well, first I told them I was a member of the South African Police Force. That made them laugh. So then I told them how much I earned by way of salary, and that made them cry. Finally, I told them I was on a recruitment drive, and that was when they all ran away."

A small salary was not the only threat to matrimonial happiness. Marital meal times were an awful ordeal both for the cook and for her victim. Marieta could string a barbed-wire fence all day, and dose cattle against Pastuerella but she could not cook to save her life. Nic had to suffer one burnt offering after another. Nor could his wife sew or do any other household chores. She had never been domesticated.

Marital bliss was out of the question because of the Alsation dog who shared their bed. For years Nic's dog had slept on his bed and bitten anyone who came into his room. Even Nic's parents. And now here was this young woman who thought that she could not only come into the Master's room but get into his bed too! Lights out time at night was a comic farce for the young Van der Merwe couple. Giggling like a school girl, Marieta would switch off the light, run for the bed and dive under the bedclothes where she was safe. Nic for his part was hanging onto the growling, struggling dog until his wife was safely in bed. A visit to the toilet during the night meant a repeat performance of the giggles, grunts and growls. If Marieta had to run the gauntlet of his dog in those days, she has since repaid Nic with interest. For the last fifteen years, she has mined his path to bed at night with lions, leopards, Cheetah, the cubs of all these species, baby baboons in nappies, porcupines and all manner of wildlife. For three years the young couple occupied a police house in Gobabis. Their first child, Nico, was born there, but it proved impossible for them to look after him properly while they were both working, and Marieta could not afford to give up her job. Nic's parents took the baby out to Nicolsrus and cared for him there. At first, the arrangement seemed to work but after a while, Nic and Marieta became unhappy about seeing their child only at weekends. Destiny which had been waiting patiently for this moment, stepped up and steered them towards Harnas. Against the security of the land itself, Nic borrowed the purchase price from the Land Bank and bought the eight thousand hectare farm from his father.

Harnas was a broad expanse of flat sandveld savanna situated about one hundred kilometres from Gobabis, and bordering Hereroland. With an average rainfall of about four hundred millimetres per annum, and a soil profile of deep Kalahari sand, one would not expect to find the land so densely treed. Indeed it could almost be described as forested with Silver terminalia (yellowwood) and Camelthorn acacias. Herds of Kudu and eland roamed the farm together with a wide variety of smaller game and although he shot for the pot Nic was careful not to over-exploit the wildlife resources. The noisy profusion of wild grasses which grew so rank between the trees were entirely of the sweetveld kind, meaning that they were nutritious and palatable for grazers. With its strong underground reserves of sweet water, Harnas was an ideal ranch for game and cattle. Nic carried on with cattle. Game farming which has become so popular in South Africa nowadays was then in its infancy. The conventional method of exploiting such a farm was to fence it, install cattle handling facilities and water points, stock it with cattle and watch the money flow in. In fact, even while he was in the Police, Nic had been slowly building up a herd of cattle on Harnas. He would go in to the adjoining tribal area (Hereroland) and buy up the tribal cattle which were always in poor condition. Then he would graze them on his father's farm, fatten them up and sell them. The profits were invested in more cows, and so the herd began to grow. Taking back Nico from Nic's parents, they moved on to Harnas and started cattle farming in earnest.

Their dwelling was a two room brick hut with a covered verandah, and they slept on the verandah. As money came in, they built on to the house, buying only the bricks and materials and doing most of the building themselves. To help make ends meet, Nic took on the job of managing the cattle for his father on the other five ranches. What with working for his father, developing his own farm and extending a house, life was hard but it was also exhilarating and they were happy. As soon as she arrived at Harnas, Marieta started to gather animals around her. At the time of her marriage, she owned a number of dogs and cats, and a tortoise, Nicodemus, who is still with her today. Nic's father bought them a Mercedes Benz car for a wedding present, but it was a gift horse whose mouth Marieta looked into, for a sedan car could not accommodate all her pets, and she eventually prevailed upon Nic to sell the car and buy a bakkie (pick-up truck).

All the love and affection bottled up inside her by a hard, loveless upbringing, was poured into her animals and she would not leave them. Everywhere she went, they went too. Her passion for animals, as well as a rancorous rebellious spirit, meant that she was a natural crusader for animal rights. If she even heard a rumour that there was, for example, a monkey being ill-treated by its owners, she would borrow the car and drive there herself. The confrontations generally went something like this: "What do you want?"

"I want your monkey."

"What? It belongs to me. Why should I give it to you?"

"Because I hear you have been treating it badly."

"So what? It is none of your business. Go away."

How often the slim young woman with her spectacles must have been underestimated in these encounters. And how formidable she proved to be.

"My husband is a Policeman. Ill-treating any animal is a criminal offence. You want to give me the animal or must I come back now with some Policemen?" Her threats to involve her 'husband in the Police' seldom failed to win the argument, and the determined slip of a woman would march resolutely out of the home clutching the poor monkey who would find that it had fallen with its bum in the butter from the moment that it was taken into her tender care.

"You can't do that," Nic would complain when the story got back to him.

"You are embarrassing me. It is against the law."

But Marieta was utterly unmoved by his complaints and the trickle of orphans into Harnas continued unabated. Nic always came around in the end. As orphaned and injured animals started to gather in numbers at Harnas, Nic protested that they did not have the money to go crusading for wild animals, and that they should rather concentrate on building up their herds of cattle and flocks of sheep before wasting money on non-economic animals. To no avail. He might as well have tried to push back the ocean tides.

Meanwhile, Schalk was born - four years after Nico - and eleven months after that, a baby girl who they named Marlize. Marlice as she later insisted on being called, was two months premature, and so small was she, that the family still calls her by the nick-name she acquired at birth - 'Vlooi' (Flea). Schalk and Marlice had the most wonderfully happy and natural childhood imaginable. Marieta did not smother her children, and Nic was always so busy that he was seldom at home during the daytime. The two children were free to do what they chose in a natural wonderland. Inevitably, their companions were the children of the Bushmen who worked for Nic. Endless sun-drenched day after day, they and their Bushman friends would roam around the veld, getting up to mischief and learning the ways of the wild. The Bushmen taught them how to speak their language. From the Bushmen they learnt how to make bows and arrows; how to make the poison for the arrows from the grubs which they dug out of the soil between the tree roots; how to stalk and shoot birds and animals and how to cook them in their skins in ovens made by scooping out the soil and burying the meat with some hot embers. They learnt how to make fires by rubbing together the sticks from the bitter berry bush and how to eat the big yellow and black beetles that cluster around the pollen in early summer, by twisting off the head and slowly and carefully pulling it to drag out the edible innards from the poisonous shell of the thorax and abdomen. How to find and draw water from the huge underground muramba root - a giant, potato-like tuber growing to more than one metre in diameter. How to suck the seeds of the tsama and narra melons; what berries were edible and which were poisonous. They were children of Mother Nature, and students of her too.

At home Nic and Marieta spoke Afrikaans, but Nico was away at school, and Marlice and her brother were seldom at home, preferring to eat mealie pap with the Bushmen at meal times. Nic was obliged to speak Bushman in order to communicate with his own daughter. Schalk picked up enough Afrikaans at home to be able to go to Gobabis Pre-primary School when he was six but it was a measure of Marlice's wildness that when her mother took her to start school at the age of six, she was refused entry. The teacher at the Kindergarten listened to the suntanned waif who could only speak Bushman and shook her head. "Classes are in Afrikaans," she told Marieta. "Your daughter will not understand and then she will fall behind. You must keep her at home for another year and teach her to speak Afrikaans."

Time marches on even - particularly - in Paradise. Summer gave Marlice and her ever-cheerful, carefree companions its crashing thunderstorms and indolent heat before passing them along to the other seasons. There is little or no autumn or spring in the Kalahari. The acacias remain green all year round, husbanding their precious leaves against the endemic droughts. The days just become milder whilst the nights grow colder, until winter is over. Then the summer heat comes blasting back and all the inhabitants run for the shade and start searching the skies anxiously for rainclouds. All too soon the rich, happy communion with Mother Africa was over and it was time for Marlice to go to the kindergarten school in Gobabis. What a shock for someone so wild and free to be ripped away from her little laughing friends, her animals, her secure and happy home, her freedom, and placed suddenly in a world she did not understand, an austere world of rules, where people did not laugh. "No wonder Nico is so serious," she thought, "after so many years in such a world." School was bad enough, but on the bare cement floors of the hostels, the time dragged by slowly while the homesick little girl cried herself miserably to sleep. She befriended a tiny little girl called Salome, someone who at least understood when she tried to share her thoughts and sadness. How she counted the unhappy weekdays until Friday afternoon arrived and Nic or Marieta was there to fetch her home. Then it was two days of gay abandonment in the veld with the little Bushmen and the animals. Sometimes Salome came home with her for weekends and the two of them would run away with the Bushman children, until Sunday afternoon loomed up against their happiness, and it was time for the long, sad drive back to the polished cement floors of the boarding hostel.

Nico and Schalk, like most brothers, were not very considerate and shied away from their pig-tailed little sister. Still, they were at least there, so that she was not totally alone. Marlice gradually adjusted and began to settle down to school life. The wild animal was becoming tame. Sharing with Schalk a natural athleticism, the two of them became good at the rough sport of karate to the point where they toured Europe with the Namibian National team. She and Schalk were Sportswoman and Sportsman of the year for several years running at Gobabis Primary School. Life was not so bad after all.

Each year, at Christmas time the whole family would go down to the resort town of Swakopmund where they owned a house. Nothing unusual in that, except this family included large carnivores, primates and other wild people. Oh, and thirteen Bushmen children once because Marieta thought it would be nice for them to see the sea. Favourite lions and cheetah were never left behind at Harnas. A few baboons for Marieta, and a monkey or two for Marlice, were loaded into cages and put on one of the large cattle trucks that Nic owned, together with a motorcycle for each member of the human family. One part of the family squeezed into a Kombi for the six hundred kilometre drive to Swakopmund, the other trundled down in the truck behind them.

Most days at the coast were spent in the same deliciously carefree way. The motorbike riders would help their passengers to climb on. Schalk had a three-wheeler A.T.V. (trot-bike) so that he could travel with a lion sitting between his legs and resting its paws on the handlebars. Baboons rode pillion-passenger style, clinging to the rider's backs. Marlice's monkeys liked to hang around her neck like a large, hairy scarf. This motley circus of Hell's Angels-meets-Noah's Ark would roar off up the endless beach of the Skeleton coast until they found a suitable spot to picnic and to spend the joyous day fishing and playing with the animals in the cold surf. Passers-by were drawn to them like a magnet at the sight of this extraordinary inter-action of humans and wild people. When someone caught a fish and brought the glistening, silvery catch to the beach, the two lions, Schabu and Elsa, would have to be held back because they would otherwise pounce upon the wiggling sea-creatures and this was not a good idea until the hook could be removed.

The Van der Merwes kept an open house in Swakopmund and there was a constant stream of visitors to see the animals and accept hospitality. And if there were animals that needed to be sheltered from the hectic pace of holiday

Schabu loved the water. Schalk on the left and Marlice in red pants

life, such as a pair of bat-eared foxes with dietary problems, Marieta was on hand to lease the house next door for the duration of the holidays. The frequent trips to the local supermarket were made with typical Harnas panache. Marieta would leave Ouma (Grandmother - her step-mother) in the car to baby-sit the lions. How that sight attracted the photographers! Elsa and Shabu or Mufasa sitting upright in their seats just like humans, accompanied by a little old lady who was chain-smoking in a blasé manner next to them. Life was indeed good. Then it got worse, very suddenly.

Nic had all these years worked for his father. They were large scale producers of beef from their ranches and it made sense to market their own meat direct to the consumer and keep the profit of both the butcher and the middle man. Nic's father decided to buy a Butchery in the coastal resort town of Swakopmund. However, this meant that Nic and the family would have to leave Harnas in the capable hands of Marieta's cousin, Rudy Britz, and go to live there. All three children were plucked out of the school to which they had with such difficulty become accustomed and taken to a place where the Atlantic Ocean borders the Skeleton coast.

Swakopmund is a testament to the human spirit. How the early German colonists could establish a quaint resort town, with its attractive houses and double-pitched roofs, in such a bleak and barren spot on the desolate Skeleton coast, is truly amazing. Molten caramel-coloured sands stretch away for hundreds of miles in every direction except to the West, where the sea-gods confront the burning land with icy Polar water swept up straight from the Antarctic by the Benguella current. Sitting on the fine divide between ice and fire, Swakopmund suffers the worst climate in the region. Every morning fog rolls over the land as the cold sea air is drawn in by the currents of hot air rising over the Namib desert. Sometimes the fog does not clear until mid-afternoon. Then the scorching heat from the desert sun beats down on the dunes and sea-sands, suffocating the inhabitants. One of the early explorers, Charles John Andersson, wrote his impressions during the 1850's, as follows: "When a heavy sea-fog rests on these uncouth and rugged surfaces - and it does so very often - a place fitter to represent the infernal regions could scarcely, in searching the world round, be found. A shudder, almost mounting to fear, came over me when its frightful desolation first suddenly broke upon my view. 'Death,' I exclaimed, 'would be preferable to banishment to such a country.'" Into this depressing world alternating between gloomy fog and oppressive heat came the van der Merwe family to run the butchery business which Nic's father had bought.

Of course, the question reared up what to do with all the orphaned and stray animals that Marieta had so assiduously collected over the early years at Harnas. These included a one-eyed eland, a kudu bull who thought he was a goat and slept in the goat-kraal every night, a large baboon and numerous other smaller animals and birds. Already by 1987, there were twenty large cages behind the house to accommodate Marieta's passion for looking after the poor

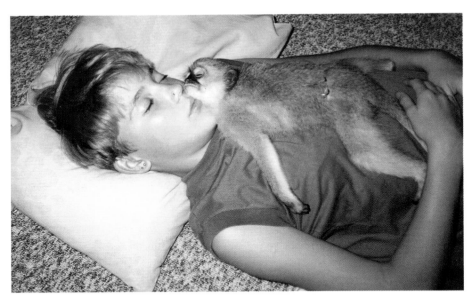

Marlice with her favourite vervet monkey

and infirm wild people of Namibia. Some sacrifices had to be made and Marlice was prevailed upon to give up, with great reluctance on her part, her favourite Vervet monkey. It was left in the care of some family friends. Marieta however, was adamant about her two Cheetah, some of the other baboons and monkeys and a meerkat (suricate) or two, which all went off to Swakopmund by cattle truck. The remaining animals were left with Rudy Britz, who had played such a leading role in the pursuit of Simba. Included in the new butchery business was a large building on a plot of some thirty hectares a few kilometres outside Swakopmund towards Windhoek. This was where the meat was prepared. The plot was situated in the dry bed of the Swakop river and so there were a few tufts of grass and even some large acacia trees to break the featureless dreariness of the desert surroundings. In the river bed Nic fenced off several hectares for Marieta's Cheetah.

There was a house in town where the family lived during the week and from where the children went to school. The new school was a nightmare for Marlice. Just as she was settling down to school life in Gobabis, she was uprooted and thrown into a school in a strange town where everyone spoke German. The school taught in three languages - German, English and Afrikaans. Once again, the ten year old girl had to learn new languages. Again, she was 'the new girl' with all the self-conscious insecurity which that brings. Her new class mates had nothing in common with her. They associated together in secretive little cliques, spoke a foreign tongue and treated her with indifference or cold disdain. How she missed her friend Salome who was now head girl at Gobabis Primary. When back at Harnas for a break she went to see Salome and her other friends, but found to her distress and growing sense of isolation that the two of them were growing apart. The family spent the next two empty, meaningless years divorced from their destiny at Harnas but with legal custody of the competitive and difficult butchery business. It was not a period of contentment or dynamic achievement for any of them, but poor Marlice probably felt the pain worst. Being a child of nature, she was too vulnerable to cruelty - not physical cruelty for she was strong and athletic - but emotional cruelty. She needed the company of animals, laughing friends, the trees and grasses of the sandveld. She needed Harnas. Just before his death in February, 1989, Nic's father had bought a house in Swakopmund to be closer to the family now that his health was failing, but in the event, he only lived there for one month before having to go in to hospital with leukaemia and he died soon after in Pretoria hospital.

Nic as his only child inherited everything, including six ranches totalling forty-six thousand hectares as well as all the cattle and improvements. A newspaper report later in the same year described him as one of the ten wealthiest individuals in the country and he certainly inherited a fortune in capital assets. With such a large and far-flung estate to look after there was no way Nic could continue with the Three Sisters Butchery at Swakopmund. The day after his father's death, he discussed the matter with Marieta and they decided to employ a manageress for the Butcher, and move back to Harnas. Nic eventually closed the business, and moved most of the butchery equipment to Harnas where it is used every day to prepare all the meat for the big cats.

In the meantime, Nic came back to Harnas to pick up the reins dropped by his father, and found himself in a hornet's nest of problems which depressed him greatly and put a strain on everyone. The problem was basically that the whole estate was run down and badly neglected. During the last few years, Nic's father had been too ill to supervise the running of the farms and too proud to ask for help. The cattle were in poor condition, and facilities such as boreholes and pumps to take water to the cattle were not working. Cattle theft was rife and they actually found wild Bushmen living on the farms. These people had to be hunted down on horseback and handed over to the Police. Nic and Marieta threw themselves into the task of getting the farms to run profitably again but it was grinding hard work, and it took its toll on the family. In this pressure-cooker of responsibility, the last thing they needed was a disaster. As the poet Longfellow says, sorrows come not singly or in pairs, but rather like vultures called by other sorrows, until 'the sky is dark with pinions'.

It happened while Marlice, now happily back at High School in Gobabis, was out riding her horse in a patch of veld where the landing strip now lies. Her father was returning to Harnas by aircraft together with Nico, who had attended a Christian school gathering. The Piper Cherokee 180 belonged to Nic who was accompanied by a young professional pilot and instructor, Alwyn Bierman. Nic was seated in the front next to the pilot while Nico was asleep in the back. The Cherokee passed low over Harnas farmstead to alert the ladies that they had arrived and the intention was then to land at Nicolsrus, the adjoining farm, where there was an airstrip. When Marlice saw the plane pass low over her head, and bank to the right, she took off at a canter for home. She had not seen Nico for some weeks and did not want to miss being in the car which she knew would be leaving shortly to fetch him. Above the muted klopping of the horse's hooves in the soft Omaheke sand, she heard the engine stutter, and looked up to see the plane falling, falling, falling, nose first towards the ground.

Meanwhile, Marieta and the pilot's wife had been cutting up meat and making biltong when they heard the sound of the aircraft passing low overhead. They watched as the plane banked right to go towards Nicolsrus. "How beautiful it looks with the afternoon sun on it," remarked Marieta as she watched the plane turn steeply, flutter for a moment, and then dive straight towards the ground. The pilot's wife was the first to realise what was happening. "They are going to crash," she warned in alarm. Marieta hardly heard her, lost in rapture at the beauty of the soft rays of the afternoon sun glinting off the little white aircraft. "They're crashing," repeated the pilot's wife, now really worried. The aircraft vanished behind the trees, about one kilometre away from them. They clearly heard the thud of the impact and the roar of the exploding fuel. Then before their shocked and disbelieving eyes rose up a mushroom cloud of smoke from the bush. Only now did Marieta realise what had happened.

At first Marlice had thought that the pilot was playing a trick on them by pretending to crash. But then she heard a sound 'like a tin being crumpled,' saw the dust and heard the fuel tank explode. Against the billowing clouds of greeny-black smoke she distinctly saw a wing with a wheel attached to it, cartwheeling over the low thorn bushes. Still hoping vainly that this was not really happening, or alternatively, that Nico and her father would be alright, she kicked the horse into a gallop. The first sight that met her when she arrived home was her brother Schalk. He was screaming uncontrollably. The Bushmen were crying and tearing off pieces of their clothing.

The Kombi, driven by Rudy Britz, was on its way towards the crash and she tried to get into the car herself but her mother, who was also in the vehicle, pushed her out, telling her to stay at the house. In the midst of all the distress and confusion, the young girl waited, believing with every minute that dragged past that she would never see her father or brother again. It was Marieta, her body covered with scratches from the thornveld, who got to the scene first, fully expecting to see her husband and child being burned to death in front of her very eyes while she stood there powerless to save them.

63

The little white plane that only minutes before had looked so proud and pretty as it played with the rays of the afternoon sun, had become a fireball. Fragments of twisted metal were strewn around the veld over a distance of seventy-five metres. Only the tailplane was intact. The fuselage was smashed open and gutted. The left wing had been ripped away, hurling aviation fuel everywhere. Sparks from the skidding, somersaulting wreck had ignited the fuel, and now there was fire everywhere. The grass was on fire, the trees were on fire, and as for the wreck of the aircraft, it was such a furnace of flame and smoke that Marieta, standing only ten metres away, was unable to see if there was anyone still inside what was left of it. Hideous shapes materialized and vanished before her as the writhing, weaving flames played tricks on her straining eyes. Above the crackling roar could be heard the loud bangs from inside the cockpit as the cartridges from two handguns exploded, and misshapen bullets whined and ricocheted about her. The terrific heat from the flames kept her back from the wreckage. There was no reply to her frantic shouts.

The pilot had turned too steeply and the aircraft was too heavily loaded. He had caught it again just before it dived into the ground and managed to bring the nose up but then it was into the trees and ploughing through the sandy veld, spinning and cartwheeling. The left wing was ripped open by trees but, unhappily, not torn off completely. It remained attached to the fuselage by shards of aluminium skin, so that when all the main components of the disintegrating aeroplane had come to rest in a cloud of dust and smoke, the left wing now lay parallel to the fuselage and next to it. The fuel in the ruptured left wing tank detonated with a roar that was heard kilometres away, and, because of the way that the wing was lying, a continuous stream of flame spewed out through the fuselage and into the veld beyond it. The effect was exactly the same as if a flamethrower had been applied to the cockpit from point-blank range. To make matters worse, the wind now blew down onto the wreckage the veld fire started by the crash. Unhurt, the pilot jumped out of the door hatch and bolted. But Nic, who had been dazed by the impact, slumped in his seat and received the full force of the fiery blast. The blaze was so intense that some of the red nylon from the seat covers actually fused onto the face of Nic's wristwatch.

Nico was awakened from a deep sleep by the impact of the crash, and his first clear recollection was being surrounded by flames, and believing he had died and gone to hell. "I remember feeling so bitter towards God," he told Marieta afterwards, "I kept saying to God how could you do this to me - send me to Hell when I have all my life been such a good Christian?" Then he realised he was still alive and in Hell on earth. In the cramped, oven-like cockpit, Nic's dazed body blocked his exit. He was trapped.

Marieta was about to put her head down and run into the crackling flames when she heard a trembling voice call out "Ma!" from behind her and she turned to see Nico standing there. He was barely recognisable as her son. All visible skin had been burned black. When he had ripped off his burning sweatshirt, it had taken off the skin from his arms and hands, and the strips of twisted, blackened skin now hung down from his fingers like tassels. One arm was shrivelled and claw-like. The pain and irritation from his burning head had maddened him to rub and worry at it until the blackened skin had come off in his hands. Tatters of skin and flesh hung from his scorched ears. But at least he was alive and out of the furnace.

They found Nic nearby behind a bush. He was deeply and extensively burned and in a state of shock. All that remained of his clothes were his socks. Virtually his whole body was coal-black. His ears had been burned off. Somehow he and Nico had got each other out. Nic has a sharp recollection of his shoes sliding as they clambered out onto the right wing, because the paint had melted and made it slippery. Had the fuel tank in the right wing blown up, there would have been no escape for anyone.

After what seemed like an age but was probably only minutes, the Kombi arrived back at the house, where Marlice was still waiting and praying. To her joy and relief she saw that Nic and Nico were still alive. She hardly noticed Nico's burns. When he saw her, he grimaced painfully and said in a hoarse whisper, "Hello, Vlooi. Come and give me a hug. I haven't seen you for a long time." Her father was clearly in a bad way and seemed to her to be very scared. He kept mumbling "I'm burning. I'm burning." Marieta could not find the keys to the medicine cupboard - she never can find her keys - and they had to smash open the door with an axe to get at the bandages.

Both men were in great pain, and Rudy wasted no time putting them into the Kombi and setting off for the hospital in Gobabis as fast as the sandy road would allow. The one and a half hour drive was purgatory for the two scorched men. Nico held his charcoaled hands out of the window to catch the cool rushing air and relieve the sensation that they were still on fire. "Blaas, Ma, Blaas," Nico kept imploring Marieta who was obliged to blow onto his burns to try to cool them.

At Gobabis hospital, there was a misunderstanding between doctor and nurse with the result that Nico received a double injection of morphine, which sent him floating away into ecstasy. Telling everyone to keep quiet, he started to pray loudly for God to spare the life of his father. Marlice looked at her father who was lying quietly on the hospital bed. His limbs were swollen and no one could stop the body fluids from running out of his burns and dripping onto the floor below his bed. When the hospital staff used side-cutters to snip off the wedding ring from his tortured fingers, she saw that the knuckles and finger-nails of his left hand had gone.

Their burns were too severe to be treated in a district hospital and they were put into the Mercedes for another long drive to Windhoek Hospital. Nic was ominously quiet and insatiably thirsty. Arrival at Windhoek Hospital brought little relief from the incessant agony and discomfort and Nico kept screaming for another injection just as soon as the effect of the previous pain-killer had worn off. The worst time for both men was when the nurses carried them into a bath of lukewarm water so that the dressings, which were stuck fast to the flesh, could be softened enough to be pulled off. Each day this exercise took place, and each day the screams of both men could be heard all over Windhoek Hospital.

66

As the journey of pain stretched into its second month, Nico began to improve, but Nic's condition deteriorated steadily until Marieta could see that he was at death's door. His blackened body and limbs swelled to twice their normal proportions and the doctors, believing that it was caused by trapped fluids, cut long incisions into his already tormented flesh which had long since gone septic and smelled putrid. The fluids seeping out of his burns dripped down forming pools under his bed, leaving him dehydrated. It was apparent that if he stayed there any longer he would die, and in October he and Nico were flown to Pretoria Hospital in South Africa, where Nic spent two weeks in intensive care. Here the standard of medical care was more first world. Antibiotic powder was sprinkled on the burned areas which were then covered by bandages soaked in Vitamin E oil. An outer wrapping of plastic prevented the oil from leaking away. Sterile conditions were applied; only sterilized water was used for cleaning and visitors were required to wear masks. Both of them responded to the more professional medical care and by the end of the year, Nico was out of hospital and Nic was out of danger.

Ten years later the skin on the left side of Nic's face and his left arm is taut and stretched with a curious marbled appearance, eloquent testimony to a very narrow escape from an ugly death. After he had recovered from his dreadful ordeal, Nico, now missing the tip of one of his left-hand fingers, went off to University at Stellenbosch, near Cape Town, to study for a B.Sc. degree. Nowadays, the puckered and discoloured skin on his arms and legs are the obvious scars of this close encounter with death. Less obvious, but just as real, are the mental scars, the nightmares and the reluctance to think, or talk about, the accident.

When the Cherokee struck the ground at Harnas, the impact spread out far beyond the crash site. Although the aircraft itself had been insured, the enormous burden of the medical bills fell upon Harnas like an avalanche. Until now there had not been any real financial stringency since the days that Nic and Marieta were newly-weds. Each of them had inherited large estates, and they were entitled to live extravagantly. They could afford it.

Marieta might not have spent a lot of money on herself but she certainly placed a high value on the lives of her animals. When her caracals (lynxs) fell ill with suspected poisoning she wasted no time in telephoning the Flying Doctor service in Windhoek and arranging for her precious wild children to be airlifted to the Vet in Windhoek. Sadly, they died anyway. And even while Nic was lying at death's door in hospital, the animals continued to flow into Harnas, and the cost of feeding them spiralled. Farmers routinely trapped Cheetah who were preying on their stock and Marieta could never say 'No' to any wildlife in need of care.

In 1995, Harnas went into the tourist business. Economic necessity had played its part in this decision. For some years, the growing number of big cats which were so expensive to feed and required such large camps had forced Nic to start selling off land. Hinda had gone, then Swakana. And still, remorselessly the costs mounted. Yanna Simon, a friend of the family, spoke to them and pointed out how many people sponged off them. Nic and Marieta had kept an open house like the generous country folk that they were, but as the fame of the Harnas Wildlife Sanctuary spread, more and more people came visiting and the stage had been reached where their home was hardly their own any longer, while the visitors ate and drank at Nic's expense. "There is only one answer," Yanna advised. "Go into the tourist industry. Put up chalets and then put the visits on a proper basis, where people can pay to come and see animals. They pay for their own food and drink and Harnas can use the profits to pay for the feeding of the animals." Neither Nic nor Marieta liked the idea, but the debts were beginning to mount, and there seemed to be no other way. By the middle of 1995, the chalets were completed.

After the horrors of the aircraft accident, fairness demanded that the Van der Merwe family be spared more misfortune for a comfortable period of time. Yet life is seldom fair, and disasters continued to arrive, as sudden and destructive as summer hailstorms. On the very day that the new chalets were due to be inspected by Department of Tourism officials so that Harnas could be registered with them for tourism purposes, Marieta made a terrible mistake. How often Life punishes us out of all proportion for the slightest error of judgment. A moment's carelessness at the wheel of a motorcar can cause a lifetime of suffering. A moment of abandonment in the heat of passion can bring an unwanted child into the world and inflict years of hardship and regret. Perhaps our journey through this world should not be called Life but rather Mistakes, for we are judged by them and they determine our every waking second.

The trouble with Marieta is that she loves all her animals. She is a spontaneous, unashamed bunny-hugger. On this occasion Marieta was walking through the small gate behind the cold room and there she caught sight of a warthog sow. She might merely have walked past without incident. But Marieta is Marieta, and this encounter called for a cuddle and a scratch. "Kom varkie, Kom" she cajoled, bending over and approaching the sow with arm outstretched. This was her mistake, for it triggered the arrival of the four horsemen of the Apocalypse in the shape of a madly jealous warthog boar who at that time was sharing the enclosure with the little sow, who, unknown to Marieta, was on heat. The first lady of Harnas did not know what had hit her. Her daily routines and mundane thoughts were rudely shattered by a cruel blow from behind which hurled her several feet off the ground. As she fell back the boar was waiting. Arms and legs flailing wildly, the middle-aged woman was flung up again and again. The spoor later revealed that she was tossed and tumbled through the air for over twenty metres before falling to the ground. Dazed, she looked up to see the boar backing away. Back he went, back further, a full fifteen metres or more. Then he tossed his head and charged. She tried to get to her feet, but her one calf muscle had been severed, leaving her unable to stand. The boar cannoned into her, chopping and slicing viciously with scything movements of his iron-hard head. Then he backed away, threw his head about and went at her again.

A warthog has two large tusks which curve up and out for perhaps ten centimetres - and these are dangerous enough - but less well known are the two lower canines which sharpen themselves on the upper tusks and cut like a knife when used to good effect. Again and again the boar charged, goring and slashing with those dreadful tusks, opening deep wounds in her chest, arms and legs. Then she tried to sit up and grab at his tusks, but presenting her face to him in this manner was another mistake. The sixty kilogram chunk of rock-hard bone and muscle smashed into her face. One tusk entered her mouth, knocked out all of the teeth on the left side and opened her left cheek to the ear. Stunned by the blow Marieta curled up in the sand and resigned herself to death. The boar continued to charge her, carving up her back and buttocks.

How long the murderous attack continued she does not know, but eventually the warthog paused and scented his victim. She lay still in the foetal position, her life blood pulsing out of all the severed arteries and countless lacerations which had been inflicted on her defenceless body. The dust cloud around them started to settle. Apparently believing that she was dead the boar knelt down and started to shovel sand over her with his snout. "Oh God," Marieta remembers thinking as she felt the sand weighing heavier and heavier on her "The twelve o'clock tour will start soon and they won't even see me. They will just walk past a mound of sand."

If Providence had over-exacted retribution for her momentary thoughtlessness it now made amends in a manner that saved Marieta's life. There is no doubt that she would have died from her frightful wounds had they not received immediate attention. It just so happened that a lorry driver from the Roads Department had - most unusually - driven to Harnas in order to collect water to pour onto some road workings. As he parked his lorry behind the sheds, he happened to look towards the house and saw what appeared to him to be a girl playing on a trampoline. When he registered that the bounces were not regular enough to be trampolining, and that the ungainly and inelegant positions of the body as it went up and down behind the wooden wall were not natural, he yelled for help. Eventually a Bushman heard him and called Max, the tour guide. Schalk arrived on the ugly scene just behind Max, and with a feeling of horror they saw Marieta's body half-covered in blood-stained sand. They ran forward to rescue her but had to turn back in order to escape the warthog who was quite prepared to play tag with any number of opponents. So full of fight was he that Schalk had to put several rifle bullets into him before he went down and they could go to Marieta's help. Max lifted her gently in his arms and carried her back to the house. "Max," she whispered weakly through her hideously damaged lips, "I am too heavy for you. Put me down."

"As soon as I get you to the doctor, Tannie (Aunt)," he replied.

Neither he nor Schalk believed at that time that she would survive her injuries, so comprehensively was her body cut up. They stemmed the copious bleeding and dressed her wounds as best they could while waiting for the Medic-Alert aircraft to fly her to Windhoek Hospital. There she spent two weeks in intensive care while her life hung in the balance. She survived the ordeal but her body remains criss-crossed with scars which flare up with infection annually when May comes around. The same phenomenon occurs with some snake bite victims, the doctors told her. Today Marieta dresses in jeans or long trousers to hide the worst scars but she laughs off the whole affair with some deprecating comment such as "That will teach me to get between a man and his woman."

As for the Tourism Inspectors, nobody gave them a thought. They arrived in the midst of the drama, and must have wondered if they had the right address or if they had strayed into someone's private battlefield, with wild beasts all around them and the wounded being airlifted to hospital. It was perhaps a fitting end to such a dreadful day that they refused to issue the Certificate and left, disgruntled and unnoticed.

A day in the life of Harnas

72

Chapter three

A DAY IN THE LIFE OF HARNAS

Each memory fades and then is gone
A small part of you now dies
And when each brittle piece is dead
This house shall feel your cries.
The cold night wind treads like a threat
Blown by wasted years
But the dust around lies undisturbed
Save for your falling tears.

Andrew Mercer

Daybreak in the biological wastelands of the first world is just something that happens with monotonous predictability. The rumble of traffic swells while the victims of modern society surrender themselves as prisoners to some clanking, swaying railway carriage, or to some stinking private mechanical beast that joins with others, coalescing into columns which march on the inner cities through a fog of continuously poisoned air. There the commuters huddle together in unnatural sedentary positions, measuring out their lives in salary cheques. What hideous prolonged sacrifices they make to their Great God Money.

Sunrise in the Kalahari is a magic time. A time when it feels good just to be alive. While the air pulsates to the enthralling symphony of the feathered choir, cool shades of night retreat before the first sunbeams which caress the land with

73

their warm and sensual touch. But even now as the sun emerges from its hiding place below the eastern horizon, the molten orb is gathering its arsenal of death-rays in order to pulverize the earth with another desiccating nine-hour assault. For now, however its greeting is warm and friendly and the natural people take full advantage. The vultures at the top of taller camelthorns spread their wings to better absorb the life-giving warmth, while on the sparsely-tufted ground the diminutive suricates sit bolt upright, fur fluffed out, presenting their bare stomachs to the bright sun.

By 7.00 a.m. the cheerful sunlight is pouring into the cages and striking through the windows at Harnas and this is the time for Nic or Marieta to push the button which activates the siren. This is a chore which is performed not without a little malicious glee especially if Staff or Volunteers are liable to be feeling the effects of some over-indulgence the night before. The siren thus roused utters a long discordant scream which wrestles with the sleeping mind, gets it in a half-Nelson and frog-marches it into the waking world. Weary from long, unbroken work spells, the staff fumble for some old clothes to put on. There is no point in wearing smart clothes; before long they will be soaked in sweat, caked with fine red dust, stained with animal excrement and very likely spattered with blood.

The side gate leading to the labourer's compound creaks open, admitting the garden staff - nine Bushman women. These Kalahari commuters travel to work in the old fashioned way, by putting one foot in front of another. With incessant chatter, laughter and smiling faces they carry their babies on their backs. As they spread out over the vast front lawn at Harnas their gay red and white robes compete with the brilliant tints of Marieta's precious flowers.

"Sleutels. Who has my keys?" calls Marieta from the kitchen door. Her cry bounces back and forth across the empty courtyard before dying a lonely, unanswered death.

"Telephone for Nic," calls out Annelie from the office. Annelie is one of the volunteers who give so much of themselves to, and learn so much from, Harnas. After completing her schooling, Annelie chanced to see a documentary on television about the wonderful work that was being done at Harnas Lion Farm in Namibia. All thoughts of University were deferred indefinitely when Harnas accepted her application to work there. After her first three-month stint, she returned home for a short time for visa purposes. Her mother was horrified at the sight of all the scars and scratches on her daughter's arms and legs, the results of close encounters of a different kind with lion cubs, baboons and other nibble-some beasts. Her brothers mockingly nick-named her 'Leeuwkos' (Lion food).

These volunteers are a very special breed of person. Ever since Harnas began to receive publicity for its work, there has been a steady stream of letters from all over the world from people offering their free services to help care for the animals. Drawn to Harnas like a moth to a candle by their love of wildlife, these young people willingly subject themselves to the rigours of slavish menial work in a strange country for no material reward. If there is any hope at all for the survival of wildlife in Africa, it is that there exists such people. The animals at Harnas would benefit even more from these stalwarts if it were not for the bureaucratic intervention of the Namibian government in the form of a three-month limit on temporary residence permits. In practice this means that just as a volunteer is starting to settle down and become useful at Harnas he or she has to leave the country for a while before returning for another three month stint. The three month limit is supposed to protect employment for local Namibians, but even the offer of normal farm wages is not enough to induce the local unemployed to come and work with wild animals, and Harnas is always short-staffed.

At this time, a slim fair-skinned girl emerges from her room and prepares to get on with her morning chores. This is Christine who, like Annelie, is a volunteer. She comes from Wolfenbuttel in Germany where she recently finished school. She has been at Harnas only one month. It is not enough that she speaks German, French and English, for Marieta requires her to learn Afrikaans too. "Morning, Marieta," she says politely as she passes on her way to collect the dirty food bowls from the monkey and baboon cages.

"Say 'Goie more'," scolds Marieta, "Where are my keys? Do you have them?"

"No, I don't, but I wanted to ask you...."

"Not now. I'm busy."

"But I only...."

"Later!"

"Telephone for Nic!" Annelie again from the office.

"Nic!" yells Marieta, "Telephone. Oh Christine. Where is Max?"

"I think he is checking the fences around the game camp. Can I ask you now about...."

"Not now. Later."

"When later?"

"Much later."

The strain of looking after over two hundred animals including forty big cats, as well as trying to run a guest farm for tourists, is evident. Christine is still trying after four weeks, to be given a coherent list of her duties and where to find what she needs to carry them out.

With her ordered Teutonic background the young girl from Wolfenbuttel places her faith firmly in a written list of duties which will guide her safely through her alien surroundings. Poor Christine! If she lasts long enough to get to know Marieta better, she will laugh at her own naivete. For Marieta, whose mistrust of books surpasses even her mistrust of the English and other 'clever people', would prefer to suffer death by hanging than to sit down and put pen to paper. Sometimes, though, this prejudice can impact upon her animals.

"Oh Marieta." This in a different tone from Christine so that Marieta can tell that she is not to be nagged yet again about the list of duties.

"What?" Suspiciously.

"When I put the tortoises away last night I think one of them was sick."

"Sick? What... I mean, how could you tell?'

"Well its head was hanging out of its shell. And it was not moving."

"Well....alright, show me. Where is it?"

Christine leads Marieta and her furry encumbrances along the flagstone path to the tortoise cage, and points to the unfortunate subject of the enquiry. Marieta kneels down to inspect it closely, adjusting her spectacles and shielding them from little groping fingers.

"This isn't sick. Its dead. Look at that. It died from bloat. How did it get bloat? What feed did you give them yesterday?"

"Lucerne. You told me to."

"Where did you get the lucerne bale? From the shed?"

"No. I cut it from that field over there!"

"What! You fed the tortoises fresh lucerne?"

"Well, nobody told me. You just said lucerne, not cut lucerne bales. How was I supposed to know?"

"Ay-ay-ay! You went to school. Did nobody teach you that fresh Lucerne is poisonous, and has to be cut and dried out for a few days before it is safe to eat?"

"No."

"Well. What did they teach you then?"

"Lots of things. But not that."

"Magtig!" Marieta's contempt for the formal education system suffers another shot of venom. "Well, you better bury this before it stinks us out. And don't forget to count the tortoises out and back in tonight."

"Every day you tell me to count the tortoises. Why? Thirty-two or thirty-four. What difference does it make?"

Marieta removes her spectacles and looks at the girl in mute astonishment. Finally.

"Don't you know?"

"No. You tell me."

"Because the Bushmen steal them and eat them. Did they not teach you that at school either?"

"No. Lots of other things. But not that either."

Nic emerges from the house, muttering, and rushes across the courtyard to Annelie's office. Nic is always rushing and muttering. After answering his phone call, he grabs the radio microphone and presses the transmit button. "Max, come in!" Sharply. No reply. "Max, Max, come in." Louder and sharper. "Ja, Oom." (Yes, Uncle) Max's voice.

"Waar is jy?"

"Checking the fences. The power went off last night and I see where Cheetah have dug out of their camp." Nic purses his lips, and shakes his head. It never rains but it pours.

"How many?"

"I see the spoor of two."

"O.K. I'm sending Schalk." Nic goes out of the office and sees Marieta at the kitchen door, festooned with baboon babies. "Marieta." Curtly. "Where is Schalk?"

"Sleutels. Do you have my keys?"

"No. Where is Schalk?"

"I don't know." She throws her head back and yells. "Christine!"

"Yes." A muffled reply from the depth of the Vervet monkey cages, about fifty metres away. A minute later she appears, her clothes dishevelled and her face and arms streaked with dirt. "Where is Schalk? Do you have my keys?"

"You ask me that already. No, I don't have them. I saw Schalk earlier at the shed. He was welding something, I think."

"Call him please."

"Alright. Can I ask you now about…."

"No, later." She turns to Nic. "What has happened?"

"That was my contact from Hereroland on the phone. He says they have captured two wild dogs, a brown hyena, and a Vaalboskat (wild cat). It is two days now. I must get there quick or they will be dead."

"Why don't you send Schalk?"

"You know Schalk does not like these jobs. He says he is too young for the blacks to pay him any respect. Anyway, the power went off again last night and two Cheetah are out. He must catch them before they kill all my goats and sheep."

78

Schalk swings around the corner from the back sheds. With his leonine mane of tousled golden locks, deep chest and broad shoulders, his resemblance to Tarzan is uncanny. He is barefoot, showing enviable contempt for the ubiquitous dubbletjie thorns (Tribulus terristris) whose bright yellow flowers carpet the ground after the first rains of the season. His only contribution to the world of sartorial elegance is a pair of rugby shorts. "What's going on, Pa?" he asks. "Christine says you want me."

"Two Cheetah escape. The power was off again last night. I have to go to Hereroland. Max is there. He can help you."

Nic, always in a rush, fires off orders like a Drill Sergeant.

"Which car should I take, Pa?"

"Take the blue bakkie. I need the long range tank and the HF radio in the Ford." Motor vehicles are not designed for countries where the next fuel station can be five hundred kilometres away. It is common place to see pick-up trucks and bakkies in Namibia which use auxiliary fuel tanks bolted into the load box behind the cab. They usually carry not one but two spare tyres. "And don't finish all the Zolitol. I need some for the animals which I will be fetching." Under Nic's critical supervision, Schalk measures out the tranquillizers and prepares four darts for the escaped Cheetah. Each dart with its perishable chemical contents costs too much for him to make more, even if it leaves him with little margin for error. Nic snatches the remains of the bottle, selects a few syringes and needles and then hurries away towards the car sheds, issuing volleys of commands at all the volunteers and labourers as he passes.

The sounds of Nic's muttering interspersed with shouted commands recedes around the corner towards the garages. After the normal noises of banging doors and the vehicle being started, there is a fresh outburst of jumbled instructions. These are caused by the leopards, Honkwe and Tai Kuli, who lie around the enclosure that surrounds the car sheds. The amount of time required for them to convert themselves from lazy, lounging leopards into fighting furies who roar out of an open gate in order to scrag some unfortunate baboon or Cheetah on the front lawn is about that of a heartbeat. This makes the opening of a gate to allow the truck out, and the hasty closing of it afterwards, a matter of some timing and teamwork, all of which requires Nic, sitting in the safety of his pick-up truck, to deal loudly and impatiently with the hapless Bushmen. They must move with urgency but not too quickly or that can provoke the leopards into undesired activity. Every day the Bushmen at Harnas must walk the tightrope and when one loses his balance, tragedy in so many different forms is lying in wait. Mufasa could testify to that. If only he still could. Eventually Nic manages to extricate his truck from the garage and all enclosures. His old Ford gurgles along easily, but thirstily, as he adjusts his sunglasses and gets comfortable in his seat. For him it is going to be a long, hot and hard day.

"Marieta." Annelie's quiet voice.

"What. Do you have my keys?"

"No. The porcupines are out."

"Bliksem! Who let them out?"

"I don't know. I just saw one of them now by the bat-eared foxes when I was checking their cages. I think they have learnt to open the gate by themselves."

"Christine!"

A distant "Yes" from the monkey cages. She re-appears, sweating and dusty. "The porcupines are out. Please put them back in their cage."

"How?"

"What?"

"How do I put them back?"

"Just chase them back. What do you think?"

"I tried before once. They don't go."

"Must I explain everything? Take a broom and push them back into their cages. Aaiiee!!" The scream at the end of the sentence is caused by a baboon jumping onto her face and stealing her glasses. Marietta seldom finishes a full sentence without some disruption from her mischievous baboon entourage.

"You monster!" She repossesses her glasses from the furry miscreant, and shakes him until he utters his chattering alarm scream, whereupon she cuddles him in her arms and smothers him with kisses.

"Marieta." Annelie's quiet voice again at her elbow.

"What now?"

"The guests have arrived for the morning tour."

"Ay-ay-ay. Where is Max?"

"He and Schalk…."

"Never mind." Marieta wades over to Annelie's office with her baboons clinging tightly to her trouser legs and takes the radio microphone. "Max. Max. Kom binne." Pause.

"Ja, Tannie." (Yes, aunt)

"Wat doen jy?"

"We are getting the Cheetah back. We found them. They have killed five goats and eaten one so their stomachs are full. We have darted one, but the other has run away."

"Your morning tour is here ready for you."

"Ooh! Tannie. I can't leave now. Get Annelie or someone to do it for me." Click. "Max. Max. Max, you jackal. I know you can hear me. I'll donder you when I see you again. Aaugh!" A baboon has jumped from the table on to her hair, jerking her head back. She disentangles her hair from his little fingers, picks up the transmitter microphone which she had dropped and throws back her head to shout. She spends a goodly proportion of each day with her voice in the raised position. "Christine!"

It takes a minute or two for Christine to arrive, sweating profusely and clutching a broom. "I tried to drive them in…." she starts to tell Marieta.

"Leave it. Take the tour."

"What?"

"Take the morning tour."

"Do I have to? Where is Max?"

"Busy."

"Why can't Annelie do it?"

"She is busy in the office. Ow..." The baboon again.

"Oh, alright then. Must I get cleaned up?"

"Quickly."

"Can I ask you now about.....?"

"No....go....hurry."

The morning tour is a leisurely stroll around the cages containing the smaller animals, while the feeding takes place. Baboons, marmosets, monkeys, mongooses, meerkats, tortoises and so on. This part of Harnas is really a little zoo. "This is the crocodile," Christine tells the guests, as she throws a lump of meat to the side of the pool. The three metre saurian, just the tip of its head showing above the green water, appears to take no notice. "He is very clever. He leaves his meat where it lies next to his pool until the crows come down to steal it. Then he catches the crow and eats it. Then he eats his meat too."

The meerkats are in an area which is surrounded by a low concrete wall. "We had to put them here, because the female meerkat is so aggressive. Whenever we try to feed her when she is free she chases us and bites us. Everybody loves the meerkats. Some of you may remember the meerkat from the film 'The Lion King'. They have so much personality. We used to have a lot of meerkats and everyone wants one for a pet because they are so affectionate. If you scratch their tummies they will lie for hours with their eyes closed. But you cannot keep them as pets like a house cat because it is cruel. They cannot be happy on their own. They need their brothers and sisters to play with and they fight all day long with each other. And scratch! They scratch the ground all day with those long front claws to get out the insects and scorpions. When they stand up on their hind legs to look around, they look so cute. But many people in Namibia like to shoot them when they do that because they say it makes an interesting target. Sick, eh? When they go foraging through the bush, they keep in touch with others in the group by making bird-like chirps. And they have a whole language which they all understand. There is so much interaction with other species when they forage. The birds, starlings and drongos, I think, follow them to pick up the insect scraps. For example, if a meerkat digs up an ant's nest the ants will attack him and bite him, so that he cannot eat all the grubs. Then the birds fly down and finish them off. And the birds warn the meerkats if there is a predator around, an eagle or a jackal. Sometimes the birds too can be clever. They wait until a meerkat has opened up a big nest full of ant grubs and then they give a false alarm call to frighten the meerkats away. Then they eat all the grubs."

These are all Max's stories. Christine has not been in Africa long enough to know if they are true or not, but she has heard Max tell them day in and day out and what she lacks in experience she makes up for with intelligence and a retentive memory. They cluster around the cages, these European visitors, fascinated by the little wild creatures therein and hungry to learn more about them. There they stand, aliens from another world, all tarmac and concrete, chrome and glass, a land where natural things have long ago been crushed and stamped out and they are childishly eager to hear the most trivial anecdotes about wild people not much larger than a rat.

Bagheera and Bengu

83

"These are banded mongooses," Christine tells them, pointing to the animals with the unmistakeable alternating dark and light vertical bands in their brown coats. "They look so friendly but they are so fierce. When they were all allowed to run free in the garden, they used to chase the Cheetahs away from their food and then steal it. Ja. Such a small animal and yet it bullies a big Cheetah like that." She points at Bagheera and Bengu who are reclining regally in a pool of shade on the lawn, sublimely unaware that their courage is being called into question. At this moment, two of the commonest and best known of all African carnivores come trotting into view. Two black-backed jackal pups, about three months old and the size of a fox terrier, move with their characteristic brisk trotting gait towards the courtyard. Their honey-coloured eyes swivel to and from the human intruders and the two Cheetah, whose heads have snapped up with interest in the newcomers. "These jackal babies," exclaims Christine. "They are so naughty. They just cause trouble all the time, for everyone. Marieta has to look out for the baboon orphans when these two are around. They tease the Cheetah and then run away. One day Bengu will catch one and teach him a lesson."

There are a number of lynxes (caracal) for the visitors to see. With their sturdy build, exquisite facial markings and long-tufted ears, they are surely amongst the most beautiful cats in the world. Also the most persecuted. They are the Nemesis of Southern African sheep farmers. It is quite usual for a Lynx to kill half a dozen sheep or goats at a time, especially when it is a mother teaching her kittens how to hunt. Some are orphans, or have been trapped. Some of them are tame, having been raised in the kitchen. "This is the tame one," says Christine, throwing pieces of meat into the cage. "He escaped once and was missing for one week. When we found him again he was very thin and Marieta used meat scraps to catch him. He cannot survive by himself in the wild. He needs his mother to teach him."

Meanwhile, Nic's route has taken him through the commercial ranching area north-east of Gobabis, where the yellow-wood sand forest forms a picturesque mantle over the dry flat landscape. A little early rain has brought out the fresh young leaves and already the forest canopy shades the earth with its summer foliage.

An hour of steady driving has brought him to a cattle grid and as the pick-up shudders over the steel bars of the grid, the countryside changes visibly. He is now in Hereroland. A trained eye can pick out at one glance the early warning signs of the presence of tribal farmers. The lovely mantle of trees becomes sparer, and bush encroachment appears in the form of swaarthaaks (blackthorns) and 'trassiebos', thick clumps of impenetrable candelabra acacia.

By midday, Nic's dust cloud has billowed into a Herero population point. The sprawling culture of tin-roofed brick buildings is interspersed with bare ground and thorn scrub all littered with rubbish and adorned by plastic bags that become caught up in the thorn branches where they flutter themselves to ribbons in the wind. The communal cattle, sheep and goats that browse the thorn-protected acacia leaves - overgrazing having long since eliminated any grass cover - are typical of peasant livestock in Africa. They boast a bewildering variety of breeds, shapes and sizes and have in common only their pitiable condition. Here at the garage Nic's contact is waiting to take him to the captured animals. Not knowing how much further it will be, he fills up the long-range tank in the back of his truck, and sets off once more, this time with his guide.

Max and Schalk have returned. At the sight of them, Marieta snatches up the nearest missile, a tomato, and hurls it, but Max is ready and dodges easily. It breaks against a wall, later to be eaten by baboons or washed up by the Bushman cleaning girl. "Max. I'll get you. You ignore me on the radio."
"No Tannie," teases Max, with mock seriousness. "We lose radio contact."
"Lose contact....," Marieta looks for another missile. Max laughs and runs away. "Max wait. Did you get the Cheetah back?"

"Ja, but only one. The other one is free. We have the four dead goats here for the cold room. Do you have the keys?"

"Keys?" Marieta raises her voice, not for the first or last time. "Sleutels," she yells at the top of her voice. "Anyone! My keys!"

"They are on your belt, behind," points out Max, grinning. Sure enough, the baboon child on her back has, in playing with the shiny keys, moved them around to the small of her back where she can neither see nor feel them. She glares at the guilty party who is clinging to her hip and sucking on his dummy He stares innocently up at her with those intent eyes.

"Christine!" Enter Christine from the back garden trailing a broom. "Here are the keys for the cold room. Help Max with the dead goats."

"Alright. Can I ask you now?"

"About what?"

"About my duties. I need to know what I have to do each day. Don't you have a list?"

"A list? No."

"Well, can we have a meeting sometime to discuss it?"

"Yes."

"When?"

"I don't know. Go now."

"Marieta." Annelie at her elbow yet again.

"What now?"

"One of the guests has lost an earring again."

"To the baboon?" Nod. "Smitty?" Nod. "I suppose he has it in his mouth." Nod. "Did you try to get it out?" Annelie holds out her hand to reveal a bleeding finger. "Oh, you people! Put some iodine on that bite. Smitty! Where is that naughty little baboon? Christine!"

A faint "Yes" from behind the bushes of the back garden.

"What are you doing with that broom?"

"You told me to get the porcupines back into their cage. I'm still trying but they run away."

"Leave it for now. Help me find Smitty. He has stolen an earring from one of the guests."

"But you told me to help Max with the goats."

"Oh, another thing, Marieta." Annelie from near the medicine cupboard in the kitchen. "There is no water in the lynx's cage."

"What? What? Max! Max! Why is there no water in the lynx's cage? That is your job." This is serious. It is something which concerns the welfare of the animals. Marieta is liable to turn nasty.

Max sticks his head out of the window of the staff quarters across the court-yard from Marieta's kitchen. "I know, Tannie. But I was busy this morning with the escaped Cheetah. So I radioed Christine and asked her to do it for me."

"Christine?"

"Max just told me to do his duties. He did not say specifically what I should do. That is what I have been trying to find out for weeks, what our duties are."

"Enough. You people will drive me mad. Max go and put water in the lynx's cage. Ouch."

Max puts his head out of the window again.

"Tannie, do you want me to shoot a horse for the afternoon feed or do you want to use the goats which the Cheetah killed this morning?" Marieta pauses for thought, recovering her glasses from the reluctant grasp of a little baboon.

"We have plenty seal meat. It is only Savannah who will not eat it. And the Cheetah. No alright, the goats will be enough. Christine, don't forget to count the tortoises before the Bushmen go off this afternoon. And Christine take the wild dog puppie for a walk."

"Oh, do I have to? I took him yesterday and he bit me very sore when I try to put the leash on him. See here." Christine points to an ugly red wound on her wrist which could really have done with a stitch or two. But if she is hoping for sympathy she is shopping in the wrong supermarket. The rock on which Harnas is founded has a heart of stone insofar as human beings are concerned. If Christine had been an animal and suffered such a cut, Marieta would have whipped her off to the Vet for treatment without any hesitation.

"It's just a scratch." Marieta's voice drips with scorn. "Go and put some iodine on it. And next time keep your hand out of the way of the wild dog. It is your fault if he bites you."

Indistinct murmurings followed by "Where?"

"Where what?"

"Where is the iodine?"

"In the medicine cupboard, where do you expect?" She turns away. "Now leave me alone, all of you. I want some peace and quiet. This isn't Harnas its Malnas (Madness)."

Seeking solace in her garden, Marieta takes up a hosepipe, and slows the day down by watering her flowers. She scans the wide undulating lawns now enjoying a soaking from the somnolent sprayers, each droplet that reaches the baked grass a triumph over evaporation. Under the divine gift of shade provided by the massive camelthorn tree near the swimming pool, she notices a small group of visitors lying on the grass, petting one of the Cheetah. It must be Bagheera, the crippled one. This is why people come to Harnas, to interact with wildlife by meeting them, shaking hands with them and getting to know them, their personalities. Where else in all of Africa can one do such a thing with such a variety of animals? Where else could one pet a Cheetah, cuddle a leopard, scratch a porcupine, and then camp in the veld with a lion? Marieta's frown starts to soften.

For most of the year, Namibia is too hot for any vigorous outdoor exertion in the middle of the day. The heat is too intense, too stunning to contemplate anything more energetic than to lie under the shade of the camelthorn trees by the swimming pool, or in the cool of the chalet. Only two sorts of creatures work tirelessly through the day at Harnas, the flies - including those nasty little Hippoboscidae horseflies referred to in Simba's story, and the overworked staff. For if the morning has not been chaotic enough, the real work begins after lunch, with the cutting up and preparation of the meat for the afternoon feed.

Every day, Marieta cuts up a carcass to feed the many carnivores.
Baboon orphans cling to her back and her foot

Thanks to the Three Sisters Butchery formerly in Swakopmund, there is no shortage of equipment at Harnas. Container fridges, cold rooms, meat saws, it is all there. Every day after lunch, Marieta, the volunteers, and the Bushmen with their wives gather at the butchery. The amount of meat that has to be prepared, cut up and placed into the correct buckets is astonishing. In quantity Harnas consumes more than one large animal - a horse or a cow - every day. Harnas gets meat wherever it can be found, buying horses and cattle from local farmers and Hereros, and even seal meat from the culling exercise at Cape Cross

Annelie and the Bushman women sorting fruit for the baboons and monkeys

north of Swakopmund. The seal meat is very rich and oily and not all the animals will eat it. Those that do benefit from its richness in Vitamin D, and their coats shine.

Outside the back door of the butchery are a number of Bushmen and their wives, all chattering away in their dialect of clicks. They are tiny, slight people - indeed the women are about the size of an average ten-year old European girl. There is a trace of the Orient in their honey-coloured faces and their wide, almond eyes. Even their rock art looks oriental. Are they the descendants of an Eastern race that settled in Africa thousands of years ago - or is the opposite possible, that early man developed in Africa and spread out to the Orient, leaving this gentle race to remain the only evidence of a great, early migration? They are bringing buckets with names on like 'Elsa', 'Schabu', or 'Savannah' to be filled with offal or seal meat. On the long table outside are a line of bins that bear names like 'Meerkats', 'Mongooses' and 'Genets', and Christine and Annelie are up to their elbows in gore cutting meat chunks into small pieces for these. Every afternoon of her life, rain or shine, Marieta stands by the saw and personally butchers a large, bloody carcass. Then she supervises its distribution. This is the engine room of the sanctuary.

Even when working Marieta is never alone. There is one orphan baboon baby asleep, dummy in its mouth, in the folds of the sash around her waist.

Annelie and Christine cutting chunks for the smaller animals

What appears to be Artic boots on her feet turn out at closer examination, to be two more little baboons. Also with dummies in their mouths, they cling tightly to her shins so that when she moves, she has to lift her feet slowly around each other, much as one would walk wearing snow shoes. All her work, all her instructions to the volunteers and Bushmen are continually interrupted by the incessant demands and boisterous play of the orphans. In the wild, baboon children maintain a close relationship with their mothers throughout their lives, and their foster mother gets no more rest from them. Her patience with these cute, demanding and troublesome orphans is quite extraordinary.

Today, the Bushmen have placed the heavy carcass of a large seal on the table of the meat saw, and Marieta braces herself, then pushes it through the thrumming blade, and a four kilogram chunk of dark red, oily meat drops into Schabu's bucket with an unctuous thump. The heavy pails of meat are hauled up onto the back of the blue bakkie, a wreck on wheels whose badly-buckled cab perches lopsidedly on the bent chassis. Max will then drive around to the different camps and enclosures and leave the buckets next to the feeding places ready for the afternoon feed.

"Look at those bliksem jackals," complains Marieta in exasperation as the two little black-backed jackal pups trot away, ignoring the seal meat that she has just put down for them. "If you go to Cape Cross, you will see plenty jackals feeding on the seal there. But my jackals, oh no, they are too proud to eat it. Oh, Christine! When you have cleaned up the butchery take this spare piece of meat and throw it outside the burrowhole of the Brown Hyenas. You know where it is? Under the back shed."

"Yes, I know. I will."

Marieta has washed up and left the butchery to check on the smaller cages and to make sure that they have all been cleaned and swept and have fresh water, when she starts at the sound of a terrifying yell from behind the building. She runs through the passageway next to the garages to see what has happened, and finds Christine, ashen-faced, standing by the gate to the small paddock behind the shed. "What is wrong? What happened?" Christine points a trembling finger in the direction of Savannah, the one-eyed lioness who is sitting on the other side of the gate, head cocked to one side, no doubt also wanting to know what is going on.

"There is a lion." she says with admirable accuracy of species identification.

"Yes. It is Savannah. So what?"

"Well. I took the food through for the hyena as you said, and then I walked into this lion. And I got a fright. l was not expecting it."

"Oh yes. We always put Savannah in this place at feeding time because she will not eat the seal meat, and we must separate her from the rest or they will fight her for her food and knock out the other eye." The young girl straight out from school in Wolfenbuttel, Germany and who has never been close to a lion before, is growing up fast at Harnas.

Meanwhile Nic and his guide have now arrived at the Herero farmhouse where the captured animals should be. The dusty track winds across a dry river bed where an ancient Lister diesel engine is throbbing away. The farmstead lies in a sea of sand, its own private desert created by the relentless overgrazing of the numerous goats and cattle. A graveyard for old iron implements forms a rusting perimeter. Outside the front door of the stark house with its peeling yellow paint and discoloured corrugated iron roof stands a deformed syringa tree pruned rather for fire wood than to create a pleasing shape. Under the little patch of shade cast by its sorry canopy is the owner. Sitting in an incongruous office swivel chair with a rifle lying at his feet, he is dressed in a white safari suit, which contrasts markedly with the dark glasses that shade his eyes. He chews on a chicken bone. The only one seated, he is surrounded by a throng of loafers, loungers, children and relatives, about a dozen in all. The throng moves aside as Nic brings his pick-up to a dusty halt in front of them. He strides purposefully up to the man and the introductions take place in Afrikaans. He asks the price of the animals and they haggle over that for five minutes with each of them trying to suggest that the other is the richer of the two and should

The brutal jaw traps which were used for the capture of the wild dogs

therefore make the greater concessions. Then Nic writes the figure in his notebook to safeguard against any future lapses of memory on what has been agreed and asks to inspect the animals. A portion of the crowd detaches itself from the main body and leads Nic nearby to a scene that would inject murder into the hearts of any animal lover.

The two wild dogs lie chained by the neck on blazing hot sand. They have been lying there for two interminable days and nights. There is no need to ask how they have been caught. The heavy iron jaw traps are lying next to them. Dried blood around the serrated jaws and the smashed and bloody forelegs of the dogs tell graphically of the horrors of capture. Nic checks the dogs. They are still alive, but so weak with shock, loss of blood and dehydration that he ponders whether to take them or to put them out of their suffering. They are too weak to require sedation so the fencing pliers are brought to cut the wire holding the

94

chain around their necks. So tight is the stranglehold of steel that the cutting notches of the pliers cannot reach the wire which is embedded in their swollen necks and has to be twisted off with the tips of the pliers. The traumatised dogs are so far gone that they offer no resistance when Nic bundles their limp bodies into the box cage on his pick-up. Nic now turns to the African wild cat, a tawny miniature lion slightly larger than a domestic cat. Neither its broken and bloody leg, nor the ordeal of being chained by its neck in the baking heat of the back of a derelict truck, has diminished its admirable spirit. Nic has to throw a fertiliser sack over the spitting, hissing little fury before he can inject the sedative and put it into his vehicle.

The brown hyena is another story. Dragged out by a heavy chain wired around its neck from under yet another old wreck of a truck where it had found some shelter from the brutal heat, it struggles, snarling, growling and biting at the chain. But as the jostling posse crowds around the normally shy animal,

The captured wild dogs lying on the hot sand in Hereroland

95

grabbing at the ears in order to subdue it and allow the pliers to unshackle him, mortal terror reaches the point of overload. With an evident conviction that the humans intend now to slaughter him, the hyena stops struggling and utters a thin, high-pitched scream sounding more like a human baby than a fierce-looking wild animal. The onlookers find this greatly amusing and they roar with laughter. Nic compresses his lips and looks grim, while he anaesthetises and loads the poor, terrified beast. When he takes his leave from the man, Nic tells him that he will not pay for the wild dogs if they die. The man, who has not left his seat throughout the entire loading exercise, turns his head, spits out a piece of well-chewed chicken bone, which is swiftly scavenged by two curs, and says brusquely. "Mister, when you load them in your truck, you pay me."

As Nic is driving back to Harnas with his maimed cargo, he has time to consider what to do next. The injured animals need the attention of the vet without delay, so that X-rays can be taken and the necessary operations, to pin and wire up the shattered bones, completed. The situation with the wild dogs is critical. They cannot drink; their dehydration is beyond that now. Their lives depend on how quickly they can be put on a drip. He also has time to consider the wider implications of the rescue. The Department of Nature Conservation in Windhoek has to be informed. In effect he is doing their job for them. The hunters who trap animals would prefer to approach him because he will pay them something whereas the Government Department will pay them nothing. On the other hand Nic is alive to the danger that by paying for trapped animals he is creating a trapping industry. The trick is in the amount of payment; it must be enough to make it worth their while to call him rather than to kill the animals out of hand, but not enough to encourage them to pick up their jaw-traps and go out looking for innocent animals in order to make money. Adjusting the sun visor against the slanting rays of the afternoon sun, he attempts to get in touch with Harnas staff by H.F. Radio but the distance is still too great. "If only," he thinks, "they would use box cages with trapdoors to catch problem animals. If only jaw traps were outlawed."

Back at Harnas, the preparation of the food and its distribution, have been completed. Now, as the volcanic heat of the afternoon sun begins to lose some of its breath-catching ferocity, it is time for Max to guide the afternoon feeding tour. He insists that Christine should accompany him, pointing out that someone has to open the gates to the camps and keep the hungry animals inside while he drives in. But that is not the real reason. Christine is a capable, well-adjusted young lady. Max has taken pity on her and decided to help her. He will teach her to escape from her well-organised and predictable existence. It will not be an easy lesson to learn. Unlike Christine who is wearing shorts, a tee-shirt and sandals, Max's long camouflage trousers offer some protection from sharp claws and clicking ivory teeth. A four-inch military webbing belt supports a silver and ebony bayonet. He wears a Lion's claw pendant, which lies against skin tanned to the colour of copper by constant exposure to the burning African sun. There are no wimpish considerations in Max's life for such things as holes in the ozone layer, skin cancer and other such things that concern ordinary people.

Max knows his animals, and has the scars to prove it. A shock of light brown hair hides a scalp wound from crown to forehead which reminds him that he once got too close to one of the half-grown male lions at feeding time. The stories of his encounters with the big cats at Harnas are written on his arms and hands, the white scars of old wounds and the reddened cuts of recent ones. Max flaunts them. "Look here," he points to the puckered wound between thumb and forefinger. "One of the Cheetah bites me here. His teeth goes right through my hand. And this here, this was Schabu. And up here, another Cheetah. There the big leopard...there Honkwe, the young leopard ....and here, my fingers, that was Simba...."

He takes his tour party, a group of a dozen or so people, most of them from Germany, to the back of the farm house where the cages are. They start with the small animals. There are the tortoises including of course, Nicodemus,

who was a full-grown tortoise when Marieta received him as her first pet at the
age of three. Fifty years later, he has not changed and one wonders how many
years - centuries perhaps - a tortoise can live. They move past the meerkats to
the bat-eared foxes. There were three but now there are only two left. At the
1998 Windhoek Show, some irresponsible mischief makers used wire cutters to
cut a hole into the Harnas exhibit enclosure with the purpose of letting out the
lions and enjoying the pandemonium that this little piece of vandalism would
have caused. Fortunately, the lions did not get out, but one of the bat-eared

foxes did, and is now missing, presumed eaten. Worse, it was an animal which had been adopted, and Marieta had the uncomfortable duty to telephone the irate benefactor and give her the bad news.

Adoption is a device for securing the future of a particular animal and is becoming a popular way to make donations. A visitor who has a special interest in one particular animal may elect to 'adopt' it. Then she usually pays a regular annual sum to meet or contribute to the cost of maintaining that animal. Harnas keeps a separate account for the animal to avoid mingling of funds, while the benefactor receives a Certificate, a photograph and regular reports. Bat-eared foxes are pretty, endearing little carnivores who shelter in underground burrows during the heat of the day. In the cool of the evening they emerge to forage for termites. Like the meerkats, they suffer high mortality from rabies, a disease introduced to Africa by the Europeans.

The spacious walk-through aviary surrounds the visitor with a kaleidoscope of colour and variety and countless small birds flutter and twitter excitedly as their grain and seed is put out for them. Marieta sometimes leaves open the wide double gates allowing the birds to leave the aviary and spend the day flying free before returning to their nesting-boxes for the night. A solitary white-backed vulture with an irreparably damaged wing, hops forward, hungrily fixing Max with his black eyes. A close look at the fierce inky eyes reveals a peculiar method of blinking, more like the contraction of an internal camera shutter than an external lid movement. Harnas has rescued many vultures over the years. The single chicks remain in the nest for at least four months and that makes them vulnerable to nest robbers, who want them for the same reason that some Orientals need Rhino horn. Their large beaks are crushed and dried to a powder and then sold as a love potion, or a cure for impotence. It is surprisingly hard to release these birds from captivity because of their need to be taught by other vultures how to find carrion and to fend for themselves. Harnas has found by bitter experience that if such a bird is simply set free without any proper release procedures it will fly around aimlessly until it dies of hunger.

The tour moves on to the Vervet monkey cages. These poor prisoners are mostly army surplus. During the border campaign when SWAPO was engaged in a guerrilla war against the South African-backed South-West Africa Administration, it became fashionable for the conscripts to acquire monkeys, usually by methods involving trapping or killing the mother. When the soldiers sought to fly back to South Africa with their 'pets' the Namibian Department of Wildlife Conservation was at the airport to confiscate the little animals. After they started to shoot them, Harnas came to hear of the killing, and Nic telephoned the Department. "Please stop shooting the little monkeys," he pleaded, "rather give them to Harnas to care for. They gave us the remaining animals," says Nic with a click of disgust, "because they believe that a captive animal is the same as a dead one."

The tour party now finds itself facing a pair of banded mongooses. Larger and heavier than the social mongoose species, groups of them have been known to chase off jackals and even climb a tree to rescue a pack mate from the talons of an eagle. "No wonder they can kill snakes," says Max as he rolls two eggs into the cage and they watch how the mongooses throw them through their back legs to break them, "they are vicious little creatures. And the eyes, they always strike at the eyes. Just like a vulture." For years Marieta had as many as eighteen of the banded mongooses running unchecked around Harnas. Their numbers gradually dwindled as they used their talent for digging under cage wires to fatal effect when such cages contained lions or leopards. The last remaining pair have been caged for their own protection and that of the visitors.

Through the butchery and behind the garages is a shed, under which a pair of brown hyena have made their burrow. Max gestures imperiously, and Christine has to stagger over to him under the weight of a foul-smelling bucket of offal which he tips onto the ground. "They will get it tonight when they come out," he explains, and relates how they nearly lost one of them recently to the young leopards. The large open area in front of the garages was shared alternatively, leopards by day and hyena at night. One morning, a staff member checked the area to make sure that the hyenas were out and seeing none, he

Max talking to the big male leopard, the father of Honkwe and Tai Kuli

opened the gate and let in the four half-grown leopards from their night cage. Nothing escapes those watchful amethyst eyes, and it was a matter of seconds before they had discovered a brown hyena resting half-hidden behind a bush. In a flash, they were on to the startled animal. Yet again it was time for the Harnas dance - four staff and Bushmen hanging on for dear life to the tails of four fighting-mad leopards, while others helped to shepherd the reprieved hyena back to the safety of his burrow.

The Honey Badger, or Ratel, is Africa's equivalent of the Wolverine. He comes out of his cage showing his teeth and Max obligingly puts out a well-used boot for the formidable little fighter to chew on. "He open his cage door once," Max tells us, "into the lions enclosure. Savannah with the one eye, and the other two lions, they all attack him. To escape, he runs into a small twenty litre steel drum which is lying in his cage. By the time we can pull the lions out and rescue him they have flattened the steel drum so badly we

101

can never use it again. Now look here. These are warthogs. You see how they fall onto their front knees so they can eat with their heads close to the ground. They look cute and you want to go and pet them. But they are hard and dangerous. Everything in Africa is hard and dangerous. Marieta, oh.. a couple of years ago, was nearly killed by one." He proceeds to relate the tale of how he found Marieta after her terrible ordeal with the warthog. "I really thought she was dead, but she is very tough."

Max reaches into a bucket, removing a hefty chunk of dripping meat. He walks slowly up to the adjoining fence. The tourists watch with bated breath. Dropping meat just over it, and then crouching beside it, he calls out, "Kom, Kom!" A piece of a large Karee tree detaches itself, and materialises into a full-grown male leopard which moves silently up to him. Max gabbles endearments in a high-pitched voice, his hand resting on the fence. The leopard responds by dabbing at Max's hand with his big, spotted paw, muttering and growling in a most conversational way. The discussion lasts for a good five minutes before the magnificent big cat gently reaches down between them for the meat and turns to disappear back into his tree. "I tame him," claims Max modestly, "Me. Every morning and every evening I come and talk to him. Takes me six months to get him to come out of his tree. He comes here full-grown so he is wild and mature and just want to kill. Nic fetch him from a hunter who traps him in Omaruru. He tells Nic you fetch him and pay N$2000 or I shoot him."

The next camp is really too small for the two handsome male lions who occupy it. These are Mufasa's brothers, and they have their own tragic story to tell. "AIDS," explains Max, as he throws offal through the hatch. The two huge cats clutch their meat between their front paws as they devour it, snarling threateningly at each other. "These two lions have feline AIDS so we have to keep them separate from the others. They go to the Vet for operation and when they come back they have AIDS. We find out that the Vet operate on a cat with AIDS on the same table before he work on our lions."

The tour party now boards an elderly Land Rover and Max signals the stalwart Christine with a jab of his finger to get the vehicle through the gates of the enclosure where the leopards are lying. It is Christine who must risk the mood of the leopards as she struggles to open the heavy steel gate, and at the same time to avoid touching the live electric wires which will give her such a painful jolt if she does. She executes the procedure nervously but without mishap and runs the deadbolt home with some relief once the vehicle is through. Christine 1, Leopards 0. But the game is not over yet.

Next to be fed are the baboons. Baboons may not be the most important animals at Harnas for the visitors, but the family spends much time with them and Marieta confesses that they are her favourites. Because she treats them like children, Nic gets impatient with her.

"Come on, Marieta," he will say sternly at dinner time while he is trying to eat and fend off three young baboons at the same time. "Put them away. Can't you see how they are worrying me?"

"Don't you like them?" Marieta will ask sweetly.

"Of course I like them. But there is a time and place for everything. Now put them away before I get angry." Later in the evening Marieta will give them to Nic to care for when he goes to bed, and he will tuck them in comfortably around him. There they will lie together, Nic with three or more orphan baboons who are sucking away at their bottles, and all of them watching T.V. An hour or so later when Marieta has completed her late night chores, she will return to her bedroom to find Nic and his foster children fast asleep together, with the T.V. still on.

There is a troop of about twenty baboons, and Marieta keeps the big male separate from the females and young orphans. Recently Harnas acquired a big male baboon whose owner had pulled out his canine teeth, because he was so aggressive. When she returned to Harnas, she placed him in the 'holding cells.' He stared at her with his intent gaze, and let one long hairy arm flop out of the cage, with the hand open. Thinking that this would be a good opportunity to make friends, Marieta reached over to hold his hand. This was a mistake. He seized her hand and pulled it violently through the bars, smashing her head against them and leaving her dazed. The following day he took over Harnas. Two Ovambo men went into his cage armed with a broom to clean it out. Instead of being intimidated by the broom he seized it and pulled the Ovambo who had been holding it, into the wall. Then he grabbed the other terrified worker by the throat and threw him into the fence. As he galloped out of the cage and across the vast expanse of front lawns, the other baboons started to bark and chatter, and the commotion alerted the Bushman women who were weeding the lawn. Seeing an ugly, great baboon bearing down on them, they fled, screaming. One of them paused to pick up her baby, and the baboon took hold of her. Fortunately, he did not bite her, but he picked her up and threw her like a rag doll into the fence of the small baboons' enclosure. Clearing fences, even electrified ones, with the utmost ease, he found himself in the area of the back garden which is used as a crèche, where some of the Bushman children are left while their mothers are working on the lawns. Taking one of the children - a little girl of about two years - by her legs, he literally flayed the ground with her, once, twice, three times before leaving her senseless on the ground. For hours, the family and staff ran that way and this trying to catch him or get away from him. The staff refused to work with such a dangerous animal on the loose, and ran back to hide in their quarters. The pursuit continued through the outer camps, and the baboon had a lucky escape when he scaled the fence of the wild dogs' camp and had to beat a very hasty retreat to avoid being torn to pieces. The game of hide and seek moved to a climax at about seven o'clock in the evening when Nic chased him through the veld in his old brown Ford until close enough to fire a tranquillizer into him. The dart contained 4 c.cs of Xylazine - enough for an adult lion - and that put him to sleep and brought the day's excitement to an end.

Luckily, no one, not even the little girl, suffered any serious injuries.

Marieta does not want to breed more mouths to feed. Max explains that Harnas is looking for a suitable place to release the baboons all together, but they cannot find a place in Namibia where the animals will be safe from persecution. Also, releasing baboons back into the wild is a complicated and tedious process. Someone has to go into the cage and live with the baboons for a while until they will follow him. This can take several months. Then the baboons must be transported to the release site, where the volunteer has to live with them for several more months, teaching them how to live off the veld, just as their mother would do if they were alive. He must teach the youngsters how to find scorpions by turning over rocks, and how to flick off the poisonous stings in the tail before they can be eaten.

"All these baboons," Max waves a hand at them, "come here as orphans. Some white people show the Bushmen money and give a 'slagyster'.. my English.. you know..." He demonstrates with his fingers the intermeshing of the teeth of a jaw trap. "They say you see here is fifty dollars. Bring me a baby baboon. The baby must be a new one..very small...or l do not pay you. Then the Bushman put out the trap and put fruit in. When they catch a mother," he indicates by the wrist "they come and kill it with sticks. If the baby is too big they kill that too. When they find a small baby they kill the mother hitting her with sticks on the head, and take the baby back for the fifty dollars. Can you believe it? White people!" He shakes his head at the callousness of a race from which he would expect better. "Then these same white people. They get tired of the baboons because they do not know what a baboon is like before they get it. A baby always stay with his mother. Always. So now they have a baby that is dirty and needs nappies. And if the woman try to put it down over there to do something, it scream like hell. So then she says too much so she give it to the Bushman to kill or she phone Harnas and say come and fetch this screaming baboon or I kill it. Oh and another thing," he says, "a baboon is resistant to tranquillizer. If we want to drug a big baboon to move him, or look at an injury, we have to give him about three times as much as a male human would need. As much as we use on a full-grown lion. I don't know why that is. I can't explain it for you, but it is so."

The venerable Land Rover now approaches the large veld camp adjacent to the visitors' chalets, and all thought of baboons vanish as Elsa and Schabu stalk majestically over to be fed, commanding attention as only lions can. Out come the cameras. Schabu, the black-maned lion, snarls at the guests and then his whole expression softens and he rubs himself affectionately against the fence by Max, who scratches his shaggy mane and chatters sweet nothings into his ear. "Schabu is my friend," announces Max, beckoning to Christine to come and wipe his hands which are now oily and dirty from contact with the lion's mane. "When he is small, he sleeps with me. We both sleep on a mattress on the floor of the hangar over there. I take him hunting in the bush. When I call to him, he comes. I use Schabu to tame that big leopard. When I go to talk to him I take Schabu with me because I know he will not attack me while Schabu is there." He goes on to recount how Schabu is too big now, but until recently, Max used to go into the camp and wrestle with him. "Sometimes the tourists want to have a go also, but I warn them, look, he breaks one of my ribs before. Anyway, some people want to try so I let them come in and wrestle with Schabu. I just hang around, making sure that Schabu will not hurt them. They love it. Soon word gets around and everyone wants to wrestle with him. Every group of tourists. They all say show us the wrestling lion." He senses that some members of his audience are wondering if this is a tall story. "I can show you photos, if you don't believe me," he says, adopting an aggrieved tone. That evening when everyone is having a drink in the bar, he appears brandishing a photograph which does, indeed, prove this story.

Tourist wrestling with Schabu whilst visiting Harnas   *Max greeting Schabu through the gate*

All the animals who are close to the house have now been fed, and the guests climb aboard the open Land Rover, to visit the outlying camps. These natural veld camps of about six hectares in extent, are surrounded by a high perimeter fence consisting of wire strands made rigid with wooden droppers and reinforced with two or three strands of electric wire. Max crooks a finger at the ever willing Christine, who has to fetch the heavy pail of seal meat, heave it onto her shoulder, and stagger over to him. Max will throw the meat through the steel hatch to the pride of young lions inside the first camp. Poor Christine. No volunteer ever delivers herself to Harnas without falling prey to Max's japes. He is an inveterate practical joker. As Christine pulls the heavy bucket up onto her shoulder, the bottom falls out and twenty kilograms of bloody, stinking chunks of seal carcass cascade over her. At the sight of her dismay as she stands there, festooned with pieces of meat and drenched in seal blood, Max collapses into fits of laughter. Click! Click! go the cameras.

"It's not funny," grumbles Christine, glowering at him. "Did you do that?"

"No, not me." Max lies easily, especially when he is doubled up convulsed with laughter. "The buckets are old. They sometimes break."

"Dear God, look at me. What a mess. Can I go and clean up?"

"Certainly not." Max recovers his composure and asserts his authority. "We must finish the tour. Come here and let me pick the pieces of meat off you for the lions."

"I can manage, thank you." Christine extracts meat chunks from her person and flicks them through the fence for the lions. Click! Click! While she is thus engaged in feeding her adornments to the lions, Max cannot resist the childish impulse to taunt them, making sudden movements and stamping his boot at them. Some flinch away, others curl their lips into a snarl.

This is wrong of Max and he should know better. Taunting wild animals may impress photo-hungry tourists who want to see the lions snarling, for the camera, but it is not fair on the lions, and can have dangerous consequences. By contrast, when Marlice takes the tour, she has a much more gentle way. She likes to wag her forefinger at the big cats and say in a stern voice: "Come on.

Marlice wants you to sing for your supper. Let's hear you." And they will lie in front of her, put their ears down and sing. The smaller ones will emit high-pitched ows and miows, while the bigger ones produce deeper oohs. Adjacent to the young lion's camp is a smaller camp containing some tuft-eared caracals. While waiting for Christine to clean herself, Max walks across the track and lobs some meat chunks over their fence. He tells how the little caracals would kill animals bigger than themselves, such as a full-grown goat or springbok. "He just catches him by the throat, and then he locks his jaws and goes into a dormant state, like a trance. There he will hang on the animal until it dies, when he will come out of his trance and eat it. But while he is in this trance, you can go up to him and catch him, you hold him up by his tail, so he cannot bite you or scratch, and then you kill him or put him in a sack, whatever. I've done it often on my grandfather's farm."

"I see this camp has live electric wire strands along the bottom of the fence," remarks one of the more observant visitors. "Do they all have it?"

"All the open camps and enclosures have electricity," answers Max. "We could not run Harnas without it. The baboons you see them testing the electric wire every day. If we have a power failure which happens sometimes in the rainy season, then we can get escapes. Not the lions, thank goodness, but the lynxs or baboons or Cheetah. One Cheetah always escape in a power failure, and he go back to his old farm fifty kilometres from here. Then the farmer trap him again and phone Nic. Nic has to pay for the same Cheetah three times now. They even put a collar on him."

"Is it dangerous, the electricity?" the same inquisitive gentleman asks.

"Ja, for small birds and things. And we have to clean the grass away by hand every year. It is a big job - all these big camps with lots of kilometres of fencing to clean. Otherwise the grass makes a short circuit from the wire to the ground when it get wet. And the big leopard once stood in water and touched the wire and he got knocked out. I have to run and switch off the power and then throw a bucket of water on him to wake him up. But lightning is a big danger, bigger than the electric wire. You see all the fences on the farm are connected with each other, and because we use wooden droppers (fence posts) the electricity cannot easily escape to the ground. So it travels along the wires. And if you are opening a gate maybe ten kilometres away from a lightning strike, you can get a shock. Maybe even fatal. Anyway let us move on, before we run out of daylight."

"Where can I sit?" enquires Christine, still plastered with bits of seal flesh and caked with dried blood. The stench is all but visible.

"On the bonnet," directs Max, placing her as far from the passengers as the design of the Land Rover allows. Away goes the tour, bumping along the dusty track that winds through the sandveld terminalia woodland. The late afternoon sun throws the shadows of the yellowwoods right across the road and the peculiar effect of driving through rapidly alternating sun and shade confuses the brain. Max stops the Land Rover at the entrance to the wild dogs' camp, and waits for Christine as she runs to unlock and pull the heavy gates open. Then he drives the vehicle through and away into the camp leaving Christine in his dust. She swings them shut and runs after him calling out "Wait for me," just as the pack of hungry wild dogs come racing out of the bush. Yipping and snickering, they mill around the vehicle, all eager to get at the food.

Christine has leapt onto the back of the Land Rover and the occupants are trapped, an impossible odour on one side and wild dogs all around. "Sorry," she apologises. "But I am frightened of the wild dogs. In my first week here, I was helping to feed the wild dogs. Max was driving the tractor, and I was sitting on the trailer with the meat. Then the trailer came loose from the tractor, I don't know why." (A close observation of Max's face would have betrayed a certain slyness in his grin.) "It came off and I fell and the meat fell on top of me. All the wild dogs were jumping over me to get at the meat. I was very frightened and I scream to Max to come and help me, but he could not hear me because of the noise of the tractor. Anyway, now I am afraid of the wild dogs, and they know it."

"Watch this," says Max, and he places a big lump of red meat on the bonnet of the Land Rover. One of the bolder dogs leaps up to snatch it before racing away with his prize. Again and again Max does his party trick, and the photographers get their money's worth. Some fifty metres away can be seen a small group of pups, their presence betrayed by several pairs of black rounded ears protruding out of the grass. "What about their food?" someone asks.

"Wild dogs is the most unselfish animals and they always look after everyone else in the pack," answers Max. "They have two stomachs, and they will fill the first stomach and then go and throw it up for the pups, or for a sick animal that can't hunt. They will never let a member of the pack go hungry. Come, Christine. It will be dark soon and we still have to feed the Cheetahs."

Once again Max reclines comfortably in his driver's seat, while Christine struggles with heavy gates, and once again he callously drives away, leaving her to close them and follow him. But this time, she is surrounded by a dozen or more spitting, feinting, mock-charging Cheetah, who rush at her, thumping the ground with their forepaws. As with the wild dogs, she has to try to make her way to the vehicle without turning her back on them, which is not easy when they are all around her. When at last she does get back to the Land Rover, there is a red stripe across her backside, and two scratch marks on the back of her calf. "Let me see," demands Max, offering no apologies for leaving her in peril.

"No - go away!"

"Oh, go on. Let us see too." This from a tourist, camera at the ready. Eventually poor Christine must hide her embarrassment and display her wound - a neat, bleeding rip on the buttock.

"Now you can see, never turn your back on a Cheetah." Pearls of wisdom from Max. As the Cheetah snatch their pieces of meat, and sprint off into the veld to enjoy their meal in peace, Max offers some more insight on how to catch them. "It is easy to trap a Cheetah. You just get an ordinary car air filter basin, fill it with fish, cover it with tinfoil and hang it in a box trap. The Cheetah smells the fish and this brings him to the cage where he sees the ball of tinfoil swinging in it. Being a cat, he wants to play and that takes him into the cage. Bingo."

"Have you ever seen such a trap work yourself?" asks a doubting visitor who knows a fishy story when he smells one. "Sure, plenty of times. I used to do it on my Grandfather's farm." One perceives from these stories that the Grandfather's farm must have been a veritable hive of activity in the field of unconventional methods of catching wild animals.

As they watch the Cheetah devour their food, the sorcerous spirits of Africa cast their spell upon them and no one speaks. Kalahari sunsets are a lingering, changing mosaic of colour, shape and atmosphere. The wind drops, stillness descends over the land, and the dust hangs heavy in the air. It is the dust and clouds that give Africa its dramatic sunsets. This evening there are only a few isolated puffs of cloud, diaphanous icebergs in an ethereal sea, always changing, wreathing, contorting, twirling, vaporising here and re-forming there. The warm evening lingers on and on long after the sun has dropped out of sight, leaving only an orange topaz line on the horizon and a translucent backdrop above it in the pleochroistic sky to silhouette the yellow woods. Ten minutes pass and the puffs of cloud, now unlit by the sun, have mysteriously joined together to become ribbons of grey islands, jagged reefs in the same lustrous aquamarine ocean. Still the ever changing, shifting sky darkens, and now it is the purple time, the ten or fifteen minutes of the evening where everything is suffused in a mauve haze - trees, soil, grass and clouds; all visible only through a mauve filter.

Then the orange backdrop in the west darkens to the colour of almandine garnet, a deep violet red behind the dense tangle of dark foliage and branches, and the sky above turns to tanzanite purple. The free-tailed bats and the nightjars flit above, harvesting Mother Nature's insect bounty and an eagle owl coos monotonously and seductively. They are entranced. Max breaks the spell by starting the Land Rover, and the harsh clatter of the engine grates on their finer feelings and drowns out the whole secret world on which they have been eavesdropping. By the time the party arrives back at the house, the pageantry of evening in the bush is over. Orion and his fellow Constellations are sparkling above them. They have glimpsed Paradise, but have chosen to return to civilisation, with its electricity and its comforts. Truly, as the prophet says, comfort enters our lives as an invited guest, and then remains as our master.

Meanwhile Annelie is getting the cages ready for the night, filling the drinking troughs with water, and laying down fresh straw on the floors. She and Marieta have already treated and injected those animals who need attention, such as a lynx that has been scratched by a young lion and requires an antibiotic. Catching the young baboons - all ten of them - after they have been released to run free around the wide lawns, is not easy, and then she has had to prepare their bottles with warm milk, put on their nappies and get them to bed. Some of the small baboons will sleep with Marieta, others with Annelie. As for Max and Christine, they seldom have time to eat after the tour arrives back, for there is the night tour to prepare for. Christine must make mealie pap for the jackal pups, bat-eared foxes, skunks, genet cats and porcupines. Max must wait for the guests to enjoy drinks and an unhurried dinner before he can guide the night tour. It is seldom before the haunting hour of midnight that the weary staff fall into bed. Every day is the same. There are no holidays or weekends when one is caring for so many animals.

Shortly after Max's return from the feeding tour, Nic arrives back and the family and staff crowd around to inspect the rescued animals. It is apparent that the wild dogs in particular will not last until morning and the decision is made to take them straight to the Vet in Windhoek, a distance of some three hundred kilometres. Schalk has just returned from Windhoek where he has been attending rugby practice but he is prepared to turn around and drive back straight away. While he is getting a quick bite to eat, Nic covers the wild dogs with a heavy blanket; in their dehydrated condition, exposure to the cool, rushing night air will be fatal.

The vehicle sets off for the arduous trip to Windhoek at about nine o'clock and the family watches the headlights as they flicker through the trees and then vanish from sight. At last Nic and Marieta can settle down and eat some food, even if it is by now cold and hard. Nic breaks off the discussion to say goodnight to Max and Christine who have just finished the night tour, and are now free - barring mishaps - to sleep until six o'clock when they must take the guests out on the early morning game drive. He phones Ulf Tubbesing, the

Vet in Windhoek, to give him notice that Schalk is bringing him some injured animals for attention. "I'll wait at my surgery," Tubbesing, conscientious as ever, tells him. "I'll put them all on a drip overnight and take the X-rays tonight so that I can operate on them first thing in the morning. Now you go get some sleep." Annelie bids him goodnight, and retires to bed, clutching an armful of baby baboons, all with dummies in their mouths and their eyes tight shut. He returns to Marieta who holds three baby baboons of her own all wearing clean whiter than white nappies. They are both tired and Nic, ever monosyllabic, has little inclination to discuss the patients who are on their way to Windhoek. Marieta takes herself and her hairy children off to bed. Nic decides to take a walk outside to clear his head of all the material concerns, and to stretch his limbs after the hard day's drive.

It is a clear night and the milky way beams down at him from the starry, starry sky. The night sounds are all around, the whine, hum and drone of the insects, the mournful whistle of the spotted dikkop, the screech of the barn owl and the distant howling of a black-backed jackal. Then Mufasa's brothers, the AIDS lions, start to roar, great OOOHs of such power and majesty that all other night sounds seem to shrink back in awe. Over by the visitors' chalets, Schabu answers them with defiant, challenging roars of his own, and then his challenge is repeated by the wild lions over in the far camp about a kilometre away. When all the lions are roaring together, and all the windows, indeed the very chalets themselves, are vibrating with the thunderous resonance, then the fortunate humans there are privileged to drink in the spine-tingling, reverberating signature of the vanishing wild Africa.

"The Harnas Lullaby," whispers Nic to himself as he turns to go to bed. He has been reminded why he and his family and staff work so hard for no material reward. Their work nourishes the soul. If there were no animal rescues, there would be no lions, and no Harnas Lullaby. And what use would all the money in the world serve when every night is silent and dead?

A mixture of sleeping babies. Cheetah, lion and meerkats

114

Chapter four

CHEETAH

So you're sitting in your man-made hell
With empty staring eyes.
The syringe on the table
Will end your broken life.
Take it in a steady hand
Put the needle to your head.
Your life is non-existent
For years you have been dead.
But now I see so clearly
Just before the shadows dance,
A vision of a child
Who never stood a chance.

Andrew Mercer

The only thing faster on land than the Cheetah is the rate at which this sublime animal and its habitat are being destroyed in Southern Africa. Whilst the Namibian tourist brochures claim that their arid country has an estimated three thousand of these big cats, the largest population of free-ranging Cheetah in Africa, the animals may nevertheless be doomed there. While this page is being read, dozens of these loveable cats are being trapped, poisoned, snared and yes, even strafed from the air by microlight hunters armed with automatic rifles and shotguns. Undeclared war is raging against them for several reasons. First, Cheetah (having been deprived of their normal prey animals by the murderous activities of the ranchers) are forced to prey on livestock - principally calves. The cattle industry is Namibia's major economic activity and it is an industry which takes no prisoners. All the lions and spotted hyena within the millions of hectares which it monopolizes have already gone the way of the bullet. Next on the list is the Cheetah. Soon there will be none left, only the haunting memory of another immaculate masterpiece of Nature which has blown away with the wind.

Second, the other large industry in Namibia is the game industry. Landowners breed antelope for consumption by the hunting fraternity. Some American, European or South African will blast the life out of them and turn their dead bodies into biltong; or a wall hanging to collect dust and spiders; or their skins into floor-mats to be walked over. Cheetah are in direct competition with these hunters for the antelope, for Cheetah do prey on antelope just as they have done since man walked on all fours. Landowners who rub their hands with glee at the value of a herd of say, sixty red hartebeest, look aghast when in the space of one year the whole herd has been eaten by a small group of Cheetah. Even large animals such as Kudu and Eland are taken. Farmers have witnessed a group of four Cheetah hunt and successfully kill two full grown kudu bulls simultaneously. Many ranchers in Namibia combine cattle ranching with game farming and therefore have double the reasons to bump off every Cheetah trespassing on their land. Furthermore there always seem to be plenty of people who will pay big bucks for a Cheetah skin; people who have no moral concerns for the original owner of the skin, and who therefore create a market which instigates the slaughter of yet more of these precious creatures. No doubt these buyers would be horrified to know that some Cheetah have been trapped, and held in that small trap for up to seven months while the unscrupulous landowner shops around for the best price for the skin. Thus the consummate sprinter is both vermin and bounty to certain farmers. Against all these reasons for landowners to shoot out their Cheetah stands only one reason to keep them alive. A sentimental reason. For the love of wildlife. It is therefore not surprising to hear many informed people in Namibia express the depressing opinion that there will be virtually no wild Cheetah left in Namibia within fifteen years.

Apart from Harnas there are other people and organizations in Namibia such as the Hansens at Okonjima and their Africat Foundation, who are doing good work to try to save the Cheetah from extinction, but for every animal rescued by them or Harnas, a hundred more perish in the box traps that litter the ranches and game farms of Namibia. Cheetah are particularly easy to trap because of their liking for Play Trees. Mothers and cubs as well as groups of males tend to visit the same favorite tree, usually one that is substantial and simple to climb. There they scent-mark, socialize and spray a mixture of urine and glandular secretions. The messages relayed by this mixture are augmented by scraping with the feet, and by clawing trees. Clawing leaves an odour-tainted, visual and olfactory mark. Faeces also have a scent-marking function. Their noses will tell them all about other Cheetah visitors to such a tree, their age, sex and breeding status, in the same way that humans read a newspaper. Thus the Play tree is a social club and notice board. But when humans discover the Play Tree it becomes a death trap. For so strong is the urge to reach the tree that if it is screened off with thorn branches so that the only passage left is through the open gate of a box trap, the landowner may succeed in wiping out all the groups in the vicinity with only one trap. Like killing several birds with one stone. The trained eye can easily identify a Play Tree from all the spoor activity and droppings that surround it.

As many ranchers ruin their land by poor grazing practices, converting open Savannah into hard woody thornveld, so the conservationists like Harnas and Africat are noticing that many Cheetah which are brought into their sanctuaries arrive suffering from eye injuries and even blindness. The reason is not hard to guess. Trying to catch prey by speed alone in thick thornbush country is asking for trouble for a wild person with large exposed eyes. The wide open scrubby plains of the semi-desert is its ideal habitat for it cannot use its speed effectively in thicker bush. Recently (1998) there has been a noticeable increase in the number of Cheetah found in Namibian ranchland, particularly in land which adjoins neighboring Botswana. As Botswana settlers move into the fragile Kalahari, so the hunting which inevitably follows is driving the Kalahari Cheetah into the traps of the Namibian ranchers. For those who will never see a wild Cheetah we may record that it is the sports car of wild Africa. It can go from naught to a hundred kilometres an hour in three seconds. Because it is built for speed, even a full grown Cheetah weighs less than fifty kilograms and has the waistline of an anorexic ballerina. It cannot compete with more powerful predators such as lion, leopards or hyenas, and Nic van der Merwe once recaptured a Cheetah which had escaped from its camp at Harnas by pulling it out by the tail from under his pick-up truck and subduing it with his bare hands. They are quite easily tamed especially when acquired young and legends abound of ancient Kings and Pharaohs keeping them as pets and employing them to hunt. Our story of the Harnas Cheetahs tells mainly of a cripple who was called Bagheera, after the much-loved character in Rudyard Kipling's famous story, the 'Jungle Book'. We all love a fairy tale because of the happy ending. Let us see how far we can get with our Namibian fairy tale before we collide with harsh reality.

One fine day in Namibia in 1996 a Cheetah who lived in the woods near a little town called Gobabis gave birth to three beautiful cubs. She had two little girls and a boy, whose human name was to be Bagheera. Like all Cheetah cubs, Bagheera bore no resemblance to his mother. Her eyes were brown while his had the bluish hue of a new-born kitten. She was cream-coloured with clearly marked spots all over her lithe body. He looked like a teddy-bear with a punk hair-do and possessed no spots as yet, just long greyish-streaked fur on the face and back, darkening to black around the legs.

In every fairy tale there has to be a wicked person for otherwise there would be no story. In this true story, there is a butcher in Gobabis, who owned the land where Bagheera was born. In order to protect his cattle, the butcher had given the Bushmen employees who looked after his ranch while he himself lived in town, strict instructions to kill any Cheetah on his land. Within a day or two of the happy birthday, the Bushmen who were following up on the mother's spoor in the sand, had found and captured the three little cubs. Bagheera's navel cord was still wet when he arrived at Harnas so we know that he was newly born. Catching the cubs was as easy as stooping to pick them up. To catch the mother, the Bushmen used dogs. A Cheetah may be the fastest animal in the world, but only over short distances, and a pack of dogs following upon the scent left by her cantering paws in the revealing sand will eventually catch her when she has become exhausted. Sometimes, the prey

Cheetah cubs and who ever else is thirsty, line up for milk in the kitchen

Cheetah will climb a tree to escape the jaws of the dog-pack. So Bagheera's mother was chased by dogs to the point of exhaustion, treed, captured and then manhandled into a steel box cage. Her three cubs were thrown in with her but in her stress and anguish she did not even recognize them and continued to dash back and forth, desperately seeking to escape. Time and again Bagheera and his two little sisters were bowled over and trodden on by their frantic mother. It must have been at this time that Bagheera's back was broken. The little cub was not even two days old. How quickly his young life had been blighted. In due course the telephone rang at Harnas, and it was the very same butcher to tell them about the captive Cheetah. Did Harnas want them or must he shoot them, was the question.

Away went Nic to collect the new foster children and for a little while, at least in regard to the cubs, we may resume our fairy tale. But not for the mother. She was so badly stressed on arrival at Harnas, that she was rigid in her limbs and could neither eat nor drink. Nic and Marieta moved her from one camp to another to try to find her a place where she could settle down but to no avail. Just before she was to be darted and force-fed liquids, she died. Before he was one week old, Bagheera was both orphaned and crippled. Here we must end our Namibian wildlife fairy tale, without the time honoured flourish. "And they all lived happily ever after."

For the first two weeks the cubs slept and slept, only waking to take milk from a bottle. They occupied a corner of Marieta's kitchen, which they shared with three lion cubs, two meerkats and a litter of dachshund pups. Even then their early stumbling attempts to walk were so comical and unsteady that it was more than a month before Marieta said to Nic, "There is something wrong with the little male cub. Look, he can't walk."

"Perhaps he is just slower to learn than his sisters," Nic replied. "Give him a little time." Marieta was not so sure. His sisters were now tumbling about and romping with the other cubs, while Bagheera could only drag his hindquarters around with his front paws. And he seemed to have an infection in his kidneys, for he leaked urine constantly. The inevitable visit to the Vet came and X-rays

Marieta, Bagheera and his two sisters

revealed the fracture to the spine, and the consequent disruption of the nerves to his back legs and kidneys. The Vet gave Marieta two choices: put the little cub down or else give him constant physiotherapy in the hope that the damaged nerves would repair themselves. For Marieta, hope was enough. She took little

121

Bagheera home and for the rest of his life, she and the staff at Harnas had to stimulate his bladder to work every morning and every evening, by pressing down on and massaging it, so that all the urine could be released. The staff built a hammock swing out of an old horse blanket and suspended it so that Bagheera's paws just touched the ground. There each day he would spend half an hour or so, with his back legs being invited to learn how to function. And then there were the swims in the swimming pool, again, to enable him to get his back legs to kick. It is one of the great regrets of Marieta's life at Harnas that none of these measures worked, and Bagheera remained paralyzed. Paralysis is bad enough in itself but of course one problem always causes another and it was not long before the constant dragging about of the hindquarters wore out the skin over the right haunch and opened a wound which would never heal. Marieta was so desperately keen to see Bagheera come right that she even sent him off to the Vet for an operation to sew a patch of leather over the wound in order to protect the open flesh from the constant abrasion. The device worked quite well for a few months but then it was pulled off and poor Bagheera had to suffer the torture of dragging his open sore along the ground every time he moved. In the meantime, the little Cheetah suffered more bereavement in his short life. One morning when they were about eight months of age Bagheera's sisters were playing together in the courtyard. Marieta was fussing about in the house when she heard a commotion outside. From the sounds of choking and growling she assumed that her animals were fighting. "Kier! Kier!" she shouted. This was her general call to all staff within earshot to come quickly and help her to break up a fight. But when she got to the cubs, she received an unpleasant shock. Not one but both of the two young Cheetah were in the throes of what appeared to be some kind of fit. Their limbs were jerking convulsively, they were drooling from the mouth and uttering peculiar choking sounds. "Snake!" thought Marieta. "Search the courtyard for the snake," she told the Bushmen. In cases of snake bite the Vet always needed to know which anti-venom to administer. Mamba venom, which is neurotoxic and causes respiratory and cardiac failure, will not be affected by an anti-venom designed for puff adders, whose venom is cytotoxic and causes tissue damage. Poly-valent anti-venoms still do not cover every species of snake. But a thorough search under every plant and bush failed to locate any snake. Marieta's efforts to revive the two Cheetah were unsuccessful and she telephoned the Vet. "It sounds like poisoning," he told her. "Keep them warm and give them each an injection of cortisone. The sooner you can get them to me, the more chance they have of surviving this." When time is of the essence for the life of one of her beloved animals any thought of financial prudence flies straight out of Marieta's mind. Without any hesitation she telephoned Med-Rescue and ordered an aircraft. Windhoek was three hours away by car and one look at the shuddering, convulsing Cheetahs told her that they would not make it by road. The aircraft arrived promptly and collected the two little spotted patients but by the time the plane touched down at Windhoek airport, Bagheera's sisters were dead.

Harnas never discovered what poison had caused their deaths. The Vet conducted his usual thorough autopsy and the internal organs were flown to Onderstepoort Veterinary Centre at Pretoria, and even to America, in order to try to isolate the poison and determine the cause of death, but to no avail. It remains a mystery that the two Cheetah should both simultaneously collapse into a coma and die so quickly. The mystery deepened when exactly the same thing happened to two of the little lynxes the very next day. One moment they were fine, playing together in the courtyard, the next they were convulsing in a coma. The same emergency flight, and the same result, dead on arrival. Again, the autopsy failed to ascertain the cause of their deaths which, from all the symptoms, could only be some kind of poison.

Bagheera was now the sole survivor of the mother and three cubs who had been trapped on the butcher's ranch. There were more than a dozen Cheetah at Harnas while Bagheera lived there. All, like him, were saved from persecution. The really wild ones were kept together in a natural, spacious camp of about eight hectares, where they could run around freely. Bagheera was one of four tame Cheetah who lived around the house and gardens and amongst the visitors. Goeters was the oldest; a haughty individual who stalked regally past the admiring visitors and paid them not the slightest attention. The two companions were called Braam and Bengu, both of whom would move off if visitors came too close. If Goeters was the most admired of the Cheetahs, the animal who stole everybody's heart was the little crippled one. Bagheera was miserable without his friends. When he was taken to the Windhoek show for people to look at and get close to, he would lie with his head down on his paws, crying that high-pitched distress call. Marieta, Marlice or Annelie would have to sit with and comfort him on these occasions, for as soon as they tried to leave, he would start his cries again. And when he was returned to Harnas after the week of the Show, what a welcome the Cheetah gave each other, with much face-licking and purring.

Right from the start, Bagheera had a strong personality, with clear likes and dislikes. The staff always warned visitors to keep their children away from Bagheera because he did not like children, but Marieta knew him best, and she always said that he disliked some children, not all of them. For instance, she would relate how Bagheera would lie in the shade near the swimming pool watching the children splashing about. He was actually assessing the children individually, for if there was a child who was considerate towards the others, and stood back to allow others a first turn on the slide, then that child was quite safe in Bagheera's critical eye. But just let one child try to bully another, or act in a taunting or unpleasant manner, Bagheera would haul himself forward, snarling, and lunge at that child. It was almost like a reprimand. In fact, Marieta relates how Bagheera actually loved some children, especially those who did not behave in a restless, excitable way. One twelve year old girl set off once across the lawns towards Bagheera. She was a plump, pleasant and cheerful girl who was very adult in her ways. "Be careful, he will bite you," warned Marieta. "No, he won't," replied that young lady with considerable self-assurance, and proceeded to pet Bagheera and make a fuss of him. Marieta was delighted to see Bagheera licking the young girl and purring. One day, a couple arrived at Harnas with their ten year old daughter who was in a wheelchair. She was painfully thin and her body was twisted like that of a polio victim. On their way to Reception, and before any of the staff could warn them about Bagheera, they came across him as he lay in the shade of a tuft of pampas-grass near the path. Leaving their little crippled girl alone with the resting and seemingly harmless Cheetah, the parents walked off to register. When they told Annelie where they had left their daughter, she dropped everything and ran out into the garden fearing the worst. She had seen Bagheera show aggression towards children before and here was a child that could not escape. When she arrived at the child's wheelchair, followed by the now worried parents, there they found Bagheera. He had dragged himself next to the wheelchair and had his head on the child's lap. He was purring loudly and every now and then would lick her frail arms as she stroked him. There they stayed, the two of them, inseparable friends until night came and the girl was wheeled off to bed. For two long days, the little crippled girl and her Cheetah remained constantly in each other's company. Again and again, amazed staff watched as Bagheera would lick the girl's arms and then rest his head on her lap. So close did the two become that when the time came for the little girl to leave Harnas she made a tearful promise to write to him. And indeed, for months after that visit, the mail always included a letter addressed to Bagheera. Marieta would have to sit with her favourite Cheetah and read to him.

"Dear Bagheera," the letter would always begin and Marieta would read to the disabled Cheetah the emotional outpourings of a young girl who, surely because of their common disability, had formed such a strong bond of affection with him.

By the middle of 1997, the sore on Bagheera's haunch was the size of a man's fist, exposed and bloody. Then Beverley, a visitor who also runs a wildlife sanctuary and rehabilitation centre in South Africa, the Kalahari Raptor Centre, took pity on Bagheera and decided to intervene. She remembered once seeing a dog whose master had made a little wheeled cart on which the dog would rest his paralysed hindquarters, and get around famously just by pulling with its forelegs. Armed with Bagheera's measurements, Bev went off to an engineering firm at Lichtenburg in South Africa. When the cart was complete, Bev drove the

Bagheera and his cart

thousand or so kilometres to Harnas and the following day, everyone gathered on the large front lawns to witness the first testing of the new cart. What a day in Bagheera's life this was. All that was needed was the theme music from St. Elmo's Fire to be blasting out. The date was Tuesday 28th October 1997. While Asian currencies collapsed and stock markets around the world crashed into turmoil, the only thing that mattered at Harnas was restoring some measure of mobility to a legend of speed. There must have been a dozen or so foreigners visiting Harnas that day, and there was an air of eager anticipation as Marieta and Schalk introduced the afflicted Cheetah to his specially designed wheelchair. Bagheera was at first suspicious of the strange contraption and grumbled and growled defensively while he was being strapped into it. But Marieta lavished him with her special brand of loving reassurance, and the operation was completed without anyone being bitten. Then - disappointment!

126

Bagheera running for the only time in his short life

A Cheetah's body is much longer in proportion to that of a dog and the cart did not fit. Try as they could, the Harnas staff members could find no way to stretch or bend or pull the cart to make it serve its purpose. They were stumped. But their gloom was soon dispelled. The tourists had their own ideas about re-designing the cart. An extraordinary scene played out that day. Arguing, gesticulating and sketching, the tourists resolved themselves into an engineering design team and various ingenious designs were proposed, discussed, if arm waving and rough sketches may be termed discussion, and then altered or rejected. A German civil engineer, an Italian graphic designer, and French film processor, each volubly passionate about his own ideas and quite unable to understand a word of what the others were trying to say, or to make himself understood. But if there were language problems, there was complete agreement on the purpose of the undertaking which was to help Baggy to run

127

free. With unity of purpose and passionate involvement, most goals can be achieved and so it happened that later in the morning a feasible working drawing finally appeared on the back of a cigarette box.

The arm-waving assemblage then moved en masse to the workshops, where Schalk set to work cutting, welding and drilling according to the multilingual directions. Not exactly computer-aided design, but the new Kalahari cart fitted Bagheera perfectly. Once again he muttered and grumbled as his immobile hindquarters were strapped into the new cart. Then, with cameras at the ready, the people stepped back and waited to see what the crippled Cheetah would do. Bagheera stood still, looking around as if to say "And now?" In this context, this is Namibian jargon for "O.K. You have tied this machine to my body. What exactly am I supposed to do with it?" Nobody had thought that he would not know what to do with his wheelchair. It seemed so obvious. A gabble of indecipherable suggestions were directed at Marieta enjoining her either to push the cart from the back to give Bagheera the idea, or to go around to the front, and pull from the biting end. No one was too keen to try taking him by the head and pulling, and the few desultory pushes from the safety of the rear merely served to make Bagheera try to turn around to see who was shoving him and to offer a nibble or two to the culprit for his impertinence. Then without any warning, he took off at a sudden rush and careered away at great speed. The cart worked like a dream. Head down and forelegs pulling like a train, Bagheera went tearing away as if in training for the next disabled Olympics. Out of nowhere, one of his companions, Bengu, appeared by his side, and bounded along next to him, no doubt astonished at his friend's unexpected burst of speed. The sight of the little crippled Cheetah running for the first time in his life had a powerful emotional effect on the spectators, most of whom swallowed lumps in their throats, and dabbed at moist eyes. The large expanse of lawn at Harnas is studded with rock gardens full of aloes, and into one of these tore Bagheera, with callous disregard for those who had worked so hard on his cart. He came to a breathless halt after a minute or two of racing, having succeeded in breaking the one wheel and bending the other. Sadly, that was the first, and as it turned out, the only time in his life that Bagheera was able to run. It took long months to get the cart repaired and by then, a further visit to the Vet revealed that he had developed cancer and would not live for much longer. Born to run, he lived only to crawl.

For Marieta this was heartbreaking news, but it was also disappointing for the tourists to whom Bagheera was so well known. Lying out on the front lawns as he did, he was always the first animal with whom a visitor came into contact on arrival at Harnas. For so many people he was the symbol of Harnas, a unique place where one could actually interact with Nature's wild animals. After the incident when Bagheera was able to run with the cart, his condition started to deteriorate as the long painful months crawled by. The cancer spread and the festering wound on his haunch started to ooze blood, so that he left a red blotchy trail as he dragged his failing body around the emerald-green lawns at his foster home. He ate less and less and became more irritable with people. Even Marieta could do no more than stroke his head. For her, this was purgatory. Her natural instinct was to cuddle and show warmth to her animals - indeed she bore the scars to prove it - and the distress of her dear Cheetah stimulated an overpowering need to bestow affection. Alas, any attempt to do so now only provoked a snarl or a snap. There seemed to be little point in keeping Bagheera alive, and more and more of her friends began to ask Marieta when she was going to let him go. "He has no dignity left," they counselled, "only pain and suffering. It is not fair to keep him alive." But still Marieta hesitated to take the final, irrevocable step, hoping against hope that some miracle would occur, the cancer would abate and Bagheera would be back to his old loveable self. Then in mid 1998, disaster! While driving the car out of the garage enclosure where the young leopards were kept, Marieta and Annelie were unable to shut the gates behind them quickly enough. In his usual place on the lawns just outside the gate, lay Bagheera, weak and feeble. Here was an opportunity for Nature to take its course. A young leopard, which had grown up beside the Cheetahs and had never shown any animosity to them before, suddenly dived through the gates as if on Nature's mission. There was a blur of spotted fur, a spring and in a heart-beat, the leopard had Bagheera by the throat. Screaming to Annelie to close the gate and help her, Marieta ran up and threw herself into the unequal contest, punching the leopard on its sensitive nose as hard as she could. Snarling, the attacker kept its grip on the Cheetah's throat. When at last help arrived and the staff managed to pull and shove the struggling, growling assailant back into its enclosure, the damage was done. Bagheera had deep puncture wounds in his neck and the bleeding and subsequent swelling made him very uncomfortable. In such a state, he was an accident waiting to happen, and Fate was not slow to play upon this weakness. On 31st May 1998 a ten year old boy went up to Bagheera to pet him as he lay on the lawn. The attention was ill-received, and the boy suffered scratches to his arm and legs some of which were deep and required stitches. Certainly this was the kind of problem Harnas could do without, and Bagheera was becoming more and more of a liability. Still Marieta hung on, hoping.......... Then on 4th September 1998 a two year old child went to pet Bagheera with the same unhappy result - he received a bite on his left leg, for which he absorbed four stitches at Gobabis Hospital. There were other minor incidents as well. Now, critical reports started to be published in the local newspapers. "Children the Prey!" shrieked one sensational headline. Marieta's hand was forced. Early one morning soon after the last incident she took the fatal step and asked Nico to put an end to Bagheera's suffering. Deliberately, she busied herself inside the house so that she would have no knowledge of when the injection was actually being administered. Nico returned in a short space of time to say that it was all over and where did Marieta wish the body to be buried. And then a very strange thing happened; something puzzling which had never occurred before or since that fateful day. Bagheera's three friends, Goeters, Braam and Bengu, got together and attacked the children in the first group of visitors to arrive at Harnas that day. Fortunately, they did not press their attack through, and so there were no injuries, but later a second group of tourists were also subjected to harassment by the three Cheetahs, who again targeted the children. "It was almost as if," remarks Marieta, "they knew that Bagheera's death was somehow

130

related to children, and they had decided to even the score." And so Bagheera departed this world leaving through no fault of his own a legacy of bad publicity. Yet it would be a mistake to think that his time here was a litany of disasters. It is true that as a paralysed orphan he faced an uncertain life with only the love of Harnas, together with the companions whom they had found for him, to give him comfort. And yet his brief life was also meaningful to the hundreds of people who petted and played with him. And if he did leave a few tooth and claw marks behind, how gently and lightly he touched and enriched so many others' lives.

Tai Kuli, the leopard as a cub

Chapter five

LEOPARDS

Detached mysterious visage
With eyes of onyx blue,
Absorbing light impenetrable
With a deep impassioned hue.
This self-imbued clarity
Extolling virtues doomed
And feeding on the ransomed prey
Whose dark thoughts are exhumed

Andrew Mercer

Amongst all of Nature's other beauties and mysteries there is a form of chrysoberyl called Alexandrite. This rare and valuable gemstone has the ability to change colour. A brilliant green stone will turn to fiery red when held under a light bulb. So it is with the eyes of a leopard. As mysterious and little-known as Alexandrite, the watchful eyes of this cat take on the colour of their surroundings. They turn to blue sapphires when he looks up into the sky. If he lies in the branches amongst the grey-green foliage of a camelthorn tree, the eyes become green tourmalines. Stalking through the pale, withered grasses of the winter savannah, the eyes change to honey-

133

coloured citrine quartz. Such is the camouflage of this the best-adapted, most secretive animal of the African veld.

It is the most deadly, most vigilant and most solitary of all the cats. It's coat is the finest, softest and most exquisite. There are true black spots on the head and limbs, but on the body, the spots are arranged in patterns, called rosettes, which are clustered around a golden khaki patch of fur. The effectiveness of the spotted fur has to be seen to be believed. In thick bush this camouflage is the ultimate but even in open Kalahari thornveld, you can watch a leopard lie down in the dappled shade of a camelthorn tree with only a sprig or two of grass on the bare sand, and there! he has disappeared in front of your eyes. Most of Africa's predators are generally alert, but here the leopard is in a class of its own. If the price of freedom is eternal vigilance, that is the creed by which the leopard survives the cruel constant persecution. Because a leopard lives and hunts alone, it can never afford to let its guard down for one moment. Lions and Cheetah make themselves vulnerable to hunters by their sociable behaviour. But a leopard lives alone, and cannot easily be found. Whether it is preying upon dassies and baboons in the rocky hills, or upon bat-eared foxes and spring hares in the deep sand, the spotted predator is infinitely adaptable. Alone but not lonely, relaxed but never lazy and unhampered by any feelings of pity or remorse, this remarkable wild person clings tenaciously to life in Southern Africa, even while its habitat shrinks and shrinks again. This is the serial killer, the silent, stealthy assassin, and also the ultimate survivor of what little remains of the African wilderness.

In November 1992 Nic applied to the Department of Nature Conservation for a permit to keep animals in cages and the list shows what was on Harnas at that time:-

Lions	14	Lynx	7
Cheetah	17	Monkeys	6
Crocodiles	5	Bat-eared foxes	7
Cranes	2	Tortoises	95
Vultures	3	Birds	Hundreds

| Warthogs | 6 | Porcupines | 4 |
| Baboons | 5 | Banded Mongoose | 18 |

The Senior Ranger who inspected the facility recommended that the permit be granted reporting that Nic was a 'well-known animal lover in the area', that the camps and cages were kept clean and that the animals were well-fed and looked after. The notable exception of animals from this list was, of course, leopards. When in May 1994 Nic heard from Max, who had just joined Harnas, of a male leopard who had been trapped the day before at Omaruru, a mountainous area about four hundred kilometres away, he jumped at the chance and arranged, through Max's father, to acquire the trapped creature for the sum of N\$2,000 (about U.S. \$400). Instead of sending Rudy Britz to fetch him, Nic decided that he would call in on his way back from Swakopmund and collect the leopard himself. To that end, he took the heavy solid-steel trunk which he used for collecting lynxes and other animals. When Nic arrived, he was relieved to find the big male leopard still inside his cage. This may sound trite, but so explosive and frantic is a trapped leopard that a man can find one in his trap, go back to his house to fetch a gun and return only to find the steel mesh torn apart and the leopard gone. Or worse still, from his point of view, the leopard has torn a hole in the wire but now lies in wait inside the cage for him to return. No, a leopard in a trap is not like a Cheetah. He is pure nitro-glycerine. "I cannot work when he is like this," said Nic to the German who had trapped the animal. The heavy steel cage was lurching and shifting as the spotted occupant sprang back and forth, crashing into the cage, while a whole medley of growls, snarls, hisses and grunts roared forth. "Put some canvas over the cage. It will calm him down." Some black plastic sheeting was found and laid over the cage, and then Nic positioned his own steel crate at its door. Then he wired the crate and the cage together, and opened both sliding doors simultaneously. The leopard saw the dark hole of Nic's box as a refuge and leapt in. Nic slammed the door shut, and they lifted the trunk with its spitting captive onto the back of Nic's pick-up. He had not even used any tranquilliser.

Now he had a male leopard, Nic put the word out on the grapevine that he was looking for a female. The scale of trapping in Namibia was such that within a month or so, he received a telephone call from a farmer in the Khomas Hochland to say that he had caught a leopardess in a cage and intended to shoot her for the skin unless Nic paid him two thousand Namibian dollars. Nic paid with alacrity and sent Rudy Britz to collect her. Rudy, knowing how badly leopards suffer from cage damage when they are trapped, telephoned the Vet in Windhoek and arranged to collect him on the way through.

The Khomas Hochland is an arid piece of rolling, rocky land lying to the west of Windhoek, between it and the Gamsberg. Where the high land (Hochland) drops down an escarpment, it presents great vistas of the sea of reddish sand known as the Namib Desert. Because the soil is thin over the rocky sub-strate, the rain is minimal, and the underground water supplies are deep and irregular, the few trees which somehow cling to existence are dwarfed and stunted. Rudy and the Vet arrived to find that they had an audience. The farmer had taken his young son and daughter out of school to see the leopard which he had trapped. He was nervous that the animal might escape and take revenge on him so he kept a shotgun in his hands, and a comfortable distance from the cage.

Rudy walked straight up to the cage in which the female leopard had spent the last three days without food or water. "Pas op," (Be careful) shouted the farmer from the safety of his bakkie fifty metres away. The two children were in the car with him. "She has been here for three days," Rudy called back to him. "She won't get out now if she has not got out before." He stooped down to see her, talking to her continuously, just prattling away in Afrikaans, saying any old nonsense that came into his head. Years of experience with the big cats at Harnas had taught him the importance of calming animals down by use of the voice. Lions, leopards and Cheetah all respond well to a monologue. After a while of introducing himself to her in this manner, she stopped spitting and snarling and striking at him, and he was able to get a good look at her. She had injured her front paws and face trying to scratch her way out of the cage, and

he drew the Vet's attention to this. It was the same with the big male leopard that Nic had collected from Omaruru. The captured animal tries to claw its way out of the cage, and the thin steel wire mesh acts like a knife, paring away the paw pads until they are raw and the nails have been torn away, and the flesh of the nose is cut. The Vet put his box of drugs down and took out an ordinary syringe which he commenced to fill with tranquilliser. Rudy watched in disbelief. "And now?" he enquired when the Vet was ready. 'And now?' in this context is Namibian jargon for 'Where is your blow gun or darting stick?'
"She is not going to present her bum to you for injection, you know."
"That's your problem, I'm here to do my job, with this needle."

It is not the easiest thing in the world to administer an injection by hand to a wild leopardess who is suffering from capture stress and who means to tear to pieces anything which comes into the cage. Rudy gave the matter some thought. "Alright," he said finally, noting that she was swishing her tail from side to side and that the tip sometimes came through the wire mesh. "You'll give it to her in the tip of the tail. Just wait there and be patient. Don't grab until I tell you." He walked back to his pick-up and took a length of nylon rope which he opened out and made into a noose. The farmer and his children watched breathlessly from the safety of their bakkie next to him. "What are you doing?" demanded the farmer. "Taking her for a walk - what do you think?" was Rudy's flippant reply. He scouted around to find a stick, not so easy in the Khomas Hochland, found one at last and hooked the noose on to it. Then he went back to the leopardess and talked to her until he was able to slide the noose gently over her ears and drop it around her neck. "Now," he said sharply and pulled her head towards him. The tail flicked out in annoyance and the Vet grabbed it. In went the injection and Rudy released her. A few more minutes of talking to her and he was able to use the stick to slide the noose back over her head. Ten minutes later she went down and Rudy checked that she was unconscious by tapping her on the nose and checking her eyes. The farmer, his two children and two Ovambo workers had by now come forward and were clustered hesitantly around the cage, curious to see what was going on. It was time to open up. Rudy walked around the cage, took hold of the drop gate and with a flourish flung it open. When he looked around, he and the Vet were alone. The Ovambos had vanished like a cloud over the Namib, and the farmer and his children were back in their bakkie, shotgun to hand. He and the Vet lifted the drugged leopardess out of the cage, and the Vet put eye drops into her eyes, to stop them from drying out, before attending to her injuries. Rudy signalled to the young boy to come forward and touch her. "Feel how soft her fur is," he invited. Fascinated, the boy began to stroke her silky, spotted coat, and in no time Rudy had her lying over the boy's lap, her head cradled in his arms. Curiosity had again drawn the farmer back and he watched his son with a tender look on his face, nursing the leopardess while the Vet worked on her. "Look here," Rudy spoke to the watching family. "You see how black and white her colour is behind the ears? And this white flash at the tip of her tail? Those are so that her young cubs can see to follow her through the grass. You never knew that, did you?" A shake of the head. "And her fur - the softest fur of all the big cats. And see how she only has spots on her head and legs. On her body she has these rosettes. Her camouflage is so good that even her eyes change colour." When the Vet was finished, and the sleeping beauty had been loaded onto the truck, the farmer approached Rudy. "You have taught me something today," he said with obvious sincerity. "I'll never shoot another leopard." They shook hands, and Rudy drove away with the mother of all the leopard cubs who now grace Harnas.

Afraid that the male might kill her if he put the leopardess into the same cage, Nic put her in to an adjoining camp, where the two of them could become acquainted without injury. In the wild these big cats have home ranges which they defend by mortal combat. The male's range is larger than that of the female and will include the home range of more than one female. The solitary male will only come together with the female for brief but frequent copulation for a day or so and then the two will separate for another year or more. Placing the two felids in the same enclosure is therefore to inflict upon them a most unnatural proximity and no one could be sure that the whole experiment would not end in bloodshed and tears. The two captives ignored each other, and so, after two days, Nic and Marieta decided to risk it and put them together in the same run. They need not have worried. The two spotted cats settled down well together, and a year later, produced a pair of leopard cubs which were named Honkwe, a male, and Tai Kuli (meaning born to kill in Ovambo) who was a female. The gestation period for a leopard is very short, about one hundred days, and six months later, the leopardess gave birth to another litter of two, again a pigeon pair who were named Ulf and Bulaya. But life is full of dangers and no one ever knows what lies around the next corner.

Next to Harnas was the farm called Nicolsrus, which had belonged to Nic's father but which Nic had sold after his father's death. The money had been needed to finance the building of more cages for the ever increasing number of animals which were being bought to Harnas to be cared for. In July 1997, the wife of the farm manager at Nicolsrus was down at the cattle post attending to the annual vaccination of the cattle against pasteurella as well as Anthrax. This is neither an easy nor a pleasant task but it is necessary in an area where the pasteurella bacteria is rife and can cause death from pneumonia. Cattle become predisposed to such an infection by stress which can variously be brought on from drought, heat or cold or even being moved from one camp to another.

Anthrax is a lethal bacteria which kills man and beast alike, and is a popular component of chemical weapons of mass destruction. The organism produces a spore in the presence of air. These spores survive for years in the soil, water or old bones. Infection usually takes place through the mouth and this would place carnivores and scavengers at the greatest risk of contagion from eating the carcasses of animals that have died from Anthrax. However, it is a curious fact that the lions of Etosha (and Kruger Park) appear to have developed a high resistance, if not immunity, to this disease, perhaps by genetic adaptation to a diet of gradually increasing Anthrax exposure, as more and more antelope, especially wildebeest and zebra, die from the disease as a result of their inability to migrate outside confining park boundaries. Acute Anthrax infection is characterised by swellings on the body, especially in the neck and face as well as congestion and oedema of the vital organs and death usually follows within a few hours. It is highly contageous because of the spores, and an outbreak of the disease can wipe out whole herds of animals. Unlike the pasteurella vaccine which comprises the normal dead organisms in quantities sufficient to stimulate the immune system to produce an anti-body, the Anthrax vaccine, which is produced inter alia at Onderstepoort Veterinary facility at Pretoria in South Africa, consists of a small number of live spores in a dose quantity sufficient to stimulate immunity but not enough to cause an overwhelming infection. It is therefore a dangerous injection to administer, because in the dusty melee of jostling, struggling cattle it is all too easy to prick oneself with the needle and cases of self-infection in this manner, and even death, are not unknown. Anyway, the Nicolsrus cattle were being innoculated when one of the beasts, a full-grown ox with an apparently cancerous infection of one eye received its jab, fell over and died. Knowing that Harnas was always short of meat for their carnivores, the wife ordered the workers to load the animal onto the back of her bakkie (pick-up) and she drove it around to Harnas where the gift was gratefully received. Never look a gift horse in the mouth is the old adage, but had Marieta done so, she might have discovered that the gift ox contained a deadly cargo of live anthrax organisms. Had she examined the spleen, she might have noticed that it was unusually red and pulpy - like strawberry jam. Similarly the kidneys, liver, heart, stomach and pancreas would all have shown congestion and/or oedema. It is so easy to be wise after the event, and there was really no reason to suspect that anything was amiss. And so it came to pass that bucket-loads of contaminated meat were happily taken around and put out to the carnivores at Harnas in the month of July 1997.

Day One. The first to die were two adult male Cheetah in their veld camp. They were found dead the next morning. While Nic, Marieta and the staff were examining the bodies and speculating on the curious swellings of the throat, they discussed the possible causes of death and agreed that a snake bite was the likeliest.

Day Two. The female leopard, the one which Rudy Britz had collected from the Khomas Hochland, was found dead, also with her throat swollen. A poignant aspect of her death was that she had given birth to two cubs only ten days before (Ulf and Bulaya) and when the staff found her, the little cubs were still attempting to suckle on her cold, still body. There was now much feverish debate on the bizarre coincidence of these occurrences but eventually, the consensus was that the same snake that had bitten the Cheetah must then have travelled the half kilometre between the leopard run and the Cheetah camp and struck the leopardess. There were obvious improbabilities in this diagnosis but the staff were at a loss to explain the coincident deaths. That same evening, the big lion - Schabu's father - lost his appetite and preferred to lie where he was rather than come out to take his food. And one of the three large lionesses in the same camp with him had the same unusual swelling of the neck. Perhaps the deaths were not caused by snake bite after all. But then what? What could possibly cause the simultaneous death of so many animals? Just to further complicate an already perplexing situation the adult male caracal in the enclosure next to that of the leopards was also found dead. The snake theory was now acquiring serpentine characteristics of its own, both in becoming stretched ever longer and in speaking with a forked tongue.

It so happened that Harnas was caring for some Cheetah belonging to the Cheetah Foundation of Namibia at this time. A Vet had, quite fortuitously, flown in to check on and innoculate these animals. He was shown the carcasses of the lynx and leopardess and, although unable to give a spot diagnosis, he agreed to take the body of the smaller animal, the lynx, back with him to Otjiwarongo for an autopsy.

Day three. The following morning, the big male lion could not be seen. A search of the camp by staff and Bushmen finally discovered his dead body lying under a bush by the perimeter fence. Also, the one lioness's throat was badly swollen. Nic was now at his wits end and without waiting for the results of the autopsy of the lynx, he phoned Ulf Tubbesing, his regular vet, who flew down from Windhoek right away. Tubbesing brought with him an interesting piece of equipment, one which had originally been developed for the rapid field diagnosis of anthrax during the Gulf War. The PA Capture chromatography Assay tester was quick and simple to use as well as effective. Taking abdominal fluid from the dead body of the lion and serum samples from the clinically ill leopard and lioness it took the Vet less than five minutes to solve the mystery. An autopsy on the corpse of the big lion confirmed the diagnosis - Anthrax. But where could the disease have come from and why were so many animals in different camps dying simultaneously? The staff were still baffled. It was now far too late for vaccinations; it had to be assumed that all the carnivores had the disease. The only remedy was broad-spectrum anti-biotics. The cost of administering massive doses of antibiotic to dozens of animals, let alone the extra work and inconvenience involved, amounted to tens of thousands of dollars. The lioness with the badly swollen throat had anti-biotic injected into her by means of a dart gun. The treatment worked and she survived the Anthrax. Sadly, only three weeks later, she died from an overdose of tranquilliser which was given to her and the other lionesses in order to move them into another camp. The other carnivores were given their medicine in the form of pills. The mass of a lion is such that it required seven of the antibiotic tablets to be administered daily for seven days. The difficulties and frustration attending this exercise can easily be imagined; lionesses receiving little balls of minced meat studded with pills would manage by careful mastication to expel some of the expensive pills whilst tucking the meat down quite nicely. One of the Brown hyenas simply refused to eat the meat which was tainted with antibiotic. He got it anyway, fired into his rump with a dart. As if this were not enough, the weary staff were obliged to clean out all the enclosures. The camps had to be combed for old bones or skins, cages had to be scrubbed out with a caustic cleaner and every enclosure had to be raked and swept. For no one knew where the infection had come from or how far it might spread. Would it wipe out all the animals at Harnas? Such a nightmare was looking at this stage like a real possibility. Tubbesing and the Van der Merwe family considered the

142

facts. The outbreak was widespread but absolutely restricted to the carnivores. No humans, antelope or other animals were showing any symptoms of the horror disease. Only the meat eaters. The source of the infection had to be the meat fed.

The origin of the epidemic was only later discovered when a telephone enquiry to the good lady who donated the ox carcass ascertained the circumstances surrounding the ox's death. One lion, one leopard, one lynx and five Cheetah died from this tragic accident. Always look a gift horse or cow in the mouth is now the standing rule at Harnas. A matter of some scientific interest was that none of the young lions, leopards or Cheetah kept at Harnas contracted the disease in spite of their proximity to infected adults and their exposure to the contaminated meat. This supports other studies which tend to show that immature animals are less susceptible to Anthrax than adults. Does this mean that children will have a higher survival rate than their parents in the germ warfare which might await us in the new millennium?

There was one amusing incident to be remembered along with all the misfortune. Tubbesing had decided that in order to administer the antibiotic more accurately to the valuable big leopard, he should be tranquillized first. When attempting to handle wild animals, the best-laid plans often go astray and what happened here was that, after getting the tranquillizer dart shot into his hindquarters, the leopard climbed to the top of his tall Karee tree where he succumbed to the drug and lay stretched out on a high branch, liable to fall any minute. He had to be brought down to safety without delay. The resolute Vet climbed up into the tree, followed by Marieta, while Nic drove the white bakkie into the cage where he and Annelie positioned a ladder. As Marieta and the Vet were manhandling the heavy leopard off his precarious perch and attempting to pass him to Annelie who had scaled the ladder, the leopard recovered slightly, let out a growl and struggled briefly, just long enough for Marieta to let him slip from her grasp. One extended claw caught in her finger as he slipped past. For an instant or two of exquisite pain, the leopard hung by one claw, which was embedded into her finger, and then the whole pack of cards collapsed and down they all came, headfirst, to crash onto the bakkie below.

143

Nic was furious as he ran his hand over the new dents on the bonnet of the old vehicle. "Always the same with you," he fumed. "Wherever you are, there goes trouble also. Go home." None of this, "Darling are you alright?" to a wife who has just fallen three metres and is now sitting, dazed and nursing a lacerated finger. This is a family that takes its knocks stoically.

The young leopard cubs had the free run of Harnas and caused mayhem wherever they went. They would sneak into the dining room and attack unsuspecting guests. Woe betide the mother who left a baby in its carry-cot next to her on the floor. In a very short space of time, the peaceful silence of the dining room would be rent with urgent yells from the baby and the frantic mother would have to separate her howling offspring from the ferocious ball of spotted fur that was wrapped around it like a blanket. Children and small people walking on the lawns were especially vulnerable to attack and strong denim jeans and shirts were sensible wearing apparel for such visitors.

The mischief of the cubs never seemed to end. When night fell and every-one went to sleep, they came awake and went hunting. Only in the hottest part of the day was there any respite from their tireless, and tiresome, importuning.

Anything that moved was attacked. When they were still a few weeks old and sleeping with puppies and other young orphans in the kitchen, the cubs showed their true colours. One night they went to sleep cuddled up to a small porcupine orphan. The next day, they killed it. That is a leopard. Rubbing itself affectionately against you one minute, killing you the next minute. Admirable it may be, but loveable it is not.

When the two sets of cubs were four and ten months old respectively, they discovered an open bathroom window and secured entrance to the house in this way. There they indulged their unrestrained mischief to the full, breaking pot plants, tearing cushions and pillows to pieces, ripping the stuffing out of the beds and upholstery and generally demolishing everything. By the time they were found, the house looked as if it had been ransacked by terrorists. Indeed, that is exactly what they were, and were known thereafter as the 'terrorists'.

Only once did Schalk and Marlice try sleeping out on the back lawn with the cubs. They often did it with the bat-eared foxes, who used to snuggle up under the blankets and sleep with them. The lion cubs were boisterous but would eventually settle down and the Cheetahs were comparatively tame to sleep with. But the leopard cubs! They never stopped. They jumped on to the children who were trying to sleep, biting, scratching and raking with their back claws. There was simply no peace to be had and in the small hours, Schalk and Marlice gave up and trailed back into the house clutching their blankets and duvets, leaving the field of battle to the spotted victors.

One morning, the older cubs chased a young cub up one of the large syringa trees behind the house. Anxious that the little cub might fall and hurt itself, Marieta decided that she would rescue it from its persecutors, and climbed up to fetch it down. Unfortunately, the branch on which she entrusted her weight proved unworthy of her trust and broke off, pitching her headfirst into one of her well-tended flower beds. She looked up from where she had fallen to see the three leopards sitting comfortably up the tree, gazing down at her with innocent curiosity.

More for the protection of the guests than any other single reason, the four terrorists were finally removed from all contact with visitors and confined to the large open area around the garages, while the four young lions, including Savannah, the one-eyed lioness who had been living there, were moved to the camp behind the monkey cages. This camp was out of bounds to guests, and only the family and some staff members were allowed in.

From this time, Schalk adopted the four terrorists and they became his consuming hobby. When not busy with other work about the farm, he spent the time playing with them and tried to take them out for a long walk in the veld at least once a day. Sometimes Max would accompany him, especially if there were visitors who had asked to go along for the experience of walking in the bush in the company of four of the most splendid of the big cats.

These 'leopard walks' became very popular especially with the keen photographers and wildlife film makers, but Harnas had to be constantly alert to the dangers of bringing together civilians and free-ranging leopards. Gradually, more by happenstance than design, Harnas became a pioneer in offering to the discerning tourist an 'interaction-with-leopards bush experience'. There was much more to the leopard bush walk than merely avoiding injury. Tourists found themselves for a few precious hours part of the Kalahari ecology with so many sights, sounds and scents to enjoy.

"I want to go too," announces Beverley, a visitor from South Africa. Several people are standing in a group by the Ford pick-up, waiting to go on the leopard bush walk. The announcement was made earlier at breakfast in the dining room, when Max stipulated that this tour was not open to children or small people. Schalk and Max are busy getting the leopards into the large cage on the back of the pick-up and pretend not to hear her. Three of the four have already leapt up onto the tailboard and gone in, displaying eager anticipation for the hunt, but Tai Kuli, the fierce little leopardess, is jibbing like a racehorse who refuses to enter the starting gate. After some fruitless attempts at persuasion, Schalk loses his patience and picks up her forequarters, while Max lifts her hindquarters and they manhandle her in to the confinement of the cage. The reason for her reluctance to enter becomes clear when there is an explosion of snarls and growling and for a few seconds she and Honkwe maul each other in a short, sharp, ugly fight. Just a few seconds. Not enough to cause any serious injury but quite enough for people to see how volatile they are, and how dangerous they can be. This is not a good start. "That is the difference between lions and leopards." Schalk tells them. "A lion is so predictable. If he is cross, you can see it. He gives you warning. But a leopard......," He shakes his head and waves towards the four felines who by now are quietly seated on their haunches looking like so many commuters in a bus.

"Can't I come too?" Beverley again. She is desperately keen to see the leopards in action. Max and Schalk look at each other and hesitate. Then Max answers.

146

Schalk with Honkwe and Tai Kuli, about eighteen months old

"No, Bev. Sorry. You are just too small."

"I'm not so small," she protests, drawing herself up to her full height of four feet eleven inches. "And look, Laura is going. She is the same size as me."

Laura smiles. At five feet and two inches she is definitely bigger than Bev. "I have to help the cameramen." She points at the American film men fussing over their photographic equipment. Schalk takes the leopards and the camera crew follow behind in a bakkie driven by Max. The two vehicles trundle down the Harnas runway and at the end, they pass the dam, the pool of water where Marlice used to bring Mufasa. Then they are on a sandy bush track which winds like a footpath around any obstruction, from a Vaalbos shrub or an antheap to a fresh antbear burrow thoughtfully excavated in the centre of the road. A family of warthogs, tails erect, trot stiffly across the path in front of them and Schalk drives on. "If we stop here," he says, "the leopards will run after those warthogs and kill some. So we must go on a little."

147

"Tell us about leopards, Schalk. What can we expect?" One of the walkers wants to know.

Schalk considers his answer. "They are very intelligent. They have already sized you up and made up their minds who they will try to catch. And they will ignore everyone else. Like with the Bushmen. We always tell them look, you must not taunt these leopards or they will remember, and later even when you have forgotten, they will hurt you. But one or two of the Bushmen, they do not listen so nicely and we see them stamp their foot or wave their arms at the leopards when they walk past the cage. Then the leopard will wait for his chance. Sometimes they bite a Bushman and we wonder why and then someone remembers that he used to bait them, maybe long ago. But the leopard never forgets."

"Are these leopards under your control, when we are walking in the veld?" Schalk shakes his head emphatically. "Leopards is ungovernable. They do exactly what they want. No pity. No remorse. Alright, lions and Cheetah, they are like dogs and want to be friends and to please you. But a leopard does not care. He is just looking for a weakness. All the time. That is why we must be careful. If you are attacked, stand still. Do not run. If you run you are in trouble. But if you don't want to take the risk, stay in the pick-up. This is your choice." A few kilometres pass and then, near the northern boundary of Harnas which separates it from Hereroland, Schalk pulls over and finds some shade under a yellowwood tree. The bakkie arrives and creeps into the miniscule amount of remaining shade. The photographers wish to film the release of the leopards from their cage. While the equipment is being set up, the four cats pace eagerly around and their movements become more sudden and nervous. Clearly, they know what is about to happen. "O.K. let them go," calls out an American voice, the accent sounding so alien in Africa. Max pushes the gate wide, and the leopards seem to flow down onto the ground with sinuous ease. One of them stalks carefully up to the people and Schalk tenses. "Stand still," he calls out. "He is only sizing you up." Just like a housecat rubbing itself up against a chair leg, the leopard, his face perfectly expressionless, runs the whole length of his

148

body against each of the visitors. Then, without any apparent effort, he takes a few bounds, and in no time has vanished from sight. His siblings have already melted away into the surrounding bush, bombshelling in different directions. A barely discernible track leads off into the veld and Schalk leads away. Then come the professional photographers and close behind is Laura who is attached by an umbilical cord of cables leading from her backpack to their cameras. Having to be alert to the most cryptic and peremptory of hand signals, Laura has no chance to keep watch for stalking leopards. This is a bad time to be a phographer's assistant. With Max bringing up the rear, the people move slowly along the path in this manner, dividing their time between keeping a proper look-out for the four-legged terrorists and learning something about the ecology of the Kalahari. It is mid-morning and the hot sun is not yet unbearable. Rank tufts of savanna grasses lie sprawling in an untidy way while the trees and shrubs which are dotted about in the grassland offer some more cover for the hunters.

This is the real Africa. And there is real danger here. The adventurers are not flashing past in air-conditioned buses or vehicles, crossing off the list of big five as they spot the animals, and then flying back to Europe to tell their friends how they have been to Africa. No, they are interacting with Africa, right down to the worrisome flies who must be continuously brushed away from the face, the grass seeds in the socks which make walking uncomfortable and the sweat which runs down into their eyes, making them smart. But the rewards are everywhere, for those who thirst for nature, those whose souls must drink in the whole orchestration of sights, sounds and smells. The sandy earth is redolent with the bewitching blend of primal scents which emanate from the very soil, together with the cocktail of odours from the vegetation. Every bush they walk past infuses them with its own distinct aroma. Drawn by the moisture on a damp patch of ground a cluster of butterflies drink, their upright triangular wings of light green and cream edged with black lace making them look for all the world like a gathering of yachts at a distant harbour. Here and there are seen diggings, smaller and shallower than a teacup, where meerkats and other small mammals have dug for beetle larvae. A fresh animal dropping has even now attracted the attention of several dung beetles. They roll the dung into a ball the size of a large marble and then, putting their heads down and using their back legs, they roll the dung ball down the track. Struggling over loose twigs and other small obstacles until they find a piece of ground which their instinct tells them is right, they dig down into the sand for six inches or so to bury the dung ball along with an egg which will hatch into a larva which in turn will live off the dung. Here on a tuft of love grass a jackal has deposited his droppings. These are full of reddish-black berries. He has been eating the fruit of the wag-'n-bietjie thorn (Zizyphus mucronata). So even when there are no carcases to scavenge, the cunning little jackal adapts his diet and survives a little longer.

"There! Leopard." Schalk is pointing away to the right. They glimpse him. Just the flicker of a spotted form about sixty metres away in the grass and then it is gone. But where are the others? "The game begins," says Max softly. "They always run away and hunt for small animals to kill. When they find there is none, then they get bored and they hunt us. We must be careful now. Close up, we must keep together."

They pass under an old camelthorn and scan the rough, fissured branches carefully for spotted ambushers. The ageing camelthorns that frown down on predator and prey alike, are hundreds of years old. Such a tree only reaches maturity, judged from production of the edible pods, at about one hundred years of age and it may either live on for centuries naturally, or be felled in two minutes by a chainsaw. In their lifetime these trees have seen and provided food for elephants and buffalo by the thousand. Now their pods lie rotting on the ground, nibbled on only by the furtive Kudu or small mammals who have survived the onslaught of Man upon Nature. Tsamma melons peep out from under the creepers which surround them, and elsewhere, the swelling earth conceals the presence of the giant tuber of the maramba bean. Hairline cracks in the ground together with deeper than usual excavations show where a bat-eared fox has scented the food of the gods, Kalahari truffles - what the Bushmen call N!abba. European truffles may have a stronger aroma but they cannot compete with N!abba for taste. Food everywhere, all around them. The Bushmen and the animals know it but these people are only beginning to understand. Suddenly there is a rush from right under their feet, and their hearts stop. The bobbing white tail of a scrub hare weaves away through the tangled grass. Their flagging attention is now most wonderfully refocussed. But not for long. For as the morning dawdles towards midday, all the most successful inhabitants of the Kalahari turn their thoughts towards siesta. Over the drowsy hum and buzzing of the myriads of insects comes the monotonous Ka-karra-ka-karra of the turtle dove, and the soft, seductive cooing of the laughing dove. "Tricky-tricky-tricky," calls the little Ashy Tit persistently while the melodious thin song of the Karahari Robin adds its own tone to the soporific symphony. Even the shrieking of a nearby Grey Lourie, "Go Away. Go Away," warning all other creatures of their intrusion, and the staccato "Kok-kok-kok" of a yellow hornbill, cocking a bright yellow eye at them as they trudge past, cannot pull them out of their lethargy. The languid heat; the heavy tranquillity; the somnolent sounds all around; they all conspire together like so many skilled hypnotists, to lull the indolent senses to sleep.

"Daar! Ek sien jy! Ek sien jy!" (I see you). Max's stentorian shout takes the adrenalin channel straight to the fight-or-flight side of the brain, dispelling reverie and daydreaming as if by a stun grenade. The skin on the back of their necks crawling, the walkers swing round to see Max advancing on a small Vaalbos shrub, arm outstretched, tanned brown finger pointing. Like an image crystallizing onto a screen the bush dissolves into two halves, one of which becomes a crouching leopard. What surreal camouflage. It is Tai Kuli. Her tail flicks in annoyance, she utters a little growl and then dashes away, bounding through the grass with the ease and grace of some terrestrial dolphin. "Look out now. . . the others. . . . ," calls Max. Hardly are the words out of his mouth when there is an hysterical shout of "I see you. I see you" from one of the photographers, pointing towards the veld on the opposite side of the track.

151

Another ambusher bounds away. Foiled again. "Now we must not sleep. Once they start they will not stop," Max warns.

The people find themselves moving along in exactly the same manner as a counter-insurgency patrol, with Schalk scouting ahead, then a knot of photographers, then the tourists and finally, turning around and walking backwards much of the time, Max is doing the tail-end-Charley duty. There is something infinitely elating about patrolling through the veld and pitting one's wits against so skilful a stalker as a leopard. The rules of the game are clear and the hunters do not cheat. If they are seen and pointed out before they can get close enough to launch their final spring, then they must go away and try again. For all their skill, the bush is open and the sparse tufts of grass afford the hunters little cover. Several more times that morning the electrifying yells of "I see you" ring out, sending the adrenalin streaming into the veins. And thus is spent a most memorable three hours. A disparate group of humans doing what their ancestors had to do every day; trek through the bush while running the gauntlet of their own predators. All their senses have come alive. They are consciously using sight, sound and scent to locate the stalkers and the mind is wonderfully sharp and focussed. The party has come almost full circle and can see the sunlight glinting off the vehicles through the bush ahead when something happens. There is a crash, a scuffle and then an angry bellow from Max. The leopardess's spring takes her directly onto Laura's back. Anyone who had had the experience of being the target of a playful house cat who emerges unexpectedly from under the dining room table to sink his fangs and claws into one's calf, should be able to imagine the extreme unpleasantness of the arrival by air of fifty kilograms of concentrated trouble, which celebrates its arrival by imbedding some serious fangs and claws into one's upper body parts. The impact of Tai Kuli's hurtling form makes an audible thump as it slams into the unprepared body of the victim. Laura goes down like a ninepin. Sensibly, she does not scream or struggle. She lies prone in the dust with her assailant clinging with all claws and savaging the backpack. Before anyone else has time to react, Max has run forward and flung himself headlong into the fray with the reckless

152

fervour of an All Black rugby forward entering a loose scrum during a grudge match. Muttering in Afrikaans, he wrestles with the leopardess until, with Schalk's help he can prise her away from Laura who is still playing possum. And then we see the stuff that a leopard is made of. The moment that Tai Kuli has been hauled off her quarry, she is immediately calm. She sits sedately and licks her paws as if nothing has happened. Laura is helped to her feet. A little shaky and bleeding from scratches on her back and shoulders, she is otherwise unhurt. No doubt she will dine out on this story for years. Perhaps her grandchildren will also hear about it. "Oh thanks, Max." She is breathless.

"It's my job." With a smile like a hyena on Max's guileless face, the pride and satisfaction are not well concealed. "You do the right thing by lying still. If you struggle she will hold you harder. And you never scream. That was a good thing. I think your rucksack save you from some more scratches." He points to her torn canvas backpack which has definitely born the brunt of the assault.

The other leopards now show themselves. It is as if some signal has told them that the game is over, and besides, they can see the cars. It is time to go home. Schalk takes Tai Kuli by the tail and she walks along unresisting until we reach the vehicles. How docile she now seems. Although the visitors have had a magic bush experience the cars with their promise of comfort are still a welcome sight. For even hiking through the veld in the distinguished company of the Crown Prince of Cats has its drawbacks. There are thorns in Paradise they say, and this is true also of the Kalahari, which never takes with one hand without giving with the other, and vice versa. For if she takes the rain away, she pays us for our loss. The drought destroys all the pathogens and dangerous micro-organisms. There is no disease. No ticks (except the sand tampans). No parasites. No roundworms, tapeworms, hookworms or wireworms to further burden the poor creatures who must endure the terrifying dust storms. Yet, when she sends rain in abundance, the creatures rejoice with cau-tion, for along with the lifegiving liquid come plagues of locusts, caterpillars, moths, flies and mosquitos. Sometimes even malaria. Always two sides to the coin in Africa.

153

The long hike has taken its toll. The soft sand gives underfoot, and it requires ever greater effort for the hikers to drag themselves on. The grass seeds in their socks are driving them mad.

Yet if they do not wear socks, then the long trek will give them blisters. If they sit down, remove their shoes and try to pick out the torturous, pricking seeds, then they must contend with the ubiquitous biting ants that play the role of taxman to an entrepreneur - keep moving or he'll catch up with and bite you. Thus it is a hot, thirsty band of stragglers who wend their weary way back to where the vehicles were left, having sampled the discomforts as well as the delights of the African bush. One of the leopards has not returned. The people seek shelter from the wilting heat while Schalk and Max must go back, calling, to look for him. Laura seems cheerful despite the blood on her shirt. The photographers are happy, excited by the footage they have shot. Names fall out of their animated conversation like gemstones out of an orebody. National Geographic, Discovery Channel.... The three leopards are lying down in their cage, awaiting the ride home. The humans will never forget them. But will the leopards even spare anyone another thought?

Marieta is waiting in the courtyard when the hikers return. She and Bev are bottle-feeding two lion cubs. "Ay-ay-ay..." she exclaims at the sight of Laura. "And now?" 'And now?' is Namibian jargon for 'What happened?'
"Leopard." Schalk, like his father, is never one for long explanations.
"Which one?"
"Tai Kuli."
"That one! She is a little terror!" Marieta laughs. She always laughs when her animals bite someone. She is not being nasty. She just thinks that it is funny, and being such a spontaneous person, will laugh out loud. "Come on, Laura. Let's put some iodine on those scratches." She feels for the kilogram of keys that should be hanging on her belt. "Keys. I need to open my medicine cupboard. Where are my keys? Max. . Schalk. . .Annelie. . . Christine. . . anybody?"

Chapter six

LIONS

Please let him know I loved him
And I wish I had been there,
To laugh with him just one last time
To let him know I care.
These memories are so poignant
I hold them in my heart,
More precious than my life itself
So we shall never be apart.
He was my friend and confidant
I watched him slip away,
Like sand between my fingers
Like a child thats lost his way.
In dreams I hear him calling
As if from far away,
He's telling me how proud he is
Of what I am today.
So let me cry one more time
Then dry these lonely tears,
And ask him for the courage
To face my final years.
He'll be waiting when I get there
Its only now I feel,
The struggle will be over
And at last my scars can heal.

Andrew Mercer

The lion is Mother Africa's largest carnivore and arguably her most significant. In direct competition with farmers for their livestock, it is the sentinel species for wild Africa. What befalls the lion today may be tomorrow's fate for all other life. The sheer size and strength of this wild person is intimidating to feeble humans; how terrifying he must have been to early hominids before they were able to invent weapons against which muscular strength could offer no answer. To put the majesty of the King of Beasts in its true perspective, compare him to the American mountain lion, which weighs between one hundred and twenty and one hundred and eighty pounds (50 - 80 kilograms). A full-grown male African lion can weigh four times as much - three hundred kilograms. In ancient times these marvelous cats roamed the whole of Europe, Asia and Africa.

Every year the shadings on the distribution maps of the Southern African lion population grow smaller and thinner, smaller and thinner. The greatest tragedy of all is that many can see what is happening but very few are doing anything about it. Even in their final retreats, like the Kruger National Park, lions are dying from terrible man-introduced diseases, such as bovine tuberculosis.

It is against this tragic background that Nic decided in 1991 to bring some lions to Harnas. He was recovering from his near-fatal aircraft crash when his attention was drawn to an advertisement in the newspaper for someone to take over a group of four lions which had originally come from Zimbabwe but were then being cared for at a private zoo at Patensie, near Port Elizabeth in South Africa. The funds to maintain them had run out, and if no one could be found to take responsibility for them then.......... Harnas was already looking after dozens of animals including Cheetah. So why not lions? The first obstacle Nic had to overcome was the formal one of obtaining the necessary transport and import permits from the Department of Nature Conservation. Bureaucratic arguments are always circular and there is therefore no way to resolve them logically. Their ultimate basis is always 'Policy'. The wearying task of squeezing permits out of Nature Conservation departments usually runs something like this:

"I want to apply for a Permit to introduce lions from South Africa to my sanctuary."

"You need three Permits, an Import Permit, a Transport Permit and a Permit to keep animals in captivity. All these Permits have different requirements. We cannot issue an Import Permit. At a recent meeting of Government Ministers from SADC it was agreed that no animals may be imported or exported to or from any country in the region. It has nothing to do with you."

"What is the reason for freezing all imports and exports?"

"I don't know. Its Policy."

"What about the transport permit?"

"We cannot give that to you either."

"Why not?"

"The animals might be diseased and introduce disease into this country."

"But I can import all the cattle and sheep or goats I want to from South Africa. Aren't they also capable of bringing disease?"

"Ah, but you would require a Veterinary Certificate that they were free from disease."

"Well, let me get a Veterinary certificate to say that the lions are free from disease. I'll get ten such Certificates from ten different Vets if that is your real concern."

"That won't help you. There are the possibilities of genetic pollution."

"What?"

"They might breed with local lions and cause genetic problems, including recessive genes."

"But recessive genes are caused by inbreeding, not by widening the gene pool. That is why we cattle farmers cross European and African cattle, to get crossbreed vigour. Besides there are no wild lions for hundreds of kilometres around me and these lions will be confined to a camp. How are they going to copulate with wild lions?"

"Nevertheless its Policy. Anyway they might escape."

"It's Policy to cause inbreeding and recessive genes?"

157

"It's Policy." And so it goes on..

But, somehow Nic pleaded and bullied the permits out of Nature Conservation, and was able to turn his attention to the logistics of transporting four lions nearly two thousand kilometres to Harnas. This task was delegated to the able manager, Rudy Britz. Rudy welded a makeshift pen on the back of Nic's Ford pick-up truck, using a steel frame and corrugated iron. He left a gap for ventilation about three inches high all around the sides of the loadbox but otherwise closed in the pen completely. Wild animals are always transported in closed containers where they feel safer and suffer less stress. Loading the lions at Port Elizabeth presented few problems. The poor creatures were being confined in a brick room with a sliding steel gate. Rudy dropped the tailboard of the truck and reversed hard up against the gate, which was then slid open. The lions were sprayed with water from a garden hosepipe. They scrambled through the opening into the shelter of the truck, and Rudy was on his way back to Namibia in no time.

The journey of seventeen hundred kilometres required a number of stops for fuel and at one of these pit stops Rudy pulled up beside a petrol pump next to which there was a red sedan vehicle. By this time it was already dark. He opened the petrol cap on the side of the truck and went off to relieve himself. Returning from his ablutions, he was just in time to see some spectacular action. A half-asleep petrol attendant had shuffled over, picked up the pump nozzle and inserted it into the filler neck when, not a metre from his bowed head there was a roar and a crash as one of the lions sprang at the side of the pen. The flimsy corrugated iron sheeting flattened and then bulged out. A huge paw rimmed with thick, ugly claws shot out through the ventilation gap and stopped inches short of his face. The attendant rolled back the ages to the dawn of time with a blood-curdling yell such as many a Neanderthal must have uttered when pounced upon by the King of Beasts. Quite forgetting his duties both to his employer and to his customer, he dropped the petrol hose, and performed a back somersault, one which would have brought applause from any Olympic gymnast, onto the bonnet of the red car which was parked behind him.

The somersault was followed by a flying leap out into the darkness wherein he vanished. After Rudy had recovered from a sustained fit of mirth, he completed the refuelling himself, pushed the money under the closed, locked door of the attendant's kiosk into which the other pump attendant had fled, and drove away, leaving the owner of the red car looking thoroughly bewildered.

The Ariamsviei border post between South Africa and Namibia lies in the middle of a salt pan in one of the driest parts of the Kalahari Desert. With not a tree or blade of grass in sight, to approach it is like driving up to an outpost of the French Foreign Legion. When Rudy arrived there with his royal leonine cargo the place was in darkness and deserted, save for two officious and unsmiling Customs Officers.

"What have you got in the back?" demanded one of the South African border guards sourly.

"Lions."

The officer looked more closely at Rudy and his sour expression deepened. "What have you really got?"

"Lions. Look for yourself."

Keeping a careful three metres or so between himself and the vehicle, the Customs man shone his torch into the ventilation gap. Four pairs of wicked citrine eyes reflected the torch light back at him. The officer froze. He looked back and calculated that the nearest building was thirty metres away. He did some mental arithmetic, distance divided by seconds. He made a critical assessment of the obviously homemade canopy and could not fail to notice the bulge in the one side. "Go," he said to Rudy in a choked voice. Breathing had become difficult.

"Don't you want to stamp my...?"

"I said go. Go now."

Rudy went. On the Namibian side, a corpse in uniform held out a rubber stamp and let it fall onto Rudy's proffered passport, after which it resumed its state of death. No doubt it came back from the dead regularly every pay day and was

Elsa always preferred the head of the carcass

therefore allowed to occupy a seat under a sign which read 'Customs and Immigration.'

Twenty-two hours after leaving Port Elizabeth, four lions including Elsa's mother and the father of both Schabu and Mufasa, arrived at Harnas. The off-loading of the Patensie lions at Harnas gave Nic a number of worries. He had constructed an enclosure for them near the house using his usual materials, gumpoles and wire mesh. Was the fence high enough? Was it strong enough? He knew that it was strong enough to contain Cheetahs but lions were a whole new story and he had visions of them jumping off the truck, smashing through the fence and disappearing into the veld in order to start a reign of terror over the cattle farms in the area. In the event, his fears proved groundless. The much-travelled felines were obviously used to fences for they did not even test them, and were content to stalk around the perimeter, calmly sniffing and scent-marking their new territory. However as Nic would learn later when he tried to release Simba into an open-air fenced enclosure, wild lions who are unused to fences will tear them to pieces even when they are reinforced with electric strands. The four lions - there were in fact one lion and three lionesses - settled down well at Harnas.

Every year the Van der Merwe family used to holiday at Swakopmund for a few weeks over Christmas. They made a point of returning to Harnas on Christmas Day in order to bring presents for the Bushmen who worked there. On the afternoon of Christmas Day 1991, and after a long, hot drive of six hundred or so kilometres, the family arrived back from Swakopmund and parked in front of the lion's enclosure. Nico was getting out of the car, his arms full of presents, when he distinctly heard a voice say "Ow." Puzzled, he stopped and looked around. "Ow," repeated the voice. Nico had never heard such a sound before. He set out to search the grass next to the fence from where the sound seemed to come. Imagine his surprise when he came upon a tiny bundle of buff-coloured fur which was lying dusty and bedraggled in the sand. The back and ears were covered with black blotches just as if someone had sprinkled coal dust onto it and then wiped his sooty hands on the teddy-bear-like ears. That was Elsa, named after Joy Adamson's famous 'Born Free' lioness. Somehow the little mite had struggled out of the enclosure, squeezing through the space offered by the diameter of the wire mesh. Newborn cubs are laughably small considering the size that they will attain, and can comfortably fit into the palm of one's hand. Nic and the family wasted no time in searching the lion camp for the other cubs in the litter and found another two. But to everyone's disappointment both of them were dead and although there was no apparent cause of death, it is quite common for lionesses to inadvertently cause the death of their newborn by lying on them. Afraid that the same fate would befall Elsa if she were placed back into the camp under the dubious care of her mother, the decision was made to remove and hand-rear her, a task which Marieta no doubt instigated. Poor Elsa. No one in Namibia had any experience of hand-rearing

161

lion cubs and she bore the brunt of the learning curve. Marieta had hand-raised so many animals, wild and domestic, that she did not expect any problems. She simply prepared warm milk and gave it to the newborn cub three times a day. The cub responded in a most unexpected manner by puking, having convulsions, and moaning with pain. Marieta, steeped in guilt, rushed her precious bundle off to the Vet, a hundred kilometres away, but he had no experience with lions and his best efforts were ineffectual. After Christmas, the family members travelled back to Swakopmund to resume their holiday but spent most of their time sitting at the local Veterinary surgery trying to determine the cause of the sickly little cub's illness. They tried everything, and nothing worked. If they gave her cow's milk, she had diarrhoea. If they fortified it with egg yolk, she became constipated. They tried skimmed milk, and she starved; full cream milk and she scoured. Several times, she went into convulsions and they half-expected her to die. Then one of Nic's numerous, frantic phone calls around the region paid off. He spoke to a man named Kleynhans in South Africa who had owned lions, and during the conversation, it came out that Harnas was only feeding the cub three times a day. "You can't do that, you'll kill her," Kleynhans told him. "Lions have a very strong digestive system, so there must be something in the stomach all the time. In the wild, they suckle frequently. You have to feed the cub every hour." First it was poor Elsa, now it was poor Marieta. Every hour, morning, noon and night, she pushed the baby bottle into the cub's mouth.

The nights were the worst and to make it easier for herself, she brought the cub into bed thereby starting a bad habit. For several weeks, Marieta kept up the feeding vigil until she was tottering around like a zombie, yawning.

Now that her foster parents had discovered that the secret lay in the frequency of feeding, Elsa thrived. She spent her waking hours exploring her surroundings and getting up to mischief. Her favourite sport was to climb into the medicine cupboard and attack the crepe bandages, scattering them all over the house and chewing up all the shoes that she could find. When the family began to run short of shoes to wear, it became apparent that lion cubs are just

The medicine cupboard never looked the same after Elsa had played there

like children, who need friends to play with or else they become nuisances. Clearly she needed companionship so Marieta looked around the district and found two Pug dogs for her. The three animals became inseparable friends. Thereafter, all the cubs who were born at Harnas received their own companion puppy. While the animals were still young the system worked very well. But when they were older, this mingling of dogs and lions could become a recipe for tragedy.

Having so nearly lost the cub, Marieta employed a Bushman woman as a nanny, whose sole task was to follow little Elsa around and see that she came to no harm. In fact, the cub was spoilt rotten not only by Marieta, but by the whole family, to the point that discipline was compromised. Schalk and Marlice clamored for Elsa to be allowed to sleep with them, and they would put mattresses down on the floor so that they could all sleep together, the children, Elsa and the Pug dogs. Elsa with her dummy in her mouth or someone's finger to suck on. If the Gobabis rugby football club wanted a mascot to run onto the field of play in front of the team, who else but a lioness dressed in a rugby jersey of the local colours would do? The novelty wore off quite soon, however, when the mascot caused delays in the game by exuberantly chasing the ball. Every weekend Nic and Marieta went to Gobabis to collect the children from school and take them home. They would sometimes go to the local dam for a picnic and Elsa became fond of splashing around and romping in the water with all the local schoolchildren.

Harnas was discovering that one cannot generalise about lions. They are not one-dimensional characters, but are intelligent beings with fully developed personalities. They say lions hate having to swim, but Elsa loved the water. Wheelbarrows terrified her. No one remembers exactly when or how this fear became apparent, or what caused it. One imagines that this harmless garden tool could well have been perceived as a terrifying monster as it creaked and clanked towards a tiny cub. Whatever the reason, this fear was detected by the family and staff at Harnas and they capitalised on it. The mundane machine became the tool of choice for protection, training and discipline. All the other cubs which were later born at Harnas, and grew up there, had the same fear of wheelbarrows. Before Harnas became a tourist facility these cubs who had since grown into young lions, used to roam freely around the house and garden, and importune anyone arriving at Harnas. A visit to the van der Merwes was only a little less dangerous than say, running with the bulls at Pamplona. The miscreants did not deal out injuries with harmful intent, but rather in an excess of joyful high spirits. Still, an injury was an injury and Nic and the family had to devise a way for bona fide visitors to get from the car park to the house without being knocked over. The system evolved where a large stock of these harmless garden machines were kept next to the car park, so that the people arriving there could pick up a barrow and wheel themselves safely past the roving lions. "Don't forget your wheelbarrow," became the standard Harnas farewell so that departing visitors could get themselves back to their cars without a too-close encounter with the young lions. Elsa never lost her fear of wheelbarrows, although some of the other lions, such as Schabu, did. Whenever the high-spirited lioness was up to mischief someone would run for the nearest wheelbarrow and the mere sight of this fearsome object rumbling towards her would send her scurrying back to her camp. Motor cars held an irresistible fascination for Elsa. She could never see a car without jumping up to explore it. It was bad enough when she was smaller and only capable of scratching the paintwork, leaving dirty paw prints and chewing on the softer rubber and plastic components. Later on, when she weighed one hundred and fifty kilograms, when each paw print became a dent and when she could collapse the roof of the car into a nice comfortable concave shape to lie in, then it was not so funny any longer. Some visitors were perfectly content with the shape of the roof as designed by the manufacturer and were less than impressed with the new hammock shape and the concomitant fact that there was no longer any headroom in the car except for a dwarf. In fact some visitors showed such a deplorable lack of interest in the comfort of the young lioness, that they took to parking their cars ever-greater distances from the house, even if it meant a longer, more arduous slog pushing a heavy wheelbarrow through hostile country where danger lurked behind every bush. The matter came to a head one unfortunate day when the local schoolmaster had occasion to visit Harnas. It so happened that he had recently purchased a brand-new motorcar of which he was especially proud. Unaware of the special hazard to motorists, he parked close to the house and went in. Marieta went to greet him and saw the car parked close by, all new and shiny. "I think you should move your car," she warned, "Elsa will tramp on it."

"Oh, I'll only be a minute," was his fateful reply. As so often happens when one is in a hurry, distractions arise and so it was not until an hour later that he left to return to his car. Marieta walked out with him. Schoolmasters are important people in the lives of mothers, and she did not want him to be bowled over by her boisterous four-pawed children. Then they stopped in disbelief. There, where he had parked his new car, was a wreck. Elsa had indeed tramped on it. The roof had collapsed and the boot and bonnet were severely dented. The rubber trim surrounding the windscreen had been hooked out and chewed. The rear view mirrors were lying on the ground, along with the license plates and crumbs of rubber from the tyres. The windscreen wipers had been eaten. Stretched out in languid comfort on the bowl of what had been the roof, was the author of this misfeasance, her chin resting on her forepaws. After the first few moments of shocked silence, Marieta with her voice at full throttle screamed at Elsa, yelled for help from the staff and offered effusive apologies to her guest, all at the same time. Elsa, unaware of quite what she had done to deserve the acrimony, but sensitive enough to know that her shares with her foster mother were lower than the Dow Jones Index after Black Friday, slunk away on her stomach with a woebegone, backward look. As for the schoolmaster he was to be seen walking heavily around his car, making inarticulate moaning sounds, his eyes sunken and misty. No doubt he rushed off to consult his attorney and received a Latin lesson. More specifically, the ramifications of the phrase "Volenti non fit injuria." After this, he must have hurried with equal celerity to his insurance broker to make a claim. Cause of Damage: "Lioness."

For Elsa, the outcome was that she was given her own car to play with. This was only the body-shell of an old Austin Mini from the local car breaker, but Elsa was as thrilled with it as if it were a brand-new Rolls-Royce. She took to living in it and insisted on getting her food delivered to her while she sat upright behind the steering wheel, making Harnas look as if it offered drive-in restaurant facilities to any local wild motorists. As Elsa grew up and her personality developed, the family noticed that she was very dog-like in her devotion to them. Perhaps because lions are social people and therefore emotionally dependent upon others, she felt insecure if anything happened to disturb the harmony of the group. If she was scolded for one of her many misdemeanours, she would cringe and crawl away on her stomach; look back with the most pitiful hang-dog expression and whimper so miserably that their anger soon melted and was replaced by sympathy for her obvious unhappiness. Then the family would forgive her and pat her and reassure her with tidbits

166

Elsa loved her car

and endearments until her normal cheerful disposition had been restored.

Once again, this trait was peculiar to Elsa, for any attempt to scold other lions, such as Schabu, would provoke a warning snarl. Yet it would have been a bad mistake to think of Elsa as a large, playful dog. Time and again she would remind everyone that loveable or not, she was a lioness, and not to be trifled with. When half-grown she had the free run of the large area which was fenced off for the sheds and garages. On the other side of the high fence was the pen where the sheep were kraaled at night and there were a number of dogs, including four Australian Khalpies who were there to protect the sheep from predators such as jackals or caracal. These Khalpy sheep dogs, not surprisingly, regarded Elsa as a predator and would rush up to the fence and bark furiously whenever they caught sight

167

of her. The other dogs, including a dachshund, ignored her and minded their own business; for this courtesy, they were to be rewarded with their lives. But Elsa would later show the four Khalpies that, like humans, lions can also harbour grudges. One day Elsa got through the gate which separated them. Lions are more intelligent than dogs and Schabu for example could open a deadbolt latch from both sides of a gate, using his claws and his nose. In any event, she gained access to the sheep kraal where there was no fence to protect the dogs from her resolve. Paying no attention to any of the other dogs including the dachshund which pluckily attached itself to her tail, Elsa single-mindedly set about the four Khalpies and in a few seconds had killed them all. Having settled her score with them and bearing no ill will towards the others who had left her in peace, she stalked proudly back to her camp, with the courageous little dachshund still clinging to her tail.

On another occasion, Nic arrived back from a business trip in his Cessna 210, to find that Elsa had wandered out onto the runway. Grazing peacefully on the short grass of the runway were a number of Nic's tollies, young oxen, and they made the fatal mistake of taking an interest in the tawny intruder. Sniffing and snorting they crowded around her in a semi-circle. Whack! Down went an ox, stone dead with a broken neck. Whack! Whack! Whack! in quick succession three more oxen dropped dead, all felled by a crushing blow from that formidable front paw, in size and weight the equivalent of a gumpole studded with steel teeth. Marieta who had come out of the house to greet Nic after hearing his aircraft arrive, was on hand to act as scorer. The game ended with the score on Elsa - 4, Oxen - 0, when Marieta's high-decibel commands brought Bushmen and staff on the double, all armed with wheel-barrows, to drive the errant lioness back into her camp. Nic was left sitting in his aircraft to reflect upon the relative values of four dead oxen versus the pleasure of a carnivore's company.

Harnas comprises eight thousand hectares of bush veld and Elsa was frequently taken out to hunt or run around there. She showed a keen interest in antelope such as oryx and springbok, but never had a chance to get close

168

enough for a successful stalk. Nico was with her once when she came across a flock of Nic's sheep, who looked up from their placid grazing to see a lioness approaching. They scattered in bleating confusion. Quite unable to resist temptation, she raced after them and pinned down one of the woolly creatures. Nico fully expected her to rip it to pieces, but she surprised him by letting it go. She repeated this two or three more times before losing interest and allowing the lucky ewe to escape with no more than a fright. Her warm personality is beautifully illustrated by her caring attitude to the new born pups of one of her Pug dog companions. Elsa carefully picked up the pups in her jaws and carried them to a spare tyre next to her car which she made their new den. Having placed them under her protective custody in this manner, she thereafter growled at anyone other than the mother who came too near. This was no isolated event. Later on, when Schabu was moved into her enclosure, a mongoose made the bad mistake of entering it. Schabu was on to it in a moment, and would have killed it but for Elsa's intervention. Using her body to shield the little animal from Schabu, she kept it between her forepaws and dribbled it back to the gate where it was able to escape. And she later saved Schalk's life.

It was only a matter of time before Elsa became a movie star. She starred in a Canadian production which was shot on a farm near Johannesburg, not far from Lanseria airport. Nic and Nico accompanied the beautiful film star throughout the weeks of filming, as did her personal Vet, Axel Hartman. His presence was necessary particularly for her Ladyship's travel arrangements. She had to be drugged, a potentially dangerous exercise, for the duration of the seven-hour flight between Harnas and Lanseria in Nic's Cessna 210. The story tells how a teenage boy falls into a ravine where there is a wild lioness, and how, trapped together, they become friends. The skill of the filmmaker becomes apparent when visuals of Elsa yawning with huge enjoyment are accompanied by the most fearsome snarls on the soundtrack. Elsa conducted herself exactly as one would expect of a professional actress. She hated the fierce spotlamps that had to be trained on her, but after considerable coaxing, accepted that her part absolutely required it! Off stage, she took an instinctive dislike to the make-up artist. After she had made her intentions towards him clear by stalking him, head held low, along the security fence, Nic drew the director's attention to the possibility of an unpleasant contretemps between actress and crew. After that, the make-up artist had to be removed from the set before the leading lady could be brought on.

Her next part took her to Cape Town in South Africa. Nic and Schalk drove her down in a pick-up truck for the five days of filming, and she stayed in an ordinary house in Hout Bay with no problems from the neighbours or their dogs. A film about the effect of lions on Bushman cattle farmers took her on location to Bushmanland. Elsa had never seen an elephant before Nic and Nico flew her up to Tsumkwe which lies to the south of the Khaodom Game Reserve. The location was next to a pan which contained water, and since the cast and crew were all sleeping rough in the veld, Elsa was not confined at night but allowed to roam free. To keep track of the peripatetic actress they hung a goat's bell around her neck. At the sound of Nico calling her, Elsa's head would go up, and the bell would tinkle. This Kalahari arrangement worked very well even if the technology could not compare with radio telemetry or satellite tracking.

One hot night, Nico was on his camp bed being kept awake by mosquitoes when he heard the distant sound of Elsa's bell. Closer and closer it came, the rapid tinkling telling Nico that she was sprinting. Into his tent she rushed, and jumped onto his bed with her paws still dripping grey mud from the edge of the pan. There she stayed all night, huddled close to him for comfort. In the morning, Nico followed her tracks to see what had alarmed her so much the night before, and in the mud of the pan he found the answer - elephant spoor. Perhaps she had thought that these were giant wheelbarrows.

Once, the script called for her to be filmed watching as a herd of cattle were driven past. The rehearsals were completed without mishap. Elsa watched the cattle with feline interest, but kept to the script. Unfortunately, when the cameras started to roll, a calf was included in the herd. The sight of the calf proved too much for Elsa to resist. She leapt up and charged into the herd, sending cattle stampeding every which way, and killed the calf with one blow to

170

the back from her mighty forepaw. Stardom seems to bring out the worst in actresses of whatever species.

For years, Elsa remained the family pet, living around the house, but there came a time when she had to be weaned and that time was when she came on heat. It is not ovulation that causes a lioness to cycle. In point of fact, the exact opposite is true. It is copulation that causes the female to ovulate, and presumably this is why a couple will mate more or less continuously over a period of three or four days. There are few things so prodigious as the sexual stamina of a lion and the matching appetite of a lioness. Until sated by intercourse, she will come on heat every two weeks. Life for the Van der Merwe family at Harnas became impossible. Because she had never known any company other than human, Elsa naturally looked for a suitor amongst her human family and she would pester Nic, Nico, Schalk or Rudy whenever she saw them. She would push and shove them against the nearest wall, rub herself against them, lie down in front of them and lift her tail. This flirting reached a stage where no one could go out of the house to do any work without having his way blocked by the demanding lioness. It was time to say goodbye to Elsa the family pet and hello to the semi-wild lioness living in her own camp, with her own mate. The only eligible male at Harnas was Schabu. He was nearly two years younger than her, but already at the age of two was an imposing masculine beast with a fine, dark mane, great head and noble bearing. Schabu was clever. As a young lion he learned to open the gate latches and this made life difficult for the staff at Harnas because he would get out and kill a horse or sheep or two. Nic would jump up and down in a rage over the dead livestock; Marieta would yell at the Bushmen, staff and volunteers about the perils of leaving gates unsecured, and those who were wrongly accused would nurse wounded feelings. Schabu could even open latches from both sides. On this side of the latch, he would push the lever up with his nose and then pull the gate open with his claws. On the other side he would pull the lever open with his claw, and then push the gate open with his nose. He had also been found as a newborn cub lying in the sand, abandoned by his mother and had also been hand-reared by Marieta. But there the similarities end. For unlike Elsa, Schabu was of an unfriendly disposition. He and Elsa shared the same father but had different mothers. All his mother's cubs were like him, bullying louts. They pushed the other cubs aside to get their food first, and snarled at people who came too close. When yet a cub, Schabu had been adopted by Max the tour guide. Thanks to his aloof character none of the van der Merwe children had grown fond of the little lion, and so there was a notable lack of protest when Max took him away and became devoted to him. Even today, Max denies that Schabu was aggressive. "Oh, he was a terrorist," Max concedes. "He was naughty and disobedient, but not aggressive."

At that time, Max's sleeping accommodation was on the primitive side, consisting of a mattress on the floor of the aircraft hangar. Sharing a bed with a growing lion made for an interesting if insomniac experience. Schabu would pad away into the veld at night to hunt the small kangaroo of the Kalahari, aptly named the Spring hare. Or a horse or a donkey. After a few nocturnal hours of dealing out death and destruction and striking fear into the hearts of the local fauna, the hunter would return to the hangar. There he would collapse like a sack of beans onto the prostrate form of his indulgent patron, and suck his thumb. Max would spend the remaining hours until dawn brought relief, trying to squirm into a position where the blood could circulate. If Schabu was the neighbourhood delinquent by night, he was always ready to spend the day bullying other people. Max the tour guide became Max the wrestling promoter and then Max the ringmaster. It all started quite by accident, with one bold tourist wanting to have a go too when he saw Max wrestling with Schabu. Then the word got around and every adventure-seeker wanted to take on the lion in the ring. Every thrill-crazy kid became a would-be gladiator. All that was needed to complete the scene was Julius Caesar and the crowds of the Circus Maximus to give the thumbs-up or thumbs-down at the end of the contest. When Schabu was nearly a year old, he was packed in the back of the family Kombi along with all the other children, Nico, Schalk and Marlice, and taken on holiday to Jeffrey's Bay near Port Elizabeth in South Africa. The long car trip to Port Elizabeth was not easy on either Schabu or the family. Not being house-trained he would simply relieve himself at will. The car would have to be hastily pulled over, and the mess cleaned out. But once there, he missed his companion, Sacha, the little cocker spaniel. Deprived of his friend, Schabu became bored and naughty, tearing the bedclothes, whining, looking for mischief, and spoiling the family's holiday. Nic was compelled to telephone Harnas and give Rudy instructions to put the little spaniel on the next flight to Port Elizabeth. They took Schabu with them when they went to collect the dog, and his delight at being reunited with his Sacha was touching. Now that he had a friend to play with, the family members could at last enjoy the rest of their holiday. Quite what the other holidaymakers thought of having a young lion romping in the surf beside them at this popular resort we do not know, but nobody complained.

Max playing with Elsa and Schabu

Little Sacha proved to be a devoted companion right up to the day she died. Schalk was taking Schabu and his dog for a walk in the veld when they came across a black mamba, the deadliest of Africa's snakes. Schabu in his ignorance tried to play with it, but Sacha kept putting herself in between him and the snake, uttering little warning cries. An aroused black mamba is one of the most frightening sights imaginable. It lifts the first third of its body off the ground and darts hither and thither, moving with incredible speed, faster than a man can run. When it finally strikes, death is inevitable, for the venom which is injected into the victim is neurotoxic. It paralyses the central nervous system. In short, the victim suffocates. By the time Schalk could kill the snake, Sacha had already been struck and she died before he could even get her back to the house. After Sacha's death and in the absence of any other suitor for Elsa's persistent affections, Schabu was duly moved into her enclosure. This move produced some wholly unexpected results. Whereas the family and Elsa were one relationship, and the family and Schabu were another, the start of a love match between the two lions introduced a fresh dynamic into the other relationships. Just as people are different depending on their company, so it is with lions too, for their emotional lives are every bit as complicated as our own. The problem was that Elsa was friendly and would run up to Nic or Nico and rub herself against them. This used to make Schabu jealous.

One hot morning, Nico made his way out of the garden towards the garages, and entered through the latch gate. The garden was home to all the new orphans, including Cheetah, baboons, jackals and foxes - all lion-prey. To keep the lions out, Nic had built a high concrete wall and stretched several strands of electrified wire along the top. Elsa heard the latch being worked, and the gate creak open. She rose and went to greet Nico in her usual affectionate way. But the lioness was on heat, her mate was jealous and lions are notoriously unpredictable in such a situation. Schabu moved in, trotting stiffly and majestically, his heavy mane shaking, head held high, intent and aggressive. Pushing between Elsa and Nico, he pinned Nico against the high wall. Then he turned on him with teeth bared and Nico knew he was in trouble. Reaching up over his head, he clasped the electric wires, ignoring the painful jolts of high-voltage electricity. Screaming and kicking, he managed to push Schabu away with his boots just long enough to pull himself up and do a back somersault over the wall to safety, falling heavily and awkwardly in the process. Badly shocked but not seriously hurt, Marieta's eldest child could be forgiven for nursing a grudge against Schabu, which still smolders today.

Perhaps it should have been foreseeable after this incident that although Elsa and Schabu could be trusted to live singly in an enclosure which was traversed by people all day, such an arrangement would not work when they were together. It took another, more serious accident before Nic was forced to make a different plan. Schalk also had occasion to walk past the lion pair. He too, could not resist automatically responding to Elsa's friendly advances by petting and scratching her. With a muffled growl, Schabu rose from his haunches and seized Schalk's leg in his massive jaws. The canines speared right through the thigh. Then Schabu shook his huge head, and Schalk felt the numbness turn to pain as he was shaken like a meerkat caught by a jackal. Desperately, he tried to fight back, pushing his fingers into the lion's cheeks so that the closing jaws would cause the lion pain too, but strong as Schalk was, Schabu was infinitely stronger. That might have been the end for Schalk had not his cries for help been answered in a most extraordinary way. Elsa, comprehending the situation perfectly, deliberately caused a diversion by attacking her mate from behind, biting his rump. To ward her off, Schabu was forced to release Schalk. Then Elsa, looking back over her shoulder, loped away, keeping her distance from the angry lion, but luring him carefully away from his victim. Schalk was able to limp away, blood pouring out of the deep wounds and haul himself agonisingly over the locked gate to safety. Having a short fuse at the best of times, the furious young man had to be physically restrained from fetching a rifle and settling the score. After this experience, Nic invested in lion-proofing an attractive piece of natural veld, about four hectares in extent, down by the entrance gate. With not a little sadness, for Elsa was really a beloved member of the family, Nic moved his favourite lioness and her disagreeable spouse to the new camp. Today Elsa and

Schabu occupy the large bush camp at the entrance to Harnas and are therefore the first lions that visitors will see on arrival. They are both alive and well.

The story of the love between Marlice and Mufasa was a fairy tale right up to the bitter end. On the one hand was the wild white Bushman girl who loved all animals. On the other was a cute, clumsy cub, all ears and paws, who grew into a huge, lazy lion. It was a match made in Heaven. Mufasa was born to the same Patensie lioness who had given Harnas their much-loved Elsa and he had the same affectionate personality. He was one of a litter of four that were born in March 1995 just as Marlice, now aged nineteen, was finishing a tardy and fragmented schooling. One weekend she arrived home from school to find the long-awaited litter of lion cubs fast asleep in the large washing basket.

Marlice, Mufasa and the dog, Serabi

One of the cubs stood out from the others, both in looks and in personality. He was small, in fact he was the runt of the litter. But his paws were enormous and as for his ears, they were so out-sized that he might have been sired by a bat-eared fox. Initially slow to take to the bottle, he made up for it once he had learned how. In fact, he became a greedy little pig and remained a glutton the rest of his life. Unlike the other cubs in the litter, he was alert, especially to the sounds of food being prepared, and was always the first to stagger forward in order to suck on his bottle. They named him Mufasa, which means 'King' in Swahili. When he was a month old, Nico came back from Pretoria with a brown mastiff-type puppy to be Mufasa's companion and the puppy was named Serabi. Because Serabi was older and therefore stronger, she became dominant over the little cub, and that dominance lasted for his whole life. Once established, the pecking order remained long after Mufasa grew big and powerful enough to have killed her with a careless blow. It was quite a sight to see Serabi robbing the huge maned lion of his food. For the first few months of their lives, the four cubs were free to wander in and out of the home, and around the court-yard and gardens. There they became a purr-fect nuisance to all workers and passers-by. A Bushman labourer would walk through the courtyard, and Serabi would chase him, barking. Mufasa would try gamely to support his friend in the attack, but he kept falling over his out-size paws and by the time he had tripped over himself a few times, the Bushman would have made good his escape. By the age of two years, Mufasa had grown into his oversize feet and ears, and was much bigger than his brothers. Because he was so big and strong, the staff were afraid to go into his camp. Except Marlice. To Marlice he was perfection on four paws and she, Mufasa and Serabi became inseparable. Marlice used to play with his chin. Even when he was older, Mufasa had this loose lower jaw which Marlice would take hold of and rattle to and fro.

"Soentjie, Soentjie," (Kiss, Kiss) she would croon and he would offer his chin for a kiss and rattle. Whether one is raising children, dogs or lions, the priciple is the same; establish good behaviour early on or the child becomes

Marlice rattling Mufasa's lower jaw

impossible when it grows up. And when the grown-up will weigh three hundred kilograms and be able to kill you without even trying to, it is infinitely more important that discipline should be instilled early on. Especially with lions, a human can only be one of two things, either master or prey.

Marlice disciplined Mufasa rigorously when he was growing up. If he jumped on her and knocked her down she would pummel his ribs with her fists and bite him on his sensitive nose. But she could not stop him from harming or teasing other animals. Because the work which Harnas was doing with wildlife was so well known in Namibia, Marlice found herself the recipient of a number of small birds and mammals which others used to bring her. Once she brought home a little fledgling dove and put it into a basket in the kitchen. The sound of the basket falling on the floor alerted her, and she went through to the kitchen just in time to see the fledgling disappear forever down the maw of her pet cub. Lions will be lions. The many tortoises at Harnas provided Mufasa with a constant field of endeavour. First, he tried to eat them but their hard shells defeated him. Then he tried to suck them out of their shells, sticking his long tongue into the orifices as the tortoise withdrew ever deeper into its shell. Finally he used to drive Marieta to distraction by picking them up and carrying them around the garden before depositing them in some corner where no one could find them, except for the Bushmen for whom tortoises are an edible delicacy. Marieta would have to dispatch the volunteers to find the missing tortoises before the Bushmen did. One of the Harnas animals was a dachshund called Lulu. Lulu had long nails which used to click against the cement walkway around the courtyard. Mufasa used to lie in wait for her on top of the concrete garden table in the courtyard. There he would lie, stretched out in the sun, until his ears picked up the sound that he was waiting for. 'Click, click, click.'

Lulu the plucky Dachsie, doing babysitting duties

He would gather himself, poised for the attack. 'Clickity-click. Clickity-click,' came the toenails on the hard cement. Then around the corner would come Lulu, and Mufasa would spring onto the luckless little sausage dog, and, clutching her to his mouth with his huge paws which completely enveloped her, he would roll over and over, pretending to savage her. He never tired of this game and poor Lulu was compelled to endure her role as lion-plaything with as much fortitude as she could. Once a spring hare got into Mufasa's camp and he promptly pounced on the little creature and pinned it down under his fore-paw. Now he faced a conundrum. He wished to inspect what he had caught but he could not see it under his huge paw. So he lifted his paw, and the spring hare hopped away, only to be pinned down again under the giant paw. This was repeated several times before the little creature made good its escape. Personalities played a big part in the relationship between lions and humans at Harnas. Marlice never felt safe around Schabu - yet Max could do what he liked with him. Unlike Schabu, who was much older than him, Mufasa was relaxed in the company of people. A person could sit down next to him and stroke him whereas Schabu would get up and move away. Nic was also fond of Mufasa and had a routine whereby every morning when he awoke, he would put on his slippers, take his cup of coffee, walk into Mufasa's enclosure and spend some time talking to and just being with him. Nic's old brown Ford, of Simba fame, was parked in the garage and although no other lions were allowed near it, Nic permitted Mufasa to get up and lie on the roof of the cab. That was Mufasa's favourite resting place. Like all cats, lions are playful and Mufasa spent every waking hour engaged in games of stalk and pounce. He had a sense of humour too. Salome was one of his victims. She was very small in stature, barely five feet tall. She became afraid of Mufasa as he grew bigger, and he knew it. If she had to enter the garage enclosure that became Mufasa's den, he would make a great show of stalking her, crouched and intent, deliberately intimidating her. Then, when her courage failed her and she fled, he would bound around his camp like a mischievous dog, jump onto his platform and off again, rush up to Serabi to give her a nip, and

180

then tear around like an idiot, thoroughly enjoying his own joke. He loved balls and could occupy himself for hours with a football, until he popped it with one of his claws. He also liked to play with toilet paper or bandages, something which would unravel and unravel, and he and Serabi used to have tugs-of-war with crepe bandages which they had stolen from the medicine cabinet. The sight of the little cub performing muscular gyrations with his jaw in order to dislodge a wad of masticated toilet paper that was now stuck to the roof of his mouth caused Marlice endless amusement.

Once Marlice was riding around on Mufasa's back as she often did, and decided to get off him and go back to the house for some reason. As she walked away, something made her turn and look back and for a fleeting instant, the memory of which remains poignantly clear even to this day, she watched as Mufasa flew gracefully through the air towards her. There was no time to avoid his spring, and the impact from his heavy body knocked her flat, and stunned her. She recovered consciousness only to discover Mufasa licking her upturned cheek with his rough tongue. Mufasa loved swimming. Marlice used to take him and Serabi for long walks through the veld, and then to the dam at the bottom of the landing strip. There the lion and the dog would gambol and play in the water. Christmas 1995 saw the Harnas tribe down at Swakopmund for their annual seaside holiday. Mufasa, being a member of the family, was there of course. Marlice would never have gone without him. He and Serabi slept in the garage. Mufasa hated the sea. It was too violent, too unpredictable, first surging towards him, then sneaking away, drawing itself up, and crashing down upon him when he was not looking. If he even got his paws wet in the cold salt water, he would shake them vigorously. Marlice used to take him for long walks into the sand dunes behind the beach. But a long walk through the hot crumbling sand tired him out, and once he sat down at the foot of a giant dune and refused to budge while Marlice and Serabi stood at the top, she beckoning to and cajoling him to come. Even tidbits of meat were scornfully ignored. Then came the fortuitous arrival of a group of holidaymakers. On their four wheel, fat-tyred ATV motorbikes, they drove in a tidy line formation into the hollow at the base of the crescent-shaped dune, and straight towards Mufasa, who stood up. The sudden and unexpected appearance of a lion at close range caused a panic reaction. The intensity of the sound of the bikes increased dramatically as the riders found their throttles and pushed them to the limit. The dust cloud from the over-revving machines spread out and caused even greater terror, because now the riders could not see each other or where the lion was. Some collided with each other, or swerved too sharply and overturned. Others attempted to surmount impossible slopes in the rough terrain, and fell off. Mufasa, who was used to motorbikes at Harnas, stood quite still and observed the pandemonium with great interest. Marlice staggered around the crest of the dune hooting with mirth as the comedy played out below her. Just as she was starting to recover her composure some other rider would crash and fall off and send her reeling around like a drunk, clutching her aching sides from fresh outbursts of hysteria. After some minutes of noisy confusion, the riders at last found each other and some kind of formation and they set off at great speed in the direction whence they had come. The brief activity provided enough adrenalin for Mufasa to haul himself up the long high slope of the dune and rejoin Marlice, who was badly weakened by laughter.

When he was two years old Marlice decided to weigh him, just as a matter of interest. Her father had a cattle scale on the farm which consisted of a large steel construction from where hung leather straps which were brought under the stomach and chest, and from which the animal was suspended as the scale read out the weight. Mufasa distrusted the scale - perhaps it reminded him of wheelbarrows, and he was a reluctant participant in the operation. Serabi was no help either, becoming excited, sniffing at the straps and generally getting in the way. How a young girl could single-handedly manoeuvre such a large lion into the leather cradle, and winch him up to read his weight, is a testimony to the trust which had built up between them. He weighed two hundred and eighty kilograms. When she let him down and released him from the straps he walked away petulantly, tail switching back and forth and refused to speak to her for hours, ignoring all her endearments and preferred titbits.

Marlice feeding Mufasa

Mufasa was incurably lazy. When Marlice went jogging to keep fit for netball, Serabi would trot with her, but Mufasa used to bound along for a few hundred metres and then get tired, whereupon he would sit down and watch her as she ran on, turning now and again to see the little sphinx with black teddy-bear ears growing smaller and smaller as the distance between them increased. Then, on her way back, he would still be waiting where she had left him, and he would deign to accompany her home, but only at his pace, a painful plod. 1996 was Marlice's year as the tour guide and she used to work with Mufasa every day. She got to know him so well that every change of mood could be read in his expression, and she would know at a glance if he wanted to be left alone, or if she could play with him.

He was well-behaved, and would take his food from her without snatching it as the other lions did. Both for Marlice and the tourists, the highlight of the afternoon feeding tour was the ten minutes spent with Mufasa. "Come on now," Marlice would say, pointing her finger up like a pedantic schoolmistress, "let's hear you sing for your supper." And the big ears would flatten, he would look at her with adoration, and sounds somewhere between a murmur and a growl would come from him. Then he would reach out and take his food from her hand without hurting her. The beautiful young woman and the great, affectionate lion should have continued to charm the tourists with their special relationship for years. But the fairy tale came to an abrupt and violent end on 18th April 1997. Mufasa was two years and one month old and not yet fully-grown. Marlice was one month short of her twenty-first birthday. The 18th April of 1997 dawned clear and bright like any other day in Namibia and the day passed uneventfully until 4.30 p.m. in the afternoon. For some reason, Marlice had to go to the Bushman camp which was on the other side of the farm but, because her stand-in tour guide was reluctant to enter Mufasa's cage, she had fed her lion and Serabi, before mounting her motor bike and buzzing away towards the Bushman camp. Marieta - ever active in her dearly-held garden - had been trimming trees and the Bushman worker had brought nine young children to help him load the cut branches onto the trailer. Here was the start of the chain of events which were to cause so much heartbreak and misery at Harnas, for instead of leading them around the house to get to the trailer, he took a short cut through the lions' enclosure, and brought a gaggle of chattering children face to face with Serabi and Mufasa who was on his raised platform, gnawing at the kudu bone which Marlice had given him.

Serabi rushed at the invading children, barking furiously. Mufasa sprang down from his platform and went for them too. The Bushman abandoned the children, ran out of the gate and slammed it so hard behind him that the latch broke off, leaving the children locked inside. By his casual thoughtlessness, the Bushman had let mischievous Fate into the situation, and by his cowardice he

184

now sealed it in. How many children might have died that afternoon had not Marieta been on hand, it is impossible to say. But she was close by and Providence allowed her to get herself in between the angry lion and the children. Alternatively pushing Mufasa back with one hand, and throwing the children over the high fence with the other - so roughly that at least one child suffered a broken arm - she managed to get eight of the nine children out. Even then, she might have been able to save the situation by talking to Mufasa and getting him to calm down but the high-pitched screaming of the children was now augmented by the shouting of the labourers and the wailing of the women who had been called to the scene by the uproar, and were pelting the lion with stones and whatever else came to hand. Enraged, Mufasa seized the boy around the waist in his massive jaws and leapt with him onto the feeding platform. With the boy's life now in real danger, Marieta tried to wrestle Mufasa away. She succeeded to the point that he turned on her instead and mauled her left arm. "Go," she shouted at the child while Mufasa was occupied with her arm. "Run!" But the terrified boy merely lay on the platform and screamed louder. With the yelling of the humans and the baboons and other animals adding their voices to the din, the noise could be heard for miles around. It was, by Marlice. Her motorbike had broken down opposite where the wild dogs are now encamped, about a kilometer away from the farmstead. While tinkering with the spark plug to get the machine re-started, she heard the commotion coming from the house and thought to herself that it sounded as if one of the baboons had got out and was causing chaos. Then as she tinkered further, completely unaware of the dismal plight that was even then being prepared for her, she heard the clear, sharp report of a rifle. "Oh dear," she thought, "another poor horse." Every afternoon at Harnas that death knell report rings out, a brutal reminder that there are forty big cats waiting for their meat. Then she realized that it was too late in the day for that to be the explanation, and was just starting to wonder what had caused the rifle shot, when a second shot split the air. And then she knew. It was as if the outraged spirit of the lion reached out to her telepathically and cried out, "Help! I'm being killed!" She knew. Without any rational expla-

185

nation she knew that Mufasa had been shot, and she began to run for home. Her overwrought mind began to play nightmarish tricks on her and she felt that awful feeling of trying to run through treacle, where no matter how hard one tries, the legs can only move at a glutinously slow pace.

It was while Marieta was being mauled by Mufasa that Nic arrived on the scene carrying a rifle. Circling around to get a clear shot, he held his fire. Mufasa then turned back to the boy and this time his jaws closed around the boy's neck. Now there really was no room for alternatives. "Skiet!" (shoot) screamed Marieta, the flesh hanging in shreds down her left arm and her clothing covered in her own blood. The heavy bullet caught Mufasa between the eyes, but a lion has no forehead, and it took off the top of his skull without killing him. It took Nic several more shots to make sure of it. The great body crashed heavily to the ground.

It must have been at least five minutes after the shooting before Marlice came running up to the farmstead, threw the gate open breathlessly and then went around the side of the shed that adjoined the garages. The uproar had ceased and there was now an ominous and unnatural silence, broken only by the car alarm of the Kombi, which was droning on unnoticed. The garage enclosure was deserted save for a tawny form which lay in a deep pool of blood near the wall of the shed. The usually clean and well swept sand had been daubed and spattered with blood as if by some demented artist. Marlice had never seen so much blood in her life and was promptly sick. Then she knelt next to Mufasa and cradled his great, smashed head in her arms. His open eyes were glazed as if in death, but she could clearly feel his heart beating. Faithful Serabi appeared from somewhere and commenced to lick the blood off her arms. Then she felt the beating of the great heart stop and knew that he was dead. He died in her arms taking her spirit with him to keep him company in the unknown beyond death. Her composure broke and the tears flowed hot and salty, mingling with Mufasa's blood. Deep down inside her body, racked by sobbing, the anger stared to burn, like something molten that was being tempered inside her. And when the tears stopped some time later, there was only the hard bright anger

186

"He never took his claws out to me"

filling the catacombs of her body and soul which had been so full of the love of Mufasa. "Why," she kept on repeating to herself, "Why? Why?" Getting to her feet, she strode across the yard towards her father's office. Her mother stood there by the gate which the Bushman had slammed shut. Her left arm had been savagely chewed by Mufasa, and strips of flesh hung down from the deep lacerations. "Why?" asked Marlice fiercely, grabbing her mother by the shoulders and pushing her back against the wall. "Why did you do it? I hate you." Marieta, also shocked, had no intelligent answer to such a question. Marlice left her and stomped into the open sliding door of Nic's office. Her father sat behind his desk, unseeing. The tears were coursing down his cheeks. "Why?" Marlice demanded hotly. "How could you do it? Why?" Nic could only shake his head, unable to speak through his tears. Mufasa had been his favourite too. "Missis, missis," came a little thin voice from the door. It was Kasupi, one of the Bushman woman. In a few sentences in the Bushman tongue she explained to Marlice what had happened. The boy was in the laundry room, she told Marlice, begging her to come and see if the boy would live or die. Angrily, Marlice brushed past her to go and see the boy whose innocent trespassing in Mufasa's enclosure had resulted in the death of her best friend. She was shown the child who was quiet now, although covered in blood and much shaken by his ordeal. "Take him," she told Kasupi roughly, "I hope he dies!"

Something drew her back to Mufasa's body and there she sat, no longer crying but consumed by rage and grief until Nic came and physically pulled her away so that he could organise for the burial of the body. The Med-Rescue aircraft arrived from Windhoek to collect Marieta and the Bushman boy, but Marieta, stoic as ever, elected to stay and to go in to Gobabis hospital by car. Nico was in Pretoria, Schalk was at rugby in Windhoek and Salome was overseas in Europe, so the only person able to take her was Marlice. There was a stony silence between them all the way to Gobabis, a hundred kilometers, a silence that Marlice was not to break for nearly three months. Marieta's lacerated arm was sewn up with countless stitches, and she returned home after only a few days. One glance at the desolate Marlice had the doctor reaching for his syringe and the sedatives, and as she sat brooding and unseeing on the hospital bed, he gave her the injection and merciful sleep blotted out the living nightmare of the worst day of her life. "He never took his claws out to me," she said as the sedative pulled her away from hideous reality, "in two years he never once took his claws out to me."

The gory details of the incident were seized upon by the Namibian Press, and widely reported. Perhaps the worst consequence of the disaster was that it drove a wedge between Marlice and her family. The wall of silence behind which she hid her outraged emotions dragged on for three dreary months, with the awkward silences at mealtimes broken only by tears. Eventually, however, it resulted in the young girl leaving home to seek her direction in the city of Pretoria.

Marlice and little Mufasa

190

Chapter seven

MARLICE

I never said goodbye to her
There always seemed more time.
To tell her what she meant to me
The essence so sublime.
I have memories of a smiling face
Of love beyond compare,
That special love a mother has,
That special love we shared.
The memories shall be with me
Although the years have passed me by,
And understanding comes with age
That love will never die.
The tears I've shed like falling rain
Lie in puddles where I stand,
She's reaching out her soul to me
I feel her guiding hand.
Andrew Mercer

Marlice had filled out and grown into a very attractive young woman. With her long blonde hair, her almond eyes and her smooth sun-tanned skin, she looked as if she belonged more on a California beach than messing around with animals. She finished school at the end of 1995. But when she got back to Harnas, everything had changed. Now there were tourists - total strangers - tramping around her beloved animals. Nic made her a tour guide. Marlice hated it. There was more work than she could comfortably handle. Marlice found herself cooking in the kitchen, running the bar and waiting on the guests. Then there were the tours which she and Salome shared as tour guides. By now there were nearly two hundred animals who needed to be fed, or medicated or nursed or bandaged. It was "Marlice do this, Marlice do that…" She tried to find time for Netball, for she was playing for the National Namibian women's team. Every Wednesday and Saturday Marlice drove the three hundred kilometres to Windhoek for practice and the game, and then back the same night. At daybreak the next day, she went back to cooking, cleaning, nursing and guiding. It was a gruelling schedule and working sixteen hours a day seven days a week was bound to tell in the end.

Harnas had never been laid out or designed to be a tourist resort, with the result that there was no separation between the guests and the family. Strangers were wandering into and around the house all day and night without respite. There was no privacy. No one had realised what a strain this would put on the family. As for the animals, Marieta complained bitterly that she no longer had any time for them because she was so busy doing stock-takes and all the other chores that go with catering to the public at large. "Look," she told Nic, "I haven't even spoken to my lions for a week. I will lose touch with them and then they will think that I am just another tourist." Nico was away in Pretoria, studying for a Veterinary degree, and living in a flat which Nic had purchased for him. Schalk had become Nic's right hand man, doing everything that his father had no time to do himself - grading the roads, welding, darting and injecting the animals when necessary, trouble-shooting whenever there was a mishap and there were plenty of those. If the power failed then the electric wires were out of action and a Cheetah or two would dig its way out of the camp and make up for lost time by killing Nic's sheep. Schalk would have to drop whatever he was doing and get the dart gun. He would have to track the escapees, dart them and bring them back. Twice a week, he travelled with Marlice to Windhoek for rugby, for he too represented Namibia at his sport.

A young Marlice with Esria, one of the Harnas youngsters

In 1996, Marieta took Marlice and Salome and flew up to Zambia to visit the Chimfunshi Chimpanzee Sanctuary. Harnas had always looked after baboons and monkeys but they had no experience of chimpanzees and besides they wished to see how the other sanctuary was run, and to exchange ideas. They loved the chimps and spent two weeks there getting to know them. But they were disappointed in other respects. The cages were small, with cement floors, and not kept as clean as the Harnas enclosures. And there were strict rules about when and how to interact with the chimps, not like the delightful informality at Harnas. The owners showed little interest in hearing about Harnas, and could not understand why all the animals could not be released. They simply could not understand how in a country as vast and underpopulated as Namibia, there could be no place to release a lion or Cheetah. But the chimps were delightful, and when she returned to Harnas, Marieta named one of her lion cubs after her favourite chimp - Schabu. Salome then left to go overseas. After a year in Europe she returned and Marlice took two w take her on holiday to Hermanus in the Cape. But in her absence, she ha' changed and differences arose. The holiday was not a success and Salome returned alone after only a week.

As for Nic, he was drowning. The root of the problem was, first, that Harnas lies off the beaten track for tourism. It was not on the way to Etosha or Swakopmund, but three hundred kilometres due east of Windhoek near the Botswana border. The package tours could not therefore include it, and they were seventy percent of the market. There were no other tourist attractions anywhere near Harnas and so only the dedicated animal lovers who specifically wished to interact closely with wildlife would take the long dusty road to visit. But whether one is catering for four or forty tourists a day, all the facilities have to be there, and Nic had spent a small fortune on building them. Now he found that there were enough visitors to make everyone work very hard, but not enough to pay the food bill for the two hundred animals. The debts continued to mount, and more farms had to be sold. Soon there would be nothing left but Harnas itself. And what then?

194

The family had never wanted to create a Zoo Park. Yes, there were some animals so badly injured that they could never be released and would have to be cared for indefinitely, but the intention was to release those who could survive back into the wild. And here came the biggest shock for Nic - there was nowhere, nowhere even in Namibia, where he could release his wild animals. Nature Conservation would have nothing to do with his animals and the wilderness areas were being so vigorously poached and infiltrated by humans that the cycle of persecution could not be broken. There he sat having to feed forty big cats - who were eating a horse a day - feeling like a Reform school headmaster trying to find a job for society's problem children.

Greatrex was the next farm to go as the debts ballooned and finally, in 1998, Marieta's own inheritance, Tennessee. The decision to sell off Tennessee was the hardest one in Marieta's whole life. She thought of her father, and how much he had put into the farm for her sake, and how he would turn in his grave at the disposal of the property. But when it came down to the stark choice, sell the farm or get rid of the animals, then sentiment had to be pushed aside. The auction of the moveable property on Tennessee was a great disappointment. Marieta opened the auction by pleading to the large crowd to be generous, for the money would all go to the animals at Harnas Wildlife Sanctuary, but she received a shock when bidding started and many of the antiques and valuable heirlooms went for $5 a piece. A number of people in the crowd were drunk and their crass behaviour made the whole procedure unpleasant. When the takings were counted up at the end of a horrid day, it was found that much of the property had been stolen, including items so large (such as steel windmills) that they could only have been taken away on big trucks. The sale of the farm itself fared no better. There were plenty of foreigners, mainly Germans, who were eager to buy the farm, only Marieta was not permitted by Namibian law to sell it to them. The SWAPO Government's election rested ultimately on the promise to take the land away from the whites and give it to blacks. The Agricultural (Commercial) Land Reform Act of 1995 laid down the procedures to be followed. Marieta had to reduce the price until it became affordable to black Namibians, who had no money of their own but could avail themselves of Bundesbank-provided funds in the Land Bank to meet the purchase price. When at last some Namibians had been found who could buy the farm, interest rates rose worldwide on the back of the Asian debt problem, and as Namibian interest rates soared into the twenty and thirty percents, the buyers took fright and resiled from the contract. Marieta was left high and dry. Other than the bare Tennessee land, there was no capital left except for Harnas itself. Twenty years of caring for orphaned and injured wild animals had cost Nic and Marieta their inherited fortunes. And what now? All the problems still remained, hovering, wheeling and circling like a flock of vultures over Harnas itself.

As if the financial problems were not enough there were other tribulations. On the 18th April 1997 there took place at Harnas the incident which rocked the van der Merwe family and captured news headlines around the country. The death of Mufasa. Unlike previous disasters which had served to bring the family together, this one had the opposite effect, especially insofar as Marlice was concerned. The whole episode, and particularly the anger and resentment which it caused Marlice to bear towards her parents, cast a pall over the family as oppressive as a summer thundercloud. Marlice herself suffered something of a nervous breakdown. It was as if the spirit of Mufasa had taken hers with him to keep him company in the great beyond, but leaving her mortal body empty. She withdrew from family life - it was nearly three months before she spoke to her parents again. She stopped guiding the tours - what was the point if the highlight of the tour, her relationship with the big lion, was no longer there? She became enervated and listless. Once she tried to take Serabi for a walk to the dam where they had all played before, but without Mufasa it was no fun and merely brought back poignant memories. Every time she shut her eyes to sleep, the face of Mufasa appeared before her in her mind's eye, vivid and compelling, and that brought yet more tears - as if enough had not been shed.

In May 1997, her twenty-first birthday arrived. The previous year, she had bought presents for Mufasa and wrapped up bits of his favourite meat in festive paper. Now her twenty-first birthday came and went with no party and no pleasure, only tears for the happy memories of the previous birthday. Not even the other two hundred animals at Harnas could lift the sombre mood. Marlice was inconsolable. She needed to get away, to find another place where there were no haunting memories. It was in this frame of mind that she went to the Windhoek Show in August of 1997. For over ten years Harnas had supported the Windhoek show, and photographs of their lions loping through the main streets of Windhoek adorn the brochures and pamphlets of the tourist industry, together with advertising slogans like 'Go wild in Namibia.' For Harnas staff and family it was gruelling hard work, loading lions, leopard cubs, Cheetah and smaller animals, transporting them three hundred kilometres to Windhoek; building enclosures for them, and then standing around for ten excruciating days, greeting visitors, talking about the animals and keeping a watchful eye on the more callous or mischievous urchins who like to taunt and bait them.

During the 1997 Windhoek show, a young man came into the animal enclosure, bent down and began to stroke the leopard cub in such a sensitive and knowledgeable way that he caught Marlice's discerning eye. The way to her heart lay through showing sensitivity and love for animals, and the way that he stroked the leopard tugged at her heartstrings. She was smitten. That was Jaco, and the beginning of a serious relationship for the vulnerable young woman, who had so much love to give and was not yet worldly enough to know that love is like money, and has to be invested wisely where it yields the best return. Just a few months after the affair began, he told her that his girlfriend from England was coming out to see him, and that they should break off for a while at least until he could make up his mind who he wanted. Her heart was broken. She struggled on with the hard work at Harnas, but was not of a disposition to put up with the constant demands. At the end of 1997, she went to her father and asked if he could afford to send her to College in Pretoria to study for a diploma in Physical Fitness and Training. He could see that his daughter was unhappy and agreed, although they both knew that there was a crying need for new camps to be built for the Cheetah, and Marlice felt guilty about dipping into those funds for her own purposes. Meanwhile Nico was four years into his Veterinary degree course at Pretoria. On the 18th November 1997 he was doing some last-minute revision for the Pathology examination on the following day, when he took a late night stroll with his two little dogs. He was attacked by two knife-wielding thugs and after a ferocious struggle, in which he sustained a deep knife wound in the shoulder, he succeeded in driving them off. After spending the rest of the night at hospital he was in no fit state to concentrate on his exam and failed Pathology miserably. For him it was the last straw. The traffic, the crowds and pollution were already getting him down and he gave up his studies to return home, another victim of South Africa's high crime rate. In this unfortunate manner, Nico's flat in Pretoria North became available for her and in January 1998 Marlice went off to the big city. The day she left, Jaco phoned her and they made up. With a lighter mind for making up, but a heavier heart for leaving him and her animals, she threw herself into her work, studies and netball hoping to cure whatever it was that frustrated her at Harnas. "She will be back soon" Nic told Marieta, "She will never live in a big city. Wait and see."

As cities go Pretoria is relatively liveable. The highveld climate is pleasant and the stately Union Buildings overlook dwellings which cluster among rolling hills. The streets of the suburbs are lined with Jacaranda trees and the sidewalks are carpeted with their lilac-blue flowers in Autumn. But it is still a city, where people gather together to compete with one another for material gain. All the ingredients of hell are there; crowds, traffic noise, pollution and crime. The flat which Nico had left for Marlice lay in the suburb of Pretoria North. The Zambesi Rylaan (highway) ran along one side of the block of flats. This busy road kept Marlice awake at nights. She was used to waking up to the sound of the birds, not the rumble of traffic. And when the truck drivers had to slow down to stop at the traffic lights, the sudden change in pitch of their engines to a clattering roar as the exhaust brakes were applied, and the shrieking of metal on metal, still made her wince months after she had arrived. The fumes from the heavy traffic invaded the flat and offended her sensitive nostrils. She found the female city dwellers to be pretentious, devious and catty, and this made her realize how important it was to have the company of her family and the sincere country folk in Gobabis. There was no shortage of eager, panting suitors to visit the flat, but her heart lay elsewhere. Although her spirits were battered by the assaults of city life, Marlice took full advantage of the facilities. Her studies kept her busy during the day and there was Netball in the afternoons. Before long she found herself selected to play for the South African Combined Universities Netball team.

But it was not enough to make up for the long lonely evenings when she lay on her couch listlessly, homesick and miserably out of place. Most of all she missed the animals. After a week she could not stand the spiritual strain of being separated from them any longer, and hurried over to the Pretoria Zoo where she wandered along the cages until she came to the baboons. There they sat in small cages with cement floors, as lethargic as she was in her flat. She thought how much richer their lives would be patrolling industriously through the veld foraging for berries and beetles and her heart went out to them. "Huh," said Marlice, imitating the voice of her baboons back at Harnas. A female baboon looked up at her and cocked her head but did not answer. "Huh," Marlice repeated, and this time the female responded. Tears welled up in the girl's eyes and for twenty minutes the two prisoners-in-spirit talked to each other. A small crowd gathered around. "What's going on?" asked a young man, his brash voice jarring on Marlice's sensitivities. "It's a girl talking to the baboon," answered an onlooker. The man watched for a few seconds and then when nothing dramatic had happened, he lost interest. "Sounds crazy to me," was his parting remark as he walked off.

After that she went to the Zoo at every opportunity. So often in fact, that the staff got to know her and stopped charging her entrance fees. She bought herself a dog at the pet shop, a cute Golden Retriever puppy, but the little pup died within a week from an infection. Marlice herself found that she

Marlice asleep with Elsa

had no resistance to the waves of influenza that washed through the city, confining her to bed for days on end and increasing her feelings of isolation. Eventually she obtained a fish bowl and spent hours talking to the fish through teeth that were chattering from the flu shivers. It was merely a question of time before she sought sanctuary again, like all the other injured and orphaned wild animals, at Harnas. But what made her grit her teeth and battle on in the city was the guilt of knowing that Nic had set her up in Pretoria with money which he had been saving for the building of more camps for the Cheetah. She felt that she would be letting him down if she did not give her College education a full go. From time to time she phoned Jaco and gained support from him, but the only one at home in whom she could confide was Schalk and in July 1998 she phoned him and told him how desperately unhappy she was. "I am sick in body and in spirit," she explained to him, "I liked the person I was and I feel that I am losing her. I know now that my way lies with animals, not with people. I have learned that I belong at Harnas, not here. And before, when I became frustrated with my parents and all the restrictions they placed on my life, now I realize that they were only putting so much responsibility on me because they were overwhelmed themselves. So I ran away. I made a mistake. What do you think Pa's attitude will be if I tell him I can't finish the year and I just want to come home?"

"Ag, Vlooi," Schalk told her "Pa never expected you to stay long in the city. He just wanted to give you the chance to find out for yourself that Harnas is your life. We need you here. Come home now."

"Oh, thank God!" Marlice replied, her eyes brimming over. She had cried many tears lately. "Will you ask Pa to come and fetch me?"

"I will. See you soon."

She phoned Jaco to give him the good news. She was coming home. The dark cloud that lay over her spirit were lifting and she was feeling something that she had not felt for a long time - elation. She had even come to terms now with what had happened to Mufasa, and could see how unfairly she had treated her parents because of it. How ignorant she had been of their own suffering and grief at the death of someone that they too had loved. That weekend Nic arrived in the old pick-up truck, and she helped him to load her few sticks of furniture into the back. Then they were on their way home, driving west past the platinum mines around Rustenburg, the smoke stacks pouring sulphurous clouds into the thin highveld air. Past the Abjaterskop mountains that surround Zeerust, immortalised in Herman Charles Bosman's wonderful stories, they went, and into the Kalahari. Now that she had found herself and was free from the pain of the past, there was so much to talk about. She wanted to know all about the animals and Nic had time to tell her everything, who had arrived, who had died, who had given birth and all the other stories that spun daily out of such a meaningful and dynamic lifestyle. There was a Japanese film crew at Harnas. They were making a documentary about African wildlife and there was nowhere better in the world to film the big cats in their own natural surroundings. An American company was enquiring if Harnas could supply a Cheetah and someone to manage it for a film which was to be shot in the Namib. More and more it seemed that the film industry was going to pull Harnas out of debt. Marlice was enthralled. When the eight hundred kilometre Trans-Kalahari Highway was behind them, they crossed the border from Botswana into Namibia at Buitepos. Immediately, they climbed the long low ridge that separates the Omaheke sandveld forest from the endless flat Kalahari and just before Gobabis, by the tall radio mast, they turned right and headed along the dirt road for home, past the Ohlsenhagen camp where the family's path had crossed that of Simba. They turned right at Drimiopsis where Simba had turned left, took the left fork just before the Sandveld Research Station and then they were back on Harnas land and she was opening the gates as they drove through the cattle and game camps. At the entrance, she saw the baboons just as she had left them. And on the right were Elsa and Schabu and as Elsa sprang up at the call of her voice, and trotted quickly towards her to rub herself, purring, against the wire netting, Marlice could contain her joy no longer. The steel bands that had been constricting her heart, her whole being, broke up and dropped away, and the beautiful young woman who had travelled the hard road to self-realization wept with joy as she clung to her gentle, loving lioness in a long moment of tender reunion which only those who have felt that mystical bond between two children of Nature, could understand. Marlice had come home to stay.

Marlice with Mufusa
A match made in Heaven

203

Part two

THE VANISHING

AND MEMORIES AS OLD AS LIFE
CAUGHT WITHIN THIS FRAME.
MOZAICS OF A PROUDER TIME
DIVERSE YET STILL THE SAME.

A VOICE THAT TOLD OF CYCLES
OF GROWTH WITHIN DECAY.
WHERE DEATH AND BIRTH PERPETUATE
WHERE NIGHT CONSUMES EACH DAY.

A BALANCE FOR EACH LIVING THING
WHERE ALL THINGS PLAY THEIR PART.
WHERE THE EBB AND FLOW ETERNALLY
BRINGS THE END BACK TO THE START.

WHAT PUNISHMENT SHALL FIT THE CRIME?
FOR THE TREACHERY AND LYING.

THE HOURGLASS IS FILLED WITH BONES
WHERE SAND POURS ON THE DYING.

AND AFRICA A SKELETON
AGAINST A SICKLE MOON.
POINTING AT THIS KILLING GROUND
A PORTENT OF OUR DOOM.

THE SILENCE JUST HOLDS FRAGMENTS
STILL QUESTIONING THE PAST.
LIKE PICTURES FADE TO NOTHINGNESS
THE DREAM COULD NEVER LAST.

OUR LIVES DEVOID OF MEANING
WHATS LOST SHALL NOT BE FOUND.
UNTIL SOMEHOW OUR SPIRITS FIND
WHATS BURIED IN THIS GROUND.

WHEN THE YEARS HAVE FILLED EACH HOOFPRINT
WITH THE DUST THAT ONCE WAS BONE.
THE DRY WIND WILL STILL REMIND US
WE SHALL ALWAYS BE ALONE.

SO TELL YOUR CHILDREN FAIRY TALES
AS THE TEARS FALL ON THE PAGE.
WHEN WE KILLED WHAT MADE US HUMAN
TO EMBRACE AN EMPTY AGE.

Andrew Mercer

The killing goes on

206

Epilogue

A BRIEF HISTORY OF PERSECUTION

Can you feel through all this static
This void within your dreaming.
An empty house of bleak neglect
For a life that has no meaning.
Turn to walk through cardboard dreams
A drab landscape with no depth.
Laugh with all your damaged toys
The pain behind each breath.
The veils of doubt your only friends
Embrace you in their sadness,
And speak of things that fade with time
Whispered through this madness.
Andrew Mercer

We cannot leave the continuing saga of Harnas here. It would be like writing about a Kossovo refugee camp without going on to explain how the refugees came to be confined there, and what must be done to put them back where they belong.

The pages of history of the early colonisers in Southern Africa drip with the blood of the murdered innocents. Here the settlers found an unspoiled Paradise teeming with the most marvellous diversity of flora and fauna anywhere

207

in the world. What sublime delights of the natural world were waiting for a wiser and more compassionate species to explore and enjoy. Alas, it was not to be. Lions roared outside Cape Town when the Dutch colonised it in 1652. In present times there are no wild lions left north of the Sahara, and most parts of Southern Africa. The game population of the Cape, once so plentiful, was wiped out in a few short years. The pioneers with their pitiless, instinctive blood-lust spread into the hinterland, through the parched, arid expanse of the karoo and then into the pleasant, well-watered interior. Hunting parties of tens, sometimes hundreds of horsemen and their lackeys fell upon the defenceless game animals in an orgy of destruction that far exceeded any legitimate need for meat. The carcasses of animals shot for sport were left to rot in the veld. Look at the early photographs of these hunting parties, those familiar black and white photographs now faded to brown and beige. So many homes have these old photographs. Too many. Look at their stark depiction of the grim, bearded men clutching their Mausers, and the antelope carcasses hanging in their dozens from the branches of the thorn trees. How could anyone with an ounce of compassion fail to see in the whole bizarre scene a mute reproach to the arrogant cruelty of the conquerors?

Thirty buffalo in a day here, ten rhino in a day there, twenty elephant at a time elsewhere. On and on went the slaughter. It was as if the game would last forever, magically contriving to reproduce from their ever-diminishing herds in order to provide fresh sport and meat for their killers. Oh how the killers gloried in their own savagery. How they wrote about and relished their murderous exploits. F.C. Selous. Henry Hartley and so many others. If you have a strong constitution you can read their sickening books today. Read them and weep.

Before this onslaught fled the bewildered animals, seeking refuge in the most inhospitable places. Across the thirstland of the dry Kalahari, through the tick-infested Bushveld and into the malarial swamps of the lowveld they trekked. There they hid fearfully, suffering the heat, the torment of the mosquitoes and the lethal bite of the tsetse flies. But their tormenting allies proved powerless against a species whose instinct to kill was so strong that it

208

drew men into these dangerous and uncomfortable places; drew them into the hot, dusty Kalahari; brought them splashing through the fetid malarial swamps and drove them into the fiery cauldron of the Limpopo Valley. Nothing could stop them. Not the tsetse fly nor the sleeping sickness. Not the heat, the scorpions, nor venomous snakes. Not the mopane flies by day nor the clouds of mosquitoes by night.

And while the traumatised survivors of the colonial onslaught huddled in the dense acacia thorn thickets, sleeping fitfully and feeding warily, the main body of the conquerors settled down to farm the 'unoccupied' land of the pleasant highveld. It was certainly unoccupied now, although they no doubt regarded it as unoccupied before the carnage merely because there were few other members of their own species living there.

How the richest concentration of magnificent wildlife in the world could ever be dismissed as 'unoccupied land' speaks volumes for the callous ignorance of our colonial forefathers

And to their new farms the farmers brought something that was destined to cause more suffering to the blighted wildlife than even their cruel guns. They brought fencing wire onto their farms. Plain ordinary fencing wire, when fashioned into a noose, became a wire snare. And so began a new and vicious assault on wildlife, one which has spread out over the whole continent and poses an even greater threat to the survival of wildlife in Africa. Today we live in the age of the wire snare.

Then the colonial governments by a process of muddled reasoning decided to institutionalise the slaughter of wildlife and to lend government support to its decimation. Cattle ranches in the wild areas were called for by the great god Economic Growth and his minions, the vested interests. However these areas were hostile to cattle. Many were infected by the foot and mouth virus. Domestic stock was vulnerable to such viruses. With imperious assurance, the colonials declared war on their own resources, i.e. themselves. "The disease is infectious, the buffalo suffer from it but do not die, and therefore they are 'carriers' of the disease who must be eliminated." And eliminate them they did

209

with a vengeance. Using military helicopters and troops of game rangers with automatic weapons, whole herds of buffalo were liquidated leaving the erstwhile wilderness barren and sterile. Several rangers have testified to those horrific buffalo liquidations and more than one of these hardened hunters had a tear in his eye when describing the dreadful scenes.

The same wondrous reasoning was used for the tsetse fly, that tenacious guardian of the few remaining wild places which shelter some ragged debris of our wildlife. The game became enemies of the State because they were 'carriers' of sleeping sickness. So back to the slaughter went the Departments of 'Nature Conservation' with their helicopters and machine guns.

Today a buffalo can fetch up to US $20,000 at the game auctions. The total value of animals killed plus their progeny would be more than enough to pay off the whole region's foreign debt. We stupidly massacre our resources and then lament the fact that we become international beggars.

If the colonisation of Africa was a ruthless exploitation of the local people, it was genocide for the wild animals. All that can kindly be said for the colonial era was that its unregretted passing left at least a few well-run game reserves for the shelter of the shattered remnants of what was once the greatest show on earth. But that too, was about to change.

With half a grain of common sense and charity, all the desperate wars of liberation could have been avoided. But the colonials selfishly refused to remove the causes of terrorism and drove the oppressed blacks into the arms of the Russians and the Chinese. Shipload after shipload of automatic weapons arrived in Dar-es-Salaam for the liberation movements of Southern Africa. The poor wildlife could hardly have known what was in store for it as a veritable avalanche of weapons cascaded upon the continent, and was distributed - free - to the eagerly awaiting cadres and guerrillas. The guns may have been intended for use against their white oppressors but the guerrillas turned them, instead, against the unfortunate wildlife. The animals became the fresh provisions of the guerrilla armies operating in wilderness areas. To see the devastating effects of these human affairs on the innocents, we must turn our outraged eyes and shuddering senses to Gorongosa in Mozambique.

Inland of the coastal town of Beira and along the banks of the turbid, malarial Pungwe River lies a five and a half thousand square kilometre reserve. This world-famous park has been described as the most diverse game park in all of Africa. An aerial survey conducted in 1972 found more than 18,000 buffalo and 7,000 elephant revelling in the tall forests and grassy plains. The Sofala province, in which this queen of game parks lay, contained the largest and most viable eco-system in Africa with a diverse cross section of habitats. Uniting the park and the mountain and extending it all the way to the mangrove swamps at the Indian Ocean in order to preserve an ancient game migratory route covering thirty thousand square kilometres would have been the obvious land-use in any far-sighted society. Instead, during the mid -1970s Renamo Leader Alfonso Dhlakama sited his tactically-dispersed forest headquarters here among the massive hardwood trees. The distant pop of the hunting guns could be clearly heard day and night as the army lived off the wildlife of the region. The opposition Frelimo soldiers had the use of Russian helicopter gunships for their hunting pleasure and stories abound of Soviet helicopters loaded with the forlorn carcasses of antelope spattering blood over the forest canopy below.

Again it is the same depressing saga. Hundreds of thousands of exquisite wild people living in an undefiled Eden. Now there is no compassionate witness to tell of their pain, bloodshed and suffering. How the rifles and wire snares were used on them month after month, year after year until all the wild voices had been silenced and all that remained were outraged spirits in the great unknown. And the woodland giants, who can only testify to a higher court of the murder of the innocent and helpless, the deafening blasts of the automatic rifles and the cries of the wounded, the bereaved, the lost and lonely. Then the unnatural stillness. Only the giant trees now survive, spreading their great boughs wide in mute appeal to the Almighty. The tall grasses grow rank, releasing their uneaten seed heads into the warm, caressing tropical breeze.

There is nothing left. A jigsaw puzzle of a beautiful Eden with half the pieces missing. Today, a pall of eerie silence hangs over Gorongosa. The first post war aerial survey conducted in 1994 revealed the following:

Of the 18,000 buffalo just thirteen animals had survived. Elephants were down from seven thousand to nineteen, hippos from five thousand to ten and the lions and rhinos were extinct. The park is open to visitors again, but there are no animals left. It is now being marketed as a venue for bird watching safaris. Poaching is widespread and the present Chief Warden, Roberto Zolho, collected eight thousand wire snares in 1998 alone. Corrupt local government officials have given logging concessions within the park itself.

First the wildlife, then the trees. And only people privileged in time and place to have witnessed Gorongosa when the great herds of buffalo and elephant roamed in their thousands, wild and free among the forest giants and the palm thickets, only we have the memories to be able to compare the desolate reality of today with the divine magic of might-have-been.

Today there is a pandemic sweeping through Southern Africa - poaching. It has killed and continues to kill more wild people than ever died in all the wars and all the plagues in the sad history of mankind. And although countless victims die every year from this pandemic few people talk or even care about them. And why? Because the victims do not belong to the human species. They are a silent, silenced people. Like American Negroes in the old deep south or the blacks in apartheid South Africa, they exist in a selective democracy which excludes them. So little is their existence recognised that their homes are contemptuously referred to as 'unoccupied land.' Night and day - even as you are reading this page, thousands upon thousands of wonderful, valuable creatures are being systematically poisoned, snared, shot and trapped in a relentless orgy of destruction that can have only one end. Extinction.

The scope of poaching in Africa today beggars all powers of description. Farm dams are poisoned so that the people can pick up the pathetic little bundles of feathers that lie around and throw them into a cooking pot. There are cases in the Eastern Transvaal where several hundred birds, many of them rare or endangered, have died around one single dam poisoning episode. The perpetrators escape with impunity.

But by far the cruellest, the most widespread and the most destructive weapon of the poacher is the simple wire snare. A pair of poachers armed only with a roll of fencing wire and a pair of rusty pliers can set dozens of snares in one night.

Animals, like humans, tend to be creatures of habit, to frequent the same areas and the same trails and so it is easy for the poachers to see where the snares can be set to best advantage. The poachers may not return to check their snares for days, sometimes weeks. Animals caught in such a snare die the most awful death imaginable. They struggle to free themselves and this only tightens the wire. Just try it: take a piece of wire, make a noose and pull it tight around your arm or leg. It burns as if it were red hot. The pain is so excruciating that some animals may even in their angst try to bite off the limb that is caught. And when the hours of agonising struggle have subsided into shock and exhaustion, the victim must wait for death. Usually by thirst, less often by the poacher's knife.

In 1998, a young Kudu bull who had been caught in a snare in Namibia managed to break free eventually. The snare remained wound around and sunk into his face and although he could just drink a little, he could no longer feed properly. In this manner he battled on for some weeks, losing condition daily until he became too weak to walk. Lying there alive but helpless he was attacked by jackals who ate his hindquarters. When he was found by a farmer a day or two later he was still alive. Half-eaten - but alive.

The scale of the problem is overwhelming. One observer walked a fence line near Harnas whilst this book was being written, and destroyed a wire snare about every twenty-five metres along a fence line stretching for tens of kilometres. All over the civilised world, people are up in arms about the few million land mines in Africa, and rightly so. But what about the billions and billions of wire snares that cause infinitely greater suffering than even the land mines?

And then there are the fires. Every year after the summer rains have brought out the grasses there is an autumn of peace and beauty. March, April and sometimes May are the months when the grass tufts have set seed and wait for the dry frosts of winter to harden them. These are the best months of the year for the little creatures, the shy steenbuck and duiker antelope, the meerkats, mongoose and ground squirrels. With grass to eat, and grass to hide in, there is a hint of the heaven that their forbears knew. Unfortunately, it does not suit the poachers that the small animals can hide from them and their hunting dogs. And so it is that every year when winter tightens its grip on the land, and the animals and their young need the grass cover most against the bitter cold winds, that the veld fires start. Sometimes when the air is still, the fires merely crackle and hiss in an unthreatening fashion as they slowly spread from tuft to tuft. But the August winds blow the evil fire genie out of the bottle and then nothing can stop him. Fuelled by the grass cover and propelled by the high seasonal winds, the fire monster roars through the countryside like Sherman's army from Atlanta to the sea. Livid flames shoot skyward, joining with each other to form twisting, writhing fireballs being hurled along on the wind. Roaring like a thousand locomotives the fireballs sweep across roads and over walls, even buildings, lighting the night sky like an artillery barrage. Palls of dark smoke spew up into the heat-shimmering air and then mushroom higher into the atmosphere until they combine with the clouds. And the land in the wake of these infernos lies ruined for months, with all the grasses and bushes destroyed and the trees deformed and damaged. Only now that they have turned Heaven into Hell and the barren, blackened land can no longer hide such small animals as have survived the flames from the hunting dogs, only now are the poachers happy. Supine governments do nothing. And the killing goes on.

It is not merely the snaring and hunting, which are horrific enough. Africans have their own weapon of mass destruction. Disease.

In colonial times people were forced by the authorities to dip their cattle and goats regularly. If they failed to do so, they were prosecuted and their cattle could even be confiscated. Nowadays all these animal health measures have fallen into disuse. Now, diseases run rife through the millions of communal cattle that border the great game reserves. Now, without the stern hand of discipline to prevent it, the tribesmen cut the game fences and drive their live-stock into the game reserves to graze. Now, their diseased cattle come into direct contact with game animals and predators who have no immunity against these terrible diseases, such as bovine tuberculosis (BTB).

Privately, some scientists now say that with the spread of BTB to many species in the parks, it is only a matter of time before the whole of Southern Africa's wild lion population could become extinct. Kruger Park researchers have revealed that more than 90% of the lions tested in the southern part of the huge reserve are infected, and that the disease is so virulent that it has halved the lion population in one study area in only two years. Other scientists are more sanguine for the survival prospects of the Kruger Park lions but at very least, their future is uncertain. Kruger scientists have now decided to draw a disease line through the park and to shoot all the 'carriers' - buffalo and kudu - who try to cross this line. Here we go again. The wild animals never have any problems, it seems, which cannot be solved by shooting them.

We have already seen how colonial governments impoverished their own environments by implementing brutal and fruitless policies to exterminate game animals. In scenes more evocative of horror movies than scientific principles, whole herds of animals were smashed to pieces by machine-gun fire both from the air and on the ground, and massacred down to the last calf in a carnage of blood and dust. Never silent for long, the government guns are thundering again in South Africa's Game Reserves. In the Umfolozi Game Reserve, the KwaZulu-Natal 'Conservation Services Department' are culling buffalo and demonstrating that they have learnt nothing from the tsetse fly and foot-and-mouth massacres of yesteryear. In an annual operation which goes on for some weeks, the game capture crews work vigorously to trap buffalo in bomas. In these bomas the stressed animals are darted and then tested for TB. Those who test negative are sold or released. The remaining animals, whether adults or calves, are gunned down in the bomas. The dead bodies are lifted out with a crane and then slaughtered so that the meat can be given to the local communities. Currying favour with the local communities is obviously high on the bureaucratic agenda; to what extent this shapes policies and thus impacts on decisions affecting the wildlife needs to be questioned. Why does a game reserve need an abattoir at all? Is Umfolozi a game reserve or a butchery business?

There is no doubt that the spread of bovine TB in this and other reserves is an ongoing concern but in their paranoid treatment of the problem, the veterinary authorities show that the situation exceeds their intellectual capacity, and that it is time to call in some first world scientific intelligence. The reason why the policy of selective extermination is bound to fail is that the affected areas are riddled with TB and the origin of the epidemic is not understood. So, as before, their cruel policy will not have the slightest effect on the spread of the disease. Next year and thereafter they will test the surviving buffalo only to find that half of them are now infected and so it will go on, with priceless assets being butchered on the altar of expedience. Thus, like civilians caught in a cross-fire, the animals catch it from the disease on one side, and the zealous counter-measures on the other.

Kruger is not the only park under ever-increasing threat from disease. As we write the Ovambos are pushing ever harder to be allowed to put down the northern fence of Etosha and graze their diseased livestock into this wonderful game reserve. And the community living next to Ndumo in northern KwaZulu-Natal have been rewarded for their fence-cutting and political agitation by being granted land for cultivation inside the game reserve. And when the elephants who live in the game reserve start trampling the crops, there are no prizes for guessing what the department of 'Nature Conservation' is going to do.

Populist concessions such as that at Ndumo have the potential to wreck the natural infrastructure needed to support tourism. The situation in Zimbabwe is even more dangerous. Indeed, the spectre of Famine rising up in Zimbabwe, hangs like a vast approaching storm cloud over the whole region. As at the end of May 2000, sixteen hundred commercial farms in Zimbabwe had been forcibly occupied by armed thugs. High Court orders to evict them had been ignored by the Police. Some of these farms form part of conservancies such as Save and Malilangwe, where significant numbers of endangered species like wild dogs, black rhino and roan antelope are carefully nurtured for the benefit of eco-tourism. A feature of the incursions has been the gratuitous violence and killing of wildlife. Whether the land invaders will overrun and destroy these conservancies, and others like it, is uncertain but some sort of partial permanent occupation by bellicose vandals seems likely. The end of May saw the first reports of large scale movements of squatters into the Gona-re-Zhou National Park in south-west Zimbabwe. It looks as if all the animals in this wonderful game reserve are now going to follow the one hundred and twenty black rhino, which survived here ten years ago, into extinction. Such a mischievous occupation will also destroy the basis for Gona-re-Zhou to join a proposed Kruger-Banhine superpark, with dire consequences for the economy of the region.

Land invasions are likely to spread through the region. Already government ministers in Namibia are making public statements to the effect that "our people are also hungry for land". Already some farms in the Kwazulu-Natal province of South Africa are being forcibly occupied. Should the Zimbabwe anarchy spread, then the damage to the wildlife could be incalculable. Some endangered species might become regionally extinct, not in years, but in months.

The wonderful wildlife together with its magically diverse habitat will be gone forever, leaving only memories, memories to be stretched by time into fairy tales of what used to be. Like memories of Gorongosa.

Epilogue

PERSECUTION

Next to the pot-holed tarmac road lies a young duiker antelope ewe, her head lolling unnaturally to one side. She cannot move because her back has been broken. The heavy trucks roar past, whipping up the dust and swirling it into her bleeding eyes. Nearby there is a wild rabbit, hanging by his ears in a position where he can appeal to passing motorists. Crucified, but still alive. Between them lies a pelican, its beak tied with tambo, a fibre rope made from the inner bark of trees. As you watch, a cigarette-smoking hawker walks up, carrying a struggling crane. With practised ease, he snaps the poor bird's beak between his fingers, and then breaks, one after another, with audible cracks, first its wings and then its legs. Crack! Crack! Then he throws the piteously maimed bird down among the rest of his stock-in-trade.

This is Africa's equivalent of a hamburger stand. It is also the shop front for the 'sustainable use' industry. As you recoil in disgust from such a macabre sight, you manage to gasp at the roadside hawker:

"How can you do this?"

"Oh well" he answers, misunderstanding the question. "You see, if I sell chickens, I only make ten bucks and I have to feed them. If I catch these wild birds, they cost me nothing and I sell them for fifty bucks."

"No, I mean how can you break their legs and hurt them so?" you ask, turning your eyes from the horror of it all.

"Oh well. They are wild. They will run away if I do not stop them. How can I get money for them if they run away?"

You look around for a Policeman. In fact, they are sitting on the stoep of the Police station which is not a hundred yards away. This business is carried on in full view of authority.

"Why do you not kill them then, so that they do not suffer?"

"Ah no. The people will only pay half-price if it is dead."

The road between Maputo and South Africa is lined with roadside vendors, all selling captured wild birds and animals. The tranquil ponds of the nearby Umbuluzi wetlands are criss-crossed with thousands, no, tens of thousands, of wire snares. Water fowl are trapped in their hundreds. The policemen do nothing; in fact, many of them are themselves customers of the bushmeat take-away. What passes muster for a Ministry of Environment will only say:- "The people are allowed to utilise a sustainable resource, blah blah..."

The international wildlife charitable organisations stand by watching as if they were spectators at Wimbledon and are not expected to interfere in the game or even to talk too loudly while play is in progress. A representative of TRAFFIC issues a press release:

"If the wetlands are over-exploited this could cause ecological problems blah blah..." No-one does a thing. Everything is globalised today, including paralysis.

In Southern Africa, the persecution of wildlife has been institutionalised. It starts right at the top with regional government policy; it is enshrined in the Constitutions; it contaminates the law and government administration, and it runs rife through human society in the form of hunting and poaching. Even the wildlife conservation charities have fallen into the trap of aiding and abetting this evil.

Time has always been running against the survival of wild Africa, but now the clock is racing. The death-knell for collapse of wild Africa has been sounded. For the Southern African states have all adopted a common policy for wildlife utilisation.

The Policy of Sustainable Use may be summed up as follows:- There is no policy to preserve wildlife or other biological assets for their own sakes or for any moral or ethical imperative. All governments agree that wildlife is a 'natural resource' and must be 'utilised in a sustainable manner.' The policy is sometimes referred to flippantly as 'if it pays, then it stays.'

How was such a heartless doctrine ever drafted, let alone adopted? It seems that the WWF hatched this Bushmeat Traders licence with the UN. More specifically, with its Environment Programme. The whole basis of the policy is that wildlife should primarily be used to alleviate human poverty. That is obviously unfair to the wild animals. The animals did not cause the poverty. The humans did that to themselves.

Let us spell out the policy in plain words so that people may more clearly understand the enormity of it.

1. Any notion of animal rights is decisively rejected. Sentient, living, intelligent wild people are categorised as a resource, like tin or copper. These children of Nature have no more rights than a piece of cardboard.

2. Not only have they no rights, but they have had a duty imposed upon them. They must make themselves useful; i.e. they must make money for the voting public - or else they must be 'harvested.' They must all become entrepreneurs. Only then may they expect any protection from the gun and the snare.

3. The same duty - to be useful or die - is not imposed by the humans upon themselves. (If it were, one wonders nervously which of us would escape the noose!). So, a higher duty is imposed on the poor animal to conform to the laws of economics than on humans, who at least have choices which the animals do not enjoy.

How, for example, does a surviving elephant in a place like Caprivi, Damaraland or Bushmanland carry out his duty to be useful. Answer, he gets himself shot by hunters who pay money to the local hunting industry, or he gets himself photographed by tourists who pay money to the local ecotourism industry. But who wants to visit a devastated tribal area with its degraded land, litter, sprawling tin shacks and shanties? Nobody, of course. So, the humans by their own abuse of the natural resources, put it out of the elephant's power to save himself. Only where the humans have set aside a reserve for him shall the elephant be permitted to exist, for only there where the local humans have been excluded will the hunters and tourists pay for their different purposes.

So, we can re-state the policy as follows: 'Only in game reserves will wild animals be allowed to live. Everywhere else they may be destroyed.'

Those responsible for the policy will be quick to assert their good intentions, and to point out how they also drafted some guidelines so that the policy could be implemented in a 'caring and compassionate manner.' We would like to have explained to us in plain words, which we ordinary folk can understand; how can wild people be shot with rifles or strangled in a wire noose in a 'caring and compassionate manner?' In our view the policy amounts to a Declaration of War on innocent wild animals.

This 007 Licence to Kill policy has caused and continues to wreak havoc with the wildlife in Southern Africa. Because of it, the trapping, maiming and selling of birds and animals by roadside vendors near Maputo in Mozambique is condoned. Hunting is encouraged and poaching is virtually unrestrained. The policy stands for the shrugging off of any effort to discipline the behaviour of those humans whose whole business revolves around unremitting physical cruelty to innocent wild people.

Under the common law wild animals simply do not exist (Res nullius). The statutes all look as if they have been dipped in a pot of persecution on their way through Parliament. These laws are not sympathetically administered by the Government Nature Conservation Departments.

In late 1998, a nature conservation official came to Harnas, inspected the animals and facilities of this possibly the largest private wildlife haven in the southern hemisphere, and then contributed to all the valuable work that Harnas was doing to save wild animals from the neglect of authority, by slapping Nic with a substantial fine for keeping some little marmoset monkeys for which he 'didn't got a license.' The marmosets were listed on Nic's permit, but in the

221

years since the last visit from the department of Nature Conservation, their numbers had naturally increased, and it was for the newborn that Nic 'didn't got a license.'

During 1996 a pride of lions left their Kalahari Gemsbok Park without permission in quadruplicate from the higher authorities. They wandered into Namibia, where they succumbed to hunger and temptation in the form of some goats which belonged to a rancher. He executed the lions - all thirteen including the young - in one nightmare massacre. All for the sake of a few goats not in total worth the tassel on a lion's tail. The Namibian department of Nature Conservation declined to prosecute the murderer, saying that he had done nothing illegal and was perfectly justified in protecting his stock.

So on the one hand it is quite alright to cruelly exterminate a whole family of magnificent animals but, on the other hand, if you lovingly care for a few more tiny marmosets than those for which you 'got a licence' then you are in trouble.

All too frequently, nature conservation departments in Southern Africa overlook what should be the fundamental consideration in every case, namely, the best interests of the wild animals in their charge. Even stray animals are callously exploited. Recently a young elephant bull was found wandering alone and lost in the Omaheke district near Gobabis. In a more caring part of the world, the ten tonne scatterling would have been darted and transported back to his own kind in a safe place. But this is Namibia and here a bizarre clash of interests arose. The local hunting safari operators began to bid against each other to buy the great animal from Government. Harnas could offer no money but it offered to use its recently acquired darting equipment to immobilise the elephant, and then to transport the tranquillised animal to whichever wilderness area or game reserve Nature Conservation might nominate.

This unequal contest of vested interests ended in a novel form of murder. An official hand reached out for a rubber stamp. Then the stamp was driven into the space provided on the hunting permit - for one elephant. Murder by rubber-stamping. The thump of the rubber stamp on the hunting permit echoed all the way back to Harnas to convey Government's rejection of the plea to be allowed to save the young elephant's life.

Stray animals or stray humans; it makes no difference. During August of 1997, five valuable lions were executed in the Kruger National Park. It seems the lions had feasted upon a trespasser, who was seeking an informal transfer between Mozambique and South Africa by sneaking through the game reserve. Kruger Park management took the decision to shoot all five lions, who after all were only doing what comes naturally in their own territory.

More recently, a Kruger Park game ranger on a night drive stopped to relieve himself, and as ill Fate would have it, conducted his bodily functions in the path of a hunting leopard. There was a leap in the dark, a scuffle and then silence. The shaken tourists returned to their camp and notified the Warden, who responded with Teutonic promptness and efficiency. Before dawn had broken the leopard had been shot, presumably on the basis that two wrongs make a right, with a make weight that having tasted human flesh, the luckless cat had become a 'potential man-eater.'

Even in their own reserves, it seems, the poor wild animals have no right to exist.

The last two decades have seen a veritable explosion of private game farms in Southern Africa, with a consequent expansion in the numbers of game antelope. South Africa's four percent of land area proclaimed to national or provincial game reserves has now been surpassed in total extent by the private game farms which have sprouted like mushrooms after heavy rains in the Kalahari.

From less than one hundred hectares (220 acres) up to more than one hundred thousand hectares, little land fragments are being stocked with wild antelope which are purchased like cattle at the game industry auctions. Some of the antelope find their way to eco-tourism resorts. The vast majority are less fortunate. They are bought as slaves to be sold to foreign hunters. Locals too. The hunting and killing of our beautiful wild antelope is the national sport and pastime of white folk in South Africa. More popular even than Rugby.

The high camp perimeter fence generally contains more animals than the area could naturally sustain because the numbers of prisoners will perish rapidly. When the provincial Nature Conservation department has inspected the perimeter fence which has been erected and granted a 'Certificate of Adequate Enclosure,' then the rancher is not even bound by irksome restrictions such as seasons or quotas. The hunting fraternity may perfectly legally go there and shoot all the pregnant kudu or eland cows they can afford to pay for.

Game hunting farms are even established by Municipalities ostensibly to attract tourists but one suspects that the ulterior motive is more often so that municipal officials and their friends will never be short of biltong. In these enclosures canned hunting also takes place. In May 2000, a rhino cow who had been a tourist attraction at Kuruman Municipal Game Park for fifteen years was sold to a Free State farmer. He spent the whole day firing bullets into her body. More than a dozen in all. Over an eight hour period. With a heavy calibre rifle. Here was an endangered animal being tortured to death by a qualified professional hunter in a tourist park within earshot of town and metres of a busy road, and all this facilitated by the Northern Cape Nature Conservation department which had issued him an open permit to do so.

The people who pay for the use of these game farms call themselves 'conservation hunters.' They say that hunting stimulates the growth of game farms and that makes them conservationists. We would analyse the logic of that argument as follows:

All cats have four legs. My dog has four legs. Therefore my dog is a cat.

"What about the fifteen year old lion?" one hears the hunters ask. "He has had a full life; he only has a year or two left; so why should we not conserve wildlife by selling him to a rich hunter for US$20,000 and using some of the money to conserve other animals?" Oh great. Why don't we go down to the old folks home and shoot all the pensioners? By the same reasoning, they've had a good innings, they've outlived their usefulness, so let's kill them now and let their heirs inherit sooner rather than later. Selecting an old lion for an example is no argument at all. Hunters cannot be conservationists, inter alia because they destroy the genetic vigour of their targets. They always want the best trophy i.e. Nature's biggest and strongest, the most important animal and the very one who should not be shot so that he can pass on his strong genes. Moreover, particularly in the case of lions, the trophy lion is the alpha lion of the pride. Having bagged his trophy, the hunter departs to get drunk and boast his exploits leaving the pride lionesses vulnerable to other predators (hyenas) and at the mercy of nomadic lions who will fight each other - perhaps to the death - and then kill all the cubs to bring the lionesses back on heat. The hunter's 'sport' has devastated the pride and caused a number of consequential deaths. If hunters genuinely desire to be conservationists they must practice conservation. If they must hunt, let them hunt by non-lethal methods such as some do using dart guns.

The high stress levels in animals who are confined in relatively small camps and who are pursued day in and day out by trigger-happy gunmen can well be imagined. It has even been scientifically measured. At the sight of a human or a motor vehicle, the animals stampede, their panic obvious to a person with any heart at all.

Game hunting farms are an affront to morality, spiritualism and to all religions that regard brutality to living beings as atheist. By smashing up the wholeness of the natural world (most notably the magnificent predators) and recovering from the wreckage only those life forms which can be used as alternative livestock, hunting farms trivialise the exquisite; de-personalise living creatures, reducing them to mere numbers which are harvested or 'removed' at the convenience of the master species and they normalise sadism by making cruelty routine.

The reason that ranchers are turning away from cattle in favour of game animals has nothing whatsoever to do with a love of wildlife. Only a love of money. A successful game farm can be many times more profitable than ranching with cattle.

The main fault of most southern African game departments is that they place the narrow interests of a declining livestock ranching industry above all else. Including the interests of wildlife. While they sit shuffling pieces of paper around and applying policies, many of which are anachronistic or just plain wrong, the wilderness perishes. Take the problem animals as an example. To whom are these irreplaceable assets a problem? Certainly not to the growing ecotourism industry which regards them as unique tourist attractions. While the land use is changing, policies rooted in a brutal past continue to cause meaningless bloodshed and to sabotage the region's efforts to promote tourism.

We also find the latest advances in genetics being bent into tools for persecution. In a paper read to the SASOL Symposium on Wildlife Rehabilitation in October 1995 Dr. Gerhard Verdoorn, a well-known South African wildlife expert, stated as follows:

"Genetic diversity and gene pools have all of a sudden become buzz words in formal conservation circles. While animals are being saved from certain deaths and rehabilitated to a state of fitness for release, conservation authorities are often obstructive and without any guidance refuse to grant permission for the release of animals. The arguments mooted are that the genetic resources from different zoo-geographical regions should not be mixed by allowing the release of rehabilitated animals. This is acceptable in many cases, but the literature clearly indicated that certain species of animals, and in particular birds, may move over vast distances. Therefore, the idea of preserving genetic pools and identities, is at best purely fictitious. The present environment in South Africa is actually restricting the genetic diversity and sustainability of most land-dwelling animals with the fences and other man-made obstructions. While game auctions offer animals from all different zoo-geographical regions without any obstruction by the authorities, rehabilitated animals face the dilemma of having to be placed at their place of origin whether the habitat can support their survival or not."

If the wildlife is being persecuted, not protected, by some government policies, laws and officials, we look to see if any salvation lies with the wildlife conservation charities.

One of the best-known and respected conservation agencies in South Africa is the EWT (Endangered Wildlife Trust). It is a member of the prestigious IUCN - the World Conservation Union. The EWT publishes an annual called 'Visions,' which is a glossy coffee-table collection of fine nature photographs. Along with the photographs comes an overview of wildlife, ecotourism and the environment in Southern Africa. A sort of annual update on what is happening to wildlife in the region. We pick up the 1995 EWT Visions Annual. Not a word about the holocaust. Nothing about the invasion of Bushmanland and the extermination of whole prides of lions in an area of four thousand square kilometres. Nothing about the encroachment into Caprivi by settlers and the havoc that they are wreaking on the wildlife. Nothing about the persecution of the desert lions or the excessive hunting of the rare desert oryx as reported in the Windhoek Observer. Nothing about the continuous trapping of leopards and Cheetah.

Then we pick up a later Annual (1998) and we read: "its looking good." The status of wildlife in Namibia is "looking good. Poaching is reported to be under control with no rhino being taken and just a handful of elephants although subsistence poaching of other species continues."

Let us rewrite the overview of Namibia for 'Visions' and let us base our information on many months of personal research in Namibia, living in the bush, travelling through remote areas and game reserves, visiting farmers and inspecting their traps and talking to people who are intimately involved with wildlife.

Vast tribal areas are already devoid of game. In Ovamboland, Kavango and Hereroland the game has succumbed to wire and bullet and Caprivi is fast going the same way. These areas are absolutely devastated. Then comes Bushmanland where the newly resettled Hereros from Botswana are killing everything in sight. Bushmanland is supposed to be reserved for hunting by Bushmen, but they complain that Herero poachers from the south and Kavangos from the north are killing their game and depriving them of their livelihood. Farmers the length and breadth of the country all tell the same story. Their farms are dripping with wire snares and it is getting worse. The police have no vehicles or radios or manpower to spare for anti-poaching patrols, which are left entirely to the individual farmer's hard-pressed budget.

Local police turn a blind eye to the possession of the fearsome jaw-traps or gin traps which are freely sold and used with the tragic results described in Chapter Three.

And now the Namibians have developed a new horror, the X-trap, which is a sort of anti-personnel mine for animals. It consists of a square section of thin steel plate which is fixed securely over a hole in the ground. Into it has been cut an X-shaped cross. When an animal steps into the plate, the points of the cross give way allowing the hoof through but not back up again, because any attempt to withdraw the hoof drives the sharp steel points further into the poor animal's leg. There the trapped animal is held, in great pain as the points of the cross gouge themselves into the leg, until merciful death comes to end its suffering.

The incidence of fires which have always been a problem here, have increased as the steady encroachment of tribesmen into adjacent wilderness areas distributes the arsonist farther and wider across this unhappy land. Etosha, that jewel of game reserves, is now under threat both from within and without. Powerful political interests in Ovamboland have fixed their eyes on the northern areas of the reserve, and plans are afoot to open the reserve to them. In they will flow along with their calling cards, overgrazing and snares, annual fires and the infecting of game with stock diseases such as anthrax and TB. As if this is not enough, within the game department itself rages a battle for jobs, with pressure from the previously disadvantaged to oust the 'Old Guard.' Grappling with the ghosts of apartheid and colonialism, the very last thing on the minds of the new ruling elite is whether the new appointees have any knowledge of, or innate desire to help, wild animals. Allegations were even made that wire snares are now being set around the accommodation compounds within the Reserve and the tourist camps like Namutoni. The situation is so bad that during 1998 buildings at Okakuejo camp were burned to the ground by dissatisfied game department employees.

The SWAPO government has also introduced a policy that the Department of Nature Conservation is obliged to provide arms and ammunition to any rural tribesman who alleges he is having a problem with wild animals. The very department which should be protecting the wildlife against poachers is now arming people with government weapons.

The Cape griffon, one of the largest of the vultures, which used to breed in its thousands on the cliffs of Rotstock and the Waterberg Plateau, has not been seen breeding in Namibia since 1995 and is now confirmed to have gone extinct there.

Swaarthaak acacias in their millions, the product of overgrazing and poor farming practices, have closed over so much of north-central Namibia that the government is actively considering a sort of 'Agent Orange' chemical attack on hundreds of square kilometres of veld and ranch land.
We do not share the opinion that things are 'looking good' in Namibia.

It is ironical to see in 'Visions' statements like: "if the last rhino in Southern Africa is not to become a drying carcass in the bush, conservation agencies in 'the new South Africa' need international and national support."

In other words "Things are tough - send more money." If the existing South African wildlife conservation organisations were involved in bold new initiatives to save chunks of southern Africa from human encroachment, we would endorse the plea for more funds. Instead we believe that some have become part of the problem, not the solution.

Nowhere is this better illustrated than in the appalling case of the Tuli elephants, which aroused so much media attention and public interest. Baby elephants are often sold into slavery as circus animals or to Zoos. Unfortunately these young elephants have a genetically-imposed wild spirit, which, however admirable and magnificent in their own natural surroundings, must be broken by the trainers.

Enter one Riccardo Ghiazza, a heavy hitter from Italy, who traffics in elephants. In February 2000, an arrest on fraud charges revealed that Interpol was after him and that he was on the run from a six-month jail sentence for Italian drug law violations. An interesting gentleman.

On May 12th, 1998 the members of the committee of the Northern Tuli Game Reserve of Botswana received a letter from their Chairman which stated as follows:- "We have had an offer from an organisation to buy from us about 40 sub-adult elephants (15 years old), to be trained at a site near Pretoria for bush clearing work and related tasks, similar to those carried out (by elephants) in Asia. The buyers would prefer bulls, but cows would also be acceptable."

We presume that the lure of the golden money diminished the critical faculties of the Tuli land owners. No person in his right mind would try to train a 15 year old wild elephant. Taming and training could only practicably be attempted with babies. Training methods usually involve the use of a surrogate mother.

Once the necessary sacrifices had been made to the great god Money, several extraordinary things took place.

Contrary to the terms of the written offer baby elephants were darted from helicopters and kidnapped from their distressed mothers in the wild. Experts Daphne Sheldrick and Dr. Joyce Poole later assessed the ages of the captives as being between two and six years old. Further, of the thirty babies captured, twenty-four were female - just what the Zoos want.

By September 1998 Ghiazza's South African company African Game Services was holding at its premises near Pretoria thirty baby elephants. Incredibly the CITES certificates had been issued. What passes muster for Nature Conservation departments in Botswana and South Africa had granted all necessary transport, export, import and holding permits. The elephant hi-jack was complete. Now it was time for the babies to be trained. The Zoos do not want wild animals. Ghiazza brought in mahouts from Indonesia. Thanks to some good work by an environmental working group called Sekai and the wildlife unit of the NSPCA, the story of these baby elephants broke in the South African press.

The consternation caused by this unwelcome publicity can only be imagined. Many unethical practices take place in the trafficking of wild animals and the prospect of the NSPCA prying into their affairs was not welcomed by the participants. A committee - the Committee for the Training & Welfare of Elephants - was formed. Ghiazza himself and several well-known people sat on this committee and made recommendations. The only two of which we are aware were the blunting of the ankuses (training hooks) and the introduction of padded anklets around which the chains could be attached. Other than this, the committee was ineffectual and used by Ghiazza to give his elephant training project credibility.

The big three in the South African wildlife conservation industry could reasonably have been expected to rush to the defence of the victims who were being tortured on a daily basis. Unbelievably, they closed ranks and lent their considerable support to the wanted man. One and all they disparaged the efforts of the only organisation which was trying to save the babies from a fate worse than death. On 2nd October 1998, a press statement was issued which contained the following paragraphs :-

"The World Wide Fund for Nature (South Africa), the Wildlife and Environment Society of South Africa and the Endangered Wildlife Trust have prepared the following joint statement on the issue of the elephants that have been captured in the Tuli area of Botswana and are currently being tamed in South Africa prior to their being translocated to other locations.

The above three organisations are in agreement that the owners of the private game reserves in Botswana from which these elephants have been removed have not acted irresponsibly in this matter. Indeed they have acted wisely, by the only means currently available to them in this country, to reduce the numbers of elephants in the area. The reserve is privately owned and receives no state subsidy for its management. The sale of these young elephants to a professional animal trader, Mr. Riccardo Ghiazza, based in South Africa, who is taming them and will then sell them internationally to Safari Parks or to operations where they will be used for elephant-back safaris, has been carefully evaluated by the reserve 5 management team. It must be stressed that the CITES authority in each country importing these elephants is responsible for issuing an import permit. These have already been approved.

The reserve management team, and the Onderstepoort veterinarians who are working with them in this instance, are confident that Mr. Ghiazza runs a bona fide operation. The taming process is the same as is used in taming Indian elephants in south-east Asia (he uses Indonesian Mahouts and tame Indian elephants in this taming programme). The animals are tied during the initial training sessions which involve hours of stroking by the mahout. Not to tie them would be suicidal for the training team as these are not baby elephants - they are weaned, sub-adult animals with tusks, aged between 5 and 10 years. They have been carefully selected at capture as being animals that have already weakened their bonds with their mothers. Monitoring of the herd from which most of these animals have been carefully and selectively removed, shows that it is still in the same area and does not appear to have been unduly stressed by the removals.

The above three organisations do not oppose this operation.

This press release, coming as it did from the united public might of three pillars of respectability, achieved everything which the Italian could have wanted. It cast a blanket of doubt over the ugly truth long enough for him to manoeuvre around the legal obstacles which the NSPCA placed before him.

The ugly truth, when it emerged, was that these babies were stolen from their mothers in the wild and then systematically beaten, chained and tortured for months by sadistic savages who called themselves mahouts.

They were brutally attacked time and again and battered about the face with long heavy poles, and whipped with sjamboks to the point of urinating in terror and pain. During the torture sessions, weapons (sorry, training apparatus) included the ankus, which is a medieval hook, long and short handled version, with a steel pointed bit at the end. Also, the nail rod which is a truly offensive weapon consisting of a stout pole with a drill bit - a drill bit, for God's sake - protruding from the end. And the traditional South African bull whip, the sjambok. The pointed devices caused wounds and abscesses to the head and upper trunk. Bare chains and hobbles also caused raw open lesions around the ankles and legs of the orphans. Not only was physical cruelty inflicted on the babies but other methods to achieve domination were used, including deprivation of food, water and sleep.

How three such respectable wildlife conservation organisations could prostitute themselves to such an extent as to publish a litany of untruths in an obvious effort to white wash Ghiazza and thereby encourage him to continue his brutal treatment, surpasses rational parameters. Both in this statement and in their subsequent campaign to frustrate and disparage the efforts of the NSPCA, these three organisations betrayed the stolen babies.

Thanks largely to their efforts as well as those of the Rhino and Elephant Foundation, the cruelty to the elephants was largely overlooked and the NSPCA stood virtually alone in South Africa in defence of the young animals.

In October 1998 after the Brits Magistrate ruled for the first time that the NSPCA should seize the babies, Ghiazza's lawyers returned to court the following day to show due cause as to why the elephants could not be removed. Due cause was given that the young animals were suffering from sand colic which could be fatal if they were moved. In actual fact the only sand was that which was being flung in the eyes of the Court.

The case was re-convened later that month after an inspection of the elephants at African Game Services at the request of Brits Magistrate Herman Glas. Among the people sitting in the Brits courtroom every day, was a young blond woman whose presence alarmed the animal exploitation industry more than anyone else. Her name was Jane Garrison and she represented the United States-based animal rights group, PETA (People for the Ethical Treatment of Animals). PETA was to draw considerable attention to the plight of the Tuli babies with their publicity activities, and the protests which took place both in South Africa and in foreign capitals. After fifty hours of testimony over several weeks, the Magistrate ruled again in favour of the NSPCA and the elephants. Ghiazza's lawyers effectively suspended the operation of the seizure order by applying forthwith to the Supreme Court for a review of the Magistrate's decision.

The Rhino and Elephant Foundation, a wildlife charity which included some prominent conservationists, responded to the judgement by issuing a press release threatening to lay cruelty charges against the NSPCA should it try to enforce its judgement and remove the animals. The REF not only jumped onto the trafficker's bandwagon but even seized the reins, bombarding the public with press releases, letters to the media, radio and TV interviews in a sustained smear campaign against the beleaguered NSPCA. The REF set up a Web-cam site and also promoted a documentary which was shown on E-TV in South Africa, which painted a pretty picture of how well the calves were being treated.

The only organisation in South Africa that did not allow itself to be dissuaded from assisting the NSPCA, in spite of intensive lobbying and pressure, was South African National Parks. The entire capture team from Kruger National Park was on standby to assist the NSPCA to move the elephants from AGS in December 1998.

Having sidelined the courts with his review application and with his publicity campaign steaming along nicely, Ghiazza set about trading the elephants. Three went to Basle Zoo in Switzerland and two each to Dresden and Erfurt Zoo in Germany. A Japanese Zoo, to its credit, cancelled its order once it had been apprised of the true circumstance of capture. How the Swiss and German zoos could have accepted the baby elephants after all the cruelty had come to light is clearly a matter for consideration. Where on earth was CITES? In fact a senior official from the South African Department of Environmental Affairs attended the Magistrates court at an urgent hearing convened on a Sunday to confirm that the CITES certificates were in order.

Yet when the NSPCA applied to the Northern Province Nature Conservation Department for a permit to transport the last remaining five elephants to Touchstone Game Reserve which had previously been approved by the Department as a suitable destination, the application was refused. Here is a pretty irony to further demonstrate how entrenched are some of the South African Provincial Nature Conservation Departments in the animal exploitation industry.

On the one hand we have a wanted man whose whole life revolves around unremitting misery for wild people and who has been publicly shown to

234

be operating a torture camp for baby elephants, which have been stolen from their mothers in the wild. Yet all the transport and export permits needed rain down on him with the blessings of the Provincial Nature Conservation Departments. CITES certificates drop from the trees and senior officials forget their bureaucratic office hours to attend court on a Sunday to help him further his cruel trade. The local police force will even help him load and off load the animals.

On the other hand is the NSPCA which can show that it alone is acting in the best interest of the orphans who are being abused, and whom it wishes to move into an approved destination in the wild where they may recover from their hideous ordeal, and it is in possession of a Seizure order from the Court. The Northern Province Nature Conservation Department will make sure that the NSPCA 'didn't got a licence,' and that the baby elephants continue to suffer. When the licensing system is applied in such an arbitrary and capricious manner, we suggest that it needs to be reviewed.

Some of the elephants went to Sandhurst Safaris which belongs to a fellow wildlife exploiter by the name of Douglas Fletcher. This gentleman's operation was described in Gareth Patterson's expose on canned lion hunting. The remaining fourteen have ended up at Marakele National Park after being purchased from the Italian and donated to the park for wild release. Mr Ghiazza got his money after all.

What happened next was that a video of the torture camp was publicly screened on a South African T.V. magazine programme called Carte Blanche. For the first time the public was able to see for themselves video footage of chained baby elephants being battered about the face with heavy poles in what was obviously an orgy of torture. The effect was explosive. Thousands of irate South Africans spontaneously besieged the property of African Game Services in an unprecedented display of public fury.

When in February 2000 the reviewing judge finally - after fourteen months - issued his 140 page judgement, he found overwhelmingly in favour of the NSPCA and he criticised the evidence of the eminent experts who had given evidence on behalf of the trafficker. He found the cruelty charges to have been proved. This judgement only confirmed what the public already knew from the Carte Blanche video.

The Tuli elephant case opened up a veritable can of worms. First, it is quite apparent that CITES certificates were obtained with ease in completely unjustified circumstances. Then there is the question why all the wildlife conservation charities in South Africa rushed to the side of the animal trader and ignored the plight of the orphan calves. As for the provincial Nature Conservation Departments who came into contact with the enterprising Italian, they seemed to behave at all times as if they were at his beck and call. Why were his permits not cancelled after the true story came to light? The effectiveness of the law was also called into question. Notwithstanding the huge financial drain caused to the NSPCA and its donors in fighting for the calves, Ghiazza was able to treat the Courts as a side-show while he got on with his deadly business. Because our law does not allow the deprivation of ownership of animals until conviction on a criminal charge and the exhaustion of all other legal remedies (such as appeal after appeal), he was able to lose every battle and yet still win the war.

The NSPCA should never have been abandoned in such a shameful manner to stand alone. There is a clear need for unity in the interests of all suffering wild animals by all charities who accept funds from donors for that purpose. However, even the darkest cloud has a silver lining. The unforeseen beneficiary of the Tuliphant affair is undoubtedly the animal rights movement. The stubborn refusal of the existing wildlife charities to enter the field of battle against the animal exploitation complex has spawned the growth of associations of ordinary concerned citizens, such as Wildlife Action Group (WAG).

With the harrowing tale of the Tuli orphans we must bring our homily on persecution to a bitter end. Yet there is one final observation to be made. The price of wild animals at the game auctions has skyrocketed. Some of the rarer and therefore more valuable species such as Roan antelope are worth more than U.S.$ 20,000 each at the auctions. A like-sized bull or cow in a commercial cattle herd is not even worth U.S. $1,000. Kilogram for kilogram, pound for pound, some game species are more than thirty times the value of domestic livestock. Now we can clearly see how short-sighted is Southern Africa's policy on wildlife utilisation from another perspective. With the active support of all the higher authorities, starting with national governments and going right up to the UN, the people are being permitted, nay, encouraged, to eradicate whole populations of precious wild animals so that the dead can be replaced by cattle and goats, which are not even worth the boss of a buffalo's horn. Like taking over a gold mine, mining out all the gold and then throwing it away so that the mine can be filled up with lead. Does this policy make economic sense? Who will want to visit Africa when the magnificent wildlife has all been replaced by cattle and goats? When the trumpeting of the elephants and the roaring of the lions have all been substituted by mooing and bleating?

We believe that Africa has a spirit which is unlike any other place on earth; that this is infused into everything indigenous and natural and that when we destroy these things, we are destroying something of our own after-lives. For when there is no cosmic and brooding spirit left around us here on Earth, where will our spirits go when we die? To Mars? At the present rate of human devastation, Africa will get to Mars before NASA. In fact, we will confound the rocket scientists by bringing Mars back to Earth, creating a lifeless, barren desert occupied now only by the harsh scouring winds and the marching ranks of sand dunes which they drive before them, with only the dried-up watercourses to betray that our Mars continent was once a rich, bountiful and spiritual Eden.

Epilogue

PROPOSALS

Each tree life spans a thousand dreams
Soon leaves shall fall like years
Coughing on this barren earth
And choking on its tears.
And who shall end this cleansing
As the victims span the sky
Blown into a question mark
for those who wonder why.
When the axes all are silent
When every voice is stilled
No sighs will bring back memories
Of a world we will have killed.
Andrew Mercer

The most immediate action that needs to be taken is to raise money for the purchase of habitat for the wildlife. Land, land and more land is what the animals need. Our own feeling based on long experience is that private enterprise is the only thing that works in Africa. If we wish to maximise our benefit to wildlife we must confine our financial efforts to purchasing ownership of privately owned ranch land in the wild areas of the region. Our political efforts should be directed at persuading the national governments to protect un-proclaimed wilderness as well as established game reserves from human intrusion.

Let us look at some different initiatives and assess them in order to avoid past mistakes. By far the most exciting concept was the original superpark idea which was mooted in 1990 at a meeting in Maputo by Anton Rupert, then President of the WWF South Africa. His idea was to link some of the sparsely-populated and protected areas in Mozambique with their adjacent counterparts in South Africa and Zimbabwe, and to combine them into huge superparks. By far the most important proposal was that the Kruger National Park in South Africa be joined to Gona-re-Zhou in Zimbabwe and Zinane, Coutada 16 hunting area, and Banhine National Park, all in Mozambique, to create a superpark almost one hundred thousand square kilometres in extent. The few rural tribesmen living within the proclaimed boundaries would have to be resettled.

A number of such superparks is the obvious panacea to wildlife woes. Large enough to encompass even ancient elephant migration routes, and vast enough for wild populations to enjoy genetic diversity, they would be the answer to any environmentalist's prayer. As for the resettled communities, they would enjoy unprecedented employment opportunities in the eco-tourism industry, which for them offered unimaginable prosperity. It was a win-win project. How could it possibly fail?

The project was referred by the Mozambique government to the World Bank. The Global Environment Facility of the World Bank took several years to prepare its report - time running against wildlife survival with every minute that ticks past - and finally released its report in June 1996.

"No way," said the Report in essence. "If you want funding from us, there must be a whole new concept. This park must not be 'strictly protected.' It must instead be a 'Trans-Frontier Conservation Area(TFCA), which emphasises 'multiple resource use by local communities'." This is UN jargon for saying that there must be no attempt to force people to be relocated outside the superpark boundaries, and that they may kill the animals in the park. Instead, "every effort must be made to develop outreach programmes to offer the people opportunities in the tourism industry."

In an American context the UN proposes allowing people to live off the land in Yellowstone National Park. This simply won't work. To understand why requires an understanding of a rural tribesman's lifestyle and mindset which is clearly lacking on the cocktail circuit in Washington and New York.

Rural tribesmen live in isolated places with virtually no technical infrastructure. Generally speaking they are subsistence farmers whose income is supplemented by the wages of relatives who are migrant workers in, say, the South African gold mines. Their whole lives revolve around hunting (poaching) and gathering of local resources. They cut down the hardwood trees to make charcoal for their own use and to sell in the distant towns. Most are illiterate.

Where do these people come from? Those presently living within the proposed park boundaries are mostly comparatively recent immigrants from the adjacent rural areas which used to be rich in resources (trees and wildlife).

Why have they infiltrated the proposed park land? Because they have cut down all the useable trees for their cottage charcoal industry and snared all the wild animals in their original tribal land and so they are obliged to move on.

What is going to happen when the World Bank-backed conservationists bring lorry loads of elephants and game animals for which they have paid tens of millions of dollars and deposit them into such a tribesman's back yard? We believe there will be a poaching frenzy. Out of the thatched roofs of the pole-and-dagga huts will come the snares and long hidden AK47s. After the bursts of automatic gunfire have sent the forest animals fleeing helter-skelter, the deathly stillness that always follows in the footprints of these hunters will settle once more like a blood-soaked blanket over a hundred thousand square kilometres. The land which could have been the economic salvation of the whole region will lie denuded and barren, a charred reminder of yet another initiative to fall victim to naive foreigners who have no idea of local conditions. How many people will want to visit an animal graveyard where the whitening bones of poached elephants lie bleaching among the charcoal ruins of the forest hardwoods in a drab, denuded landscape?

During the ten years of government inertia since the first proposal, yes, ten long years, there has been a distressing increase in the extent of human encroachment into the proposed Park together with the inevitable consequences - poaching and deforestation. With every sordid year that hauls itself painfully over the corpses of the luckless wildlife, it becomes harder and harder to go back to the original, workable proposal.

The result of all this is that an opportunity of a lifetime has been squandered. The prosperity of the whole region may even have been lost forever. Like a derailed train, the superpark proposal was transmuted to a 'Peace Park' project. The 'Peace Parks Foundation' was established on 1st February 1997 to facilitate the establishment of the UN version of the superpark i.e. one where the wildlife is sacrificed on the altar of alleviating human poverty. Instead of continuing to ride a derailed train on a rough road that leads nowhere, the Peace Parks Foundation should publicise the failure of governments and international agencies to support its efforts by closing down and returning what is left of the substantial donations to the donors. Perhaps not enough people are aware of how much has been lost by mankind and animal alike by the failure of the Mozambique, Zimbabwe and South African governments to implement the original superpark proposal. Tens of thousands of jobs and tens of millions of dollars in annual income have been thrown away, together with the preservation of a hundred thousand square kilometres of biological wealth.

The tragedy is that it is actually in the best interests of the tribesmen themselves to agree to vacate the Pgark, for once tourism has been developed and money is flowing in, then these same people would be the first to benefit enormously from the job opportunities which that development would create. Their present nihilistic lifestyle can only end in their own extinction once they have obliterated the resource base on which their whole lives depend. Only their own resettlement could achieve the sustainable use of the park.

241

Those on the derailed train may argue with us and say that this is a bad example and that there are other Peace Parks, one of which, the Kgalagadi Transfrontier Park, is already in existence. Unfortunately, the change of name from Kalahari Gemsbok Park to Kgalagadi Transfrontier Park was much ado about nothing, since the two halves of the Park have been run as one since 1948. The change of status of the Park from de facto to de jure is hardly anything to crow about. Certainly, because of the park's remoteness, there were no difficult decisions by the Botswana government over human resettlement. The Peace Parks Foundation's major contribution to the change of formal status was to commission the design and building of an impressive entrance gate, and to fund the opening ceremony (over half a million SA rands). We have our own views about such expenses. That half-million would have bought more than a thousand hectares of land for the wild animals had it been employed as we suggest, in the buying of habitat in the Southern Kalahari.

There have been a number of initiatives within the region to try to save wildlife by giving the local communities a financial stake in eco-tourism. We cannot recommend risking capital here for a number of reasons. Consider the Ju/Hoan project in Namibia. As recently as the early 1990's the Bushmen of eastern Bushmanland were killing leopards, mainly by poisoning prey carcasses. The reason? The leopards were killing their livestock. A study by the Namibian Nature Conservation department revealed that total losses of livestock per annum amounted to a financial loss of N$9 per adult Bushmen inhabitant, and when losses due to other causes such as disease and poisonous plants had been factored out of the calculation, the total annual losses attributable to leopards was less than N$2. That is twenty English pennies. A fraction more than a U.S. quarter. Many of these priceless biological assets were being destroyed for the sake of a paltry sum. And most of those losses were due to neglect on the part of the Bushmen farmers who were leaving heavily pregnant cows out in the bush because it was too much trouble to bring them in at night.

As an experiment, a partnership was formed between the local Ju/Hoan community and the travel industry, whereby tourists were brought in for a

Bushman leopard tour. The village members showed tourists how to track leopards and then to view them from a mobile hide which was placed near a fresh kill. The Ju/Hoan community also exposed tourists to some of their traditional practices, such as collecting food from the veld and the making of poisoned arrows. Financial benefits were astonishingly high, and exceeded the cost of losses due to leopards by twelve times. But the success of the project attracted the attention of the Namibian government who condemned the eco-tourism enterprise for various political reasons, inter alia that it was 'paternalistic.' The surrounding farmers were also unhappy at the prospect of stock killers increasing in numbers. The project has fallen away, and the routine killing of priceless creatures drags on.

We cannot recommend raising money for government game reserves either, because of the prevalence of mismanagement and wasted resources. Take Marakele in the north-western bushveld of South Africa, near the mining town of Thabazimbi. A small reserve (about 40,000 hectares) it has been granted some of the most beautiful mountain scenery in the Province, courtesy of the taxpayer. If it were privately owned there would be an ethnic two hundred room lodge which would take full advantage of the incomparable views. The terrain lends itself to a novel idea - game viewing by cable car. There would be restaurants on three or four of the mountain peaks, all connected by cable car and tourists could enjoy the unique experience of seeing and photographing the big five from the quiet comfort of a swaying cable car. The reserve would be world-famous and would bring tens of millions of tourist dollars annually into South Africa's coffers. The profits could go into expanding the area of the reserve by buying up the surrounding farms. Unfortunately this is but a pipe dream because the reserve is not privately owned. Instead, the dead hand of bureaucracy is smothering it. Here is a hundred million Rand public investment with a R.O.A.M. - return on assets managed - of Nil. The reserve looks as if nobody loves it. The roads are badly maintained. A visit to the bush camp, a huddle of tents built tastefully around an ugly brick toilet, is easier with a four-wheel drive vehicle. The entrance to Reception winds past a ruined farmhouse appropriately reminiscent of Berlin after the fall of the Third Reich. The reserve is subsidised.

Only a few kilometres north of this sad testament to the high price paid by a country when the control of its assets is vested in the unproductive hands of State officials lies a private game reserve called Lapalala. Here the owners have had to find the millions to buy the land and put in all the infrastructure. Yet the roads are well maintained, the staff knowledgeable and service-oriented, and the eco-tourism facilities well-marketed and well-run. It is a leader in environmental education with its Outward Bound type school. This is one of a growing number of private conservancies which may yet prove to be the future for wildlife conservation in southern Africa.

The southern Kalahari lies in the Northern Cape province of South Africa. With a surface area of 369,000 square kilometres and a population of less than one million, the semi-arid Northern Cape is the largest and most sparsely populated South African province. The land stretching westward from Kuruman and Hotazel (aptly named; it is indeed hot as hell) to the Namibian border and north to the Botswana border is wonderful game country. The carrying capacity for livestock is severely limited by the semi-desert conditions but the wildlife thrives. Lying in the transition zone between the savannah grassland and the shrubveld of the dry Karoo the Kalahari seems to have picked out the best of both biomes. Good summer rains will support a mantle of blue buffalo, schmidtia sweetveld and waist-high silky bushman grasses. If the rains come in April then winter flowers ignite the landscape with a breath-catching display of colours; purple, lilac and tints and tinctures of colours that defy description. This is camelthorn country. Gemsbok (Oryx), springbok, red hartebeest, wildebeest, roan, duiker and the dainty steenbok live here under siege. So did the predators, lions, cheetah, hyenas, caracal (lynx) and leopard. Other than in the Kalahari Gemsbok Park, now the Kgalagadi Transfrontier Park, lions had not roared here for many years. Owing to the extraordinary commitment of one man, wild lions again roar in the southern Kalahari.

244

That man's name was Stephen Boler and to save Africa we can do no better than to follow the example of this wealthy philanthropist. After business success, Boler floated his company, the Limelight group, on the London Stock Exchange back in 1996, and walked away with a large fortune. Now he had the money and he could afford to indulge his passion. As a young hunter and later as a fierce conservationist, Boler had a love of Africa and its wildlife that transcended mere money. He was determined to do something significant to save the desert black rhino which was being massacred to near extinction. He threw his considerable fortune and his formidable entrepreneurial skills into saving some restorable wilderness. In just forty months - from 1994 to 1997- Boler had created in the Kalahari the largest individually-owned private game reserve in South Africa. Paying premiums for the land where necessary, he bought up thirty-five contiguous farms totalling 90,000 hectares (over 200,000 acres). No money or effort was spared to foster the spirit of wild Africa. Unsightly power lines spoiling the ambience of the view had to be replaced by underground lines - at a cost of millions. Unwanted farmsteads, together with their other structures, were bulldozed into the ground. Thousands of kilometres of fencing were torn out and buried.

He named his dream Tswalu Private Desert Reserve, and built superb lodges there. One lodge and a portion of the land was reserved for hunting, a cheerless reminder that there are many moneyed people who prefer to kill the animals rather than to admire and photograph them.

In November 1998, and not long after he had seen his dream come to fruition, Boler flew out to Tswalu in his private jet from England. The staff who were waiting to meet him saw the plane dip a wing and describe a wide, long circuit and then another before landing. Never before had the time-conscious industrialist done this. Perhaps he suspected what was to come and took the time for one last, lingering look over the sprawling expanse of his wilderness domain. When the plane touched down, he looked pale and the staff persuaded him to fly straight to Johannesburg, where he died of a heart attack.

Stephen Boler, we salute you. Your friends will mourn the passing of a valuable life but not half as much as the thousands of wild animals and two hundred and fifty species of birds whose world you saved and re-built. It was not only the wildlife who you saved. By preserving the wilderness, you also created hundreds of job opportunities for Africans.

In April 1999, Tswalu was purchased from Boler's estate by the Oppenheimer family. A programme to uplift the local community was started, including a new healthcare clinic. To the credit of the new owners, they are phasing out hunting at Tswalu in order to focus on the growing demand for eco-tourism and photographic safaris. It does seem that Mr Boler's monument to the Kalahari is being taken into the future with a new vision and enthusiasm.

African governments say that they want a better life for their people, free from poverty. We want a better life for the innocent wild people, free from persecution. Actually, we both want the same thing.

What can the governments of the region do to preserve the wilderness and wildlife? We can make suggestions but these are worthless if the regional states continue to demonstrate a deplorable lack of political will to stem the haemorrhaging away of their bio-treasures. The first step would be to abandon the 'sustainable use' policy, which is both cruel and unworkable.

For example, in 1998 a group of South African businessmen applied to open an abattoir for baboons in a small town north of Pretoria. The businessmen intended to produce salami, polony, ribs and canned baboon meat for human consumption in central Africa and parts of Europe. Body parts such as teeth, nails and hands were intended for export to Asia for use in aphrodisiacs. Such an abattoir would have been in perfect accordance with the policy of sustainable use and building was due to start with the approval of all the higher authorities when someone squealed and the spotlight of publicity fell like an artillery barrage on this sickening enterprise. Someone must have explained to the government how grievously insulted the great god Money would be if tourists decided to boycott South Africa. The authorities were forced to refuse the CITES permit.

What is the point of having a policy which is so wrong that it has to be abandoned every time a spotlight falls on it?

We suggest a more caring and compassionate Policy such as the following. This is proffered as can an addendum for Section 24 of the South African Constitution and the equivalents in the various regional Constitutions.

A. All wild animals shall have the following legally enforceable rights, which rights shall be written into the Constitutions of all Southern African nations:

1. The right to live free from physical or mental cruelty.
2. The right to live undisturbed in all existing proclaimed game reserves.
3. The right to share unproclaimed wilderness areas free from human persecution.
4. The right to protection of the law against any person who violates these rights.

B. The High Courts shall act as Upper Guardians of all wild animals, and may appoint curators to carry out such investigations or duties as the Court may direct in order to protect the rights of wild animals.

C. Any person shall have locus sitandi in judicio (legal capacity) to bring to the attention of the Upper Guardian any breach of the rights of animals.

D. Any order made by a Judge acting as Upper Guardian shall be binding on the State and any officials or persons who flout such order shall be subject to arrest and punishment for contempt of Court.

The adoption of a compassionate Charter such as the above is not enough in itself to save the vanishing wilderness. There is also a need for a fast-track legal procedure in poaching cases. It is not enough merely to change the rules of evidence. The whole system of justice must be brought into line with practical reality. To help the wilderness to survive the poaching pandemic, and the looming prospect of land invasions, we suggest the following changes to the law of criminal procedure and evidence.

1. In poaching cases evidence by telephone or radio should be admissible. The court can always call the ranger/landowner to give evidence if it feels this is necessary. The cost of bringing the ranger to court should be recoverable

247

from the accused in appropriate cases.

2. Game rangers and landowners should have the right to shoot at poachers who are either armed or fleeing to avoid arrest.

3. Any trespasser on any game reserve, proclaimed wilderness area or private land where there is wildlife shall be presumed to be poaching unless he can prove to the contrary.

4. Jaw traps (spring loaded gin traps), X-traps and wire snares should be banned. The sale, possession or use of these articles should be prohibited and wide powers of search and confiscation given to Police, rangers and landowners.

It is useless to ban the mere setting of the trap in terms similar to Section 2 of the South African Animals Protection Act of 1962, because it is virtually impossible to catch the trapper red-handed.

5. Any vehicle used for poaching or to transport such prohibited articles should be subject to mandatory confiscation. Land, which is being used for cruel or inhuman purposes, should be liable to confiscation, in the discretion of the Court.

6. Minimum sentences should be imposed for the use of snares and traps. The reason for this is the extraordinary cruelty of their use.

7. All exclusionary rules of evidence should be replaced by one rule which states that no relevant evidence shall be inadmissible for any other reason.

8. The right of silence of an accused person should not apply in poaching cases. Victims of crimes have no right to silence so why on earth should criminals have greater rights than their victims? In Zimbabwe this is already the law.

9. Interim orders affecting the interests of maltreated animals should not be suspended by the noting of a review or appeal. This would prevent wild animal traders from sidelining the courts pending endless legal proceedings such as occurred with the Tuli elephants.

Years of cruel neglect have earned for African governments the reputation that they are happy to talk conservation in order to milk the wildlife charities but not to do anything themselves. If international beggars like Namibia and Zimbabwe can afford to send tens of thousands of troops supported by military aircraft into the Congo, they can scarcely expect to be believed when they spread their protesting hands wide and plead lack of resources to save the dying wildlife.

If they were serious about saving their wilderness areas, and there truly was a lack of manpower (with nearly half the population unemployed!) and resources, why then have they not taken any steps to address the problem? There are thousands of people in developed countries who would happily come out and help. Harnas sits with hundreds of letters from overseas volunteers. Why have the governments failed to set up volunteer game militias? These could comprise Africans who are skilled in tracking and bush-craft as well as people from abroad with suitable military training, experience or ability. The cost of the anti-poaching militia could be born by donations from abroad. Supported by equipment such as microlight aircraft for aerial surveillance, it would not take long for the volunteer militia to catch the poachers and take control of the wilderness. The anti-poaching units could also stop the poaching in proclaimed game parks such as Khaodom in Namibia.

Or, developed nations are always looking for places to train their armed forces and to give their troops exposure to foreign conditions. How easy it would be to invite them to use their troops in joint anti-poaching operations with Africans, who could teach them bush craft. That way the wilderness areas and game reserves are saved and the bulk of the expenses are born by the military budgets of the developed countries.

There are so many ways that the regional governments could have shown a real will to save their heritage. Why have they not done so?

Turning to the departments of Nature Conservation, we believe that these arms of government should be reorganised to adapt to a changing society. Along with the changes should come a paradigm change of attitude away from being the Military Wing of the Livestock Industry. Instances of misdirected effort are every-where. In Chapter One, we saw how Dr. Stander's nature studies in Bushmanland were rudely interrupted by the land invasion there. What is the point of knowing the home ranges of the Bushmanland lions when there are none left?

249

It is not only the apex predators (and Cape Foxes) whose extinction is being presided over by these inaptly named Nature Conservation departments. Unscientific livestock farmers are turning the Kalahari into a desert. Most ranchers are guilty of overgrazing their land and the long term damage to the region is incalculable. The replacement of sweetveld grassland by impenetrable swarthaak thorn bushes will leave our children a costly legacy.

A reorganised nature conservation department would, with the assistance of the department of agriculture where necessary, be visiting the ranches regularly, analysing and recording veld character and condition, and forcing recalcitrant ranchers to de-stock where necessary. It would be formulating and implementing wiser and more far-sighted policies, with the help of scientific services from the developed world. Departmental time and manpower would be much better directed towards environmental education in the schools and at farmers' meetings; road blocks and patrols in remote areas; extension work in the field to assist in the humane trapping and re-location of so-called problem animals; anti-poaching activities; confiscating banned traps and assisting the work of the rehabilitation centres around the region. There would be less bureaucracy and a dynamic change in official mindset away from the animal exploitation industry towards a genuine concern for the well-being of the wild animals and their natural habitat.

As for the wildlife conservation charities, their support for the policy of sustainable use needs to be reconsidered. They should accept that there is no alternative but to grant rights to animals themselves in some manner such as is suggested in our compassionate charter. Granting rights over animals to the humans who own or possess them has only led to cruelty and injustice where those humans are themselves the persecutors, as with the Tuli Elephants.

In the face of the growing lawlessness and the threat to survival of wildlife from unrestrained poaching or even Zimbabwe-style land invasions, charities should consider shifting resources away from non-essential individual projects to the more fundamental strategy. By concentrating on specific projects and ignoring the land issue, organisations allow themselves to become irrelevant to the really pressing needs of wildlife. It is like the Titanic. So long as the ship is on a steady course, there is a need for compartmentalised applications. The engineers must look after the engines and the Pursers must look after the passengers. But when the ship tilts and starts to dive for the bottom, there is no longer room for compartmentalised thinking. It is a case of all hands to the lifeboats. The survival of wilderness is now so precarious that every effort should be directed at buying up private ranch land, and pressuring the governments to protect identified wild places from human encroachment. We believe that all other efforts, no matter how valuable in themselves, are peripheral.

For example, it has become fashionable to spend funds, which have been donated to benefit wildlife, on politically popular schemes for community upliftment. Important conservancies in Zimbabwe such as Save and Malilangwe spent millions on social outreach programmes to help develop their local communities. Notwithstanding all this expenditure, they have been brutalised by land invasions along with other farms in Zimbabwe. Now the wildlife, or rather the people who donate funds for conservation, might well ask how such schemes benefit them.

Rubbing shoulders with zillionaires and famous actresses at glitzy conferences and glamorous cocktail parties may help to raise funds. But the suffering animals are not being snared and shot in the foyers of the five-star hotels. It is here where we live in the Kalahari, in the remote and isolated parts of the region, where the sound of gunfire is heard, and the fencelines, festooned with wire snares all patiently awaiting the next torture-victim, stretch for thousands of kilometres. Directing those funds at the heart of the problem, namely habitat expansion, has never been more crucial.

Here too there is a dire need for a dynamic change of mindset. Too many wildlife conservation charities act as if they enjoy observer status at the war upon Nature, and that it is enough that they document and report, say, the bushmeat trade. We call upon the conservation charities to enlist and participate in the battle to save our heritage.

251

Finally we plead for unity. The animal welfare and conservation organisations in Europe and North America are politically influential. No effort should be spared to unite all environmentalists worldwide in order to encourage our regional governments to rein in their violent elements and preserve law and order. Without unity among environmental groups we see little chance of saving the vestiges of our vanishing wilderness.

The Kalahari is slipping away from us like sand between our fingers. A wide world which used to stretch in our own lifetimes for countless horizons is now artificially chopped up and dismembered. Strangled by fences and scarred by ribbons of sudden death called roads. The whole tragedy is written in the sand. The hoof prints of the multitude are gone, replaced first by blood stains and then by emptiness. Five million years of creation reduced to an almost lifeless wreck in one generation.

As we write a dozen vultures sit hunched on their low camelthorn perch looking out over the vlei to the mottled cloud-shadowed Kuruman Hills behind. All the loving care in the world cannot give them back what Mankind has taken away. They will never again glide and soar through the heavens. To those of us who live with the backwash from the tidal wave of economic activity, the flotsam of shocked and bewildered wild refugees are a constant reminder of the relentless war on our wilderness that will not stop until everything worthwhile is gone forever, and there is nothing left to live for.

THE END